HANDBOOK OF AMERICAN RESOURCES

FOR AFRICAN STUDIES

Hoover Institution Bibliographical Series: XXIX

Handbook of American Resources for African Studies

Peter Duignan

Hoover Institution Bibliographical Series: XXIX

The Hoover Institution on War, Revolution, and Peace

1967 Stanford University

The Hoover Institution on War, Revolution, and Peace, founded at Stanford University in 1919 by the late President Herbert Hoover, is a center for advanced study and research on public and international affairs in the twentieth century. The views expressed in its publications are entirely those of the authors and do not necessarily reflect the views of the Hoover Institution.

TO FRANCES

PREFACE

UNITED STATES LINKS with Africa are and have been close if only because one of every ten Americans has an African ancestor. In addition, as explorers and missionaries, frontiersmen and soldiers, tobacco farmers and mining engineers, our countrymen have helped to develop the continent. Yet the history of American involvement in Africa, to be found in a variety and quantity of library, archival, and manuscript material and of art and ethnographic collections in the United States relating to Africa, is inadequately known. Because of the extent of American commercial, missionary, philanthropic, scientific, and governmental contacts with Africa since 1619 the resources are many. The purpose of this *Handbook of American Resources for African Studies* therefore is to call attention to these resources and to encourage utilization of the scattered but rich materials held by various American institutions and museums.

A previous work which Robert Collins and I coauthored, *Americans in Africa: A Preliminary Guide to American Missionary Archives and Library Manuscript Collections on Africa* (1963), described 52 missionary archives and 47 library manuscript collections and cited only records and papers of Americans who went to Africa. The present handbook attempts to describe all materials relevant to African studies—not just archives or manuscripts dealing with Americans in Africa. Descriptions are given of the holdings of 95 library and manuscript collections, 108 church and missionary libraries and archives, 95 art and ethnographic collections, and 4 business archives. No systematic effort was made to cover North Africa, but if librarians supplied data on their North African holdings this information was left in.

To compile the handbook I reviewed bibliographic aids like Hamer's *Guide to Archives and Manuscripts in the United States* (1961), the Library of Congress *Manuscripts in Public and Private Collections in the United States* (1924) and *National Union Catalog of Manuscript Collections* (1962–), inventories prepared by the Work Projects Administration's Historical Records Survey, and, wherever possible, the calendars or registers prepared by libraries and archives such as those of the Sanford Papers, Sanford, Florida, and the Schomburg Collection of the New York Public Library. Unfortunately not all published inventories were available to me and there will be omissions. Collections with only a small amount of material on Africa were also excluded.

A major difficulty was that most guides did not indicate an African relationship. Valuable collections may have been overlooked because I did not know of an individual's or organization's activity in Africa.

Some collections were examined directly, but most information came from responses to questionnaires. Major Africana libraries are described by the curator or bibliographer concerned. The entries vary in length and content because the details provided by the institutions were so different—it proved impossible to impose a standard form on busy librarians or archivists. A draft of each entry was returned to the institution to be checked for accuracy.

Many organizations did not reply to the questionnaire. One has only to check *African Programs of U.S. Organizations: A Select Directory* (1965) to see how many groups active in Africa are not described in this handbook. There were other problems. Archivists will note flaws in the entries: they are not always specific or concrete about indicating the type of records (e.g., correspondence, minutes, reports, etc.); they do not always give the inclusive years of the records, their quantity, or what part of Africa they referred to; and they do not cover in most cases the principal subjects dealt with in the holdings. However, as editor I provided all the information I could get from as many institutions as were willing to reply. There are numerous collections which have not been inventoried or catalogued. In such cases, short of visits to the repository no analysis was possible. But this handbook is only a start; as the first attempt to describe American resources for African studies it is bound to be incomplete. It is hoped that others will be stimulated to do more scientific surveys. One such survey is already under way.

The African Studies Association in 1963 received a grant from the Ford Foundation to prepare a descriptive guide to African-related archival and manuscript sources in this country. The ASA and the Archivist of the United States, the National Archives and Records Services, have assumed responsibility for the project. Mr. Morris Rieger of the National Archives will prepare the guide. (A Hoover Institution project to have Mr. Rieger survey the African-related materials in the National Archives has been merged with the larger study.)

The Rieger guide will also serve as the United States national volume of the projected 'Guide to the Sources of African History' outside of Africa, sponsored by the International Council on Archives. Mr. Rieger will attempt a comprehensive coverage of the African archival and manuscript materials in American government agencies, commercial concerns, religious and missionary groups, and other non-commercial organizations. African-related sources held by private individuals will be included if they are in depository custody. The guide will survey the entire continent of Africa plus the adjacent coastal islands. There will be no chronological limits on coverage.

In the preparation of the handbook I have been helped by many people. My first words of appreciation must go to the Director of the Hoover Institution, Dr. W. Glenn Campbell, for supporting this expensive and time-consuming project. I wish next to thank the staffs of the missionary societies, libraries, archives, businesses, art museums, and ethnographic collections who so generously contributed information on their holdings. My debts to Mr. Morris Rieger of the National Archives are many: he read parts of the manuscript, made several useful suggestions about the form of the entries, and pointed out many additional manuscript sources. The completion of this book owes much to the careful editing and checking of Mrs. Evelyn Boyce and to the organizational skills of Miss Evelyn Love. And without the patience and encouragement of my wife, Frances, and my children this book would not have been finished. To all who have helped, my thanks; any remaining errors or inadequacies are solely my responsibility.

PETER DUIGNAN

Hoover Institution
January 21, 1966

CONTENTS

LIBRARY AND MANUSCRIPT COLLECTIONS

UNIVERSITY OF ALABAMA

The Library of the University of Alabama, University, Alabama, has papers of William Crawford Gorgas (1854–1920), U.S. Army Surgeon General and pioneer in tropical medicine, who in 1913–1914 visited South Africa as consultant to the Transvaal Chamber of Mines to advise on measures for improving the health of the African miners.

ALABAMA DEPARTMENT OF ARCHIVES AND HISTORY

The Alabama Department of Archives and History, Montgomery, Alabama, contains about 50 pieces of material concerning John Tyler Morgan (1824–1907), Alabama Senator and chairman of the Senate Foreign Relations Committee in the 1880's, who played a major role in American diplomatic recognition of Leopold II's International Congo Association and in the origins of the Congo Free State. Also at the Alabama Department of Archives are papers of Robert Ernest Noble (1870–1956), surgeon in the U.S. Medical Corps and chairman of the Yellow Fever Commission to West Africa (early 1920's), 1 file drawer.

AMERICAN ANTIQUARIAN SOCIETY

The American Antiquarian Society, Salisbury Street and Park Avenue, Worcester, Massachusetts, has a few papers on the slave trade, slaves, and shipping to Africa in the eighteenth and nineteenth centuries. Especially noteworthy are the papers of Charles W. Agard and those of Lucy Chase (slave dealer's papers, 1846–1864). The Society also has 9 boxes of papers of Samuel Hodges (1792–1827), who was consul at the Cape Verde Islands, 1818–1827.

AMERICAN GEOGRAPHICAL SOCIETY

The American Geographical Society, Broadway at 156th Street, New York, New York 10032, has an African collection of approximately 5,000 volumes, with emphasis on exploration, travel, description, history, and geography, and an estimated 137 linear feet of shelf space of government documents and 100 feet of shelf space for periodicals. The Society holds sets of maps for most African countries as well as numerous single maps for individual countries. The maps date from 1500 to the present time. Subjects covered include geology, soils, population, ethnography, economics, history, and transportation. The approximate number of single maps is 7,000. In addition, the Society has approximately 70 atlases, and a unique catalogue of maps published in periodicals and books is maintained. An example of its varied concern with Africa might include mention that the Society was a proponent of American recognition of Leopold II's International Congo Association in 1884. The Society also has archives dating from 1852.

AMERICAN JEWISH HISTORICAL SOCIETY

The American Jewish Historical Society of New York City has 7 boxes of papers of Aaron Lopez (1731–1782), who was a merchant and slave trader of Newport, Rhode Island.

AMERICAN PHILOSOPHICAL SOCIETY

The American Philosophical Society, Philadelphia, Pennsylvania, has papers of such noted figures as Sir Joseph Banks (1743–1820), scientific administrator and prime mover in the British African Association's effort to locate the sources of the Niger River, and Matthew Fontaine Maury (1806–1873), oceanographer and astronomer, who conducted oceanographic studies of the Indian Ocean and the South Atlantic.

AMERICAN SOCIETY OF AFRICAN CULTURE

The American Society of African Culture (AMSAC), 15 East 40th Street, New York 16, New York, is a membership organization composed primarily of scholars, writers, and artists of African descent. Founded in 1957, it is affiliated with the Société Africaine de Culture, publisher of *Présence Africaine*, and maintains offices in New York City and Lagos, Nigeria. AMSAC carries out its program through publications, conferences, lectures, cultural exchanges, and hospitality services.

The Society holds approximately 735 volumes on African culture, 300 volumes on the American Negro, and 100 volumes on international relations. AMSAC publishes volumes on Africa, as well as a newsletter and reports of its annual meetings.

UNIVERSITY OF ARIZONA

The Special Collections Division of the Library of the University of Arizona, Tucson, Arizona, contains the papers of Homer LeRoy Shantz (1876–1958), botanist and agriculturist, for the period 1905–1957 (10 feet). This material includes articles, notes, abstracts, notes on reading, autobiographical material concerning professional activities, printed material, photographs, and other papers. Material on Africa concerns botany in Africa, the Smithsonian African expedition (1919–1920), and the second African Education Commission (sponsored by the Phelps-Stokes Fund, 1923–1924).

ARIZONA PIONEERS' HISTORICAL SOCIETY

The Arizona Pioneers' Historical Society, Tucson, Arizona, has about 300 linear feet of papers of John Campbell Greenway (1872–1926), a mineowner whose interests extended to Africa.

ATLANTA UNIVERSITY

The Negro Collection of the Trevor Arnett Library of Atlanta University, Atlanta, Georgia, was established as a separate department in 1946 when the Henry P. Slaughter Collection was purchased. There are materials by and about Negroes from many countries.

Approximately 1,100 titles are in the area of African studies. Especially important are the 336 titles published between 1673 and 1899. West Africa and history are most frequently represented in the holdings, but all of Africa is included and among the subjects covered are travel, colonization, philology, folklore, and slavery.

For listing, see Maude Moore Pinkett, 'A Bibliography of Works on Africa in the Trevor Arnett Library of Atlanta University Published before 1900' (M.L.S. thesis, School of Library Service, Atlanta University, 1962, 53 pp.), and Julia W. Bond, 'A Bibliography of Works on Africa in the Negro Collection of the Trevor Arnett Library Published 1900–1925' (M.L.S. thesis, School of Library Service, Atlanta University, 1964, 41 pp.).

The Library of the University also has some papers of Thomas Clarkson (1760–1846), leading British abolitionist associated with the establishment of Sierra Leone, about 20 items.

THE BEVERLY (MASSACHUSETTS) HISTORICAL SOCIETY

Material covering Massachusetts commercial activity in Africa is available at the Beverly Historical Society, 117 Cabot Street, Beverly, Massachusetts.

Letters from Foreign Ports, 1784–1785—Book of Clearances, 1786–1788—Light Money, 1784–1800, Beverly Historical Society, Volume 44, 6045. The schooner *Collector*, owned by John Carnes of Beverly, received clearance from Beverly on February 11, 1786, for an unknown part of Africa. The cargo consisted of 92 hogsheads of rum, 64 hogsheads of tobacco, 1 box of European goods, and 1 chest of beads. It was an unarmed forty-ton vessel, manned by a crew of nine. This is the first evidence of a Beverly trade with Africa.

Records, Naval Office, Beverly, 1784–1800: Manifests, Volume 6, 1788–1789, Beverly Historical Society, 6698, 6705, 6706, 6710, 6711, 6712, 6714, 6716. In 1789, ships from Beverly stopped at the Cape Verde Islands on at least eight occasions. Their principal homeward-bound cargo was salt, probably serving as ballast for the trip. Salt was also a valuable commodity in a fishing community. It is curious that these stopovers occurred within a five-week period. Beverly manifest lists attest to these ventures:

1. Schooner, *Industry*, March 30, 1789; master, John Smith, II; cargo, 200 hogsheads of salt.

2. Schooner, *Hannah*, April 11, 1789; master, Brackenbury Prince; cargo, 240 hogsheads of salt, sundries (joiner's ware).

3. Schooner, *Dolphin*, April 11, 1789; master, H. Wallace; cargo, 270 hogsheads of salt.

4. Schooner, *Success*, April 16, 1789; master, Thomas Bodcock; owner, Samuel Foster; cargo, 200 hogsheads of salt.

5. Schooner, *Hawk*, April 17, 1789; master and owner, Isaac Rea; cargo, 300 hogsheads of salt.

6. Schooner, *Rambler*, April 17, 1789; master, John Hammond; cargo, 400 hogsheads of salt.

7. Schooner, *Fish Hawk*, April 23, 1789; master, Andrew Ober; cargo, 270 hogsheads of salt.

8. Schooner, *Dolphin*, April 1789; master, Andrew Gage; cargo, 250 hogsheads of salt, 130 hides.

Sea Journal of *Snow Fanny*, Beverly Historical Society, 17008. The voyage of the *Snow Fanny* began in 1796 at Boston and ended the following year at the same port. The *Fanny* visited St. Dennis, the Isles of Bourbon and France, the Cape of Good Hope, Cowes, and other ports. The journal, however, has little historical value.

Journal of Voyage of Brig *Hector*, Beverly Historical Society, 16972. The sea journal of the brig *Hector* is for a voyage from Beverly to Calcutta and the return to Beverly. The *Hector* left on June 13, 1804, visiting the Isle of Bourbon (October 3–November 10) and the Isle of France (November 14–December 4), towards Batavia. On October 2, the *Hector*

> at 3PM was boarded by the British frigate called the *Phaeton*, they demanded my papers which I delivered the Capn ordered me on board accordingly I went with an officer . . . they dismissed me and set me on board but impressed John Shanbra a sailor.

At the Isles of Bourbon and France, pilots came on board and took charge— the only comments regarding the *Hector*'s visits to the islands. The log was kept by Nicholas Thorndike.

Capt. Amos Lefavour, Jr., *Directions and Remarks on the Coast of Sumatra, So. Madagascar, Red Sea, Persian Gulf, East Coast of Africa, Glorious, Aldebra, Solomon, Zanzibar, Mombasa, and Other Islands*, Beverly Historical Society, 16977. The booklet was compiled by Amos Lefavour, Jr., one of Beverly's sea captains. It has considerable historical value. The compilation is a sequence of events from 1819 to 1833.

Account Book of Capt. George Abbott, Beverly Historical Society, 16982. The account book of Capt. George Abbott of Beverly contains shipping papers, invoices, accounts of sales, disbursements, etc., concerning four voyages to West Africa. The brig *Attentive* (1826), the brig *Sarah Louisa* (1827), and the brig *Dido* (1828) made sales at the Cape Verde Islands, St. Mary's on the River Gambia, and Fort Praya (Praga), and the brig *Roxana* (1831) visited the Cape Verde Islands, Goree, Praya, and the Isle of Mayo.

Sea Journal of Barque *Monmouth*, Beverly Historical Society, 16969. The voyage began in January 1831 at Boston. After visiting Mozambique, Zanzibar, Colombo, and Bombay, the *Monmouth* returned to Boston the next year. Amos Lefavour was master.

Journal of Ship *Robert Pulsford*, Beverly Historical Society, 17148. Beginning in 1842 at Boston, the *Robert Pulsford* visited Cape Town, as well as Hobart Town, Wellington, and Manila. The voyage ended at Boston in 1844. The master was William Caldwell. The ship remained in Cape Town from December 23, 1842, to January 10, 1843, but there was no mention of the stay.

Sea Journal of Barque *Lucia Maria*, Beverly Historical Society, 20714. The most recent sea journal found at the Society is one concerning a voyage of the barque *Lucia Maria* dated February 6, 1851. Departing from Salem, they visited Zanzibar, Mozambique, Masunge, and other ports, arriving in Beverly on November 8, 1853.   RONALD TAGNEY

BOSTON PUBLIC LIBRARY

The Boston Public Library, Copley Square, Boston, Massachusetts 02117, contains accounts of nineteenth-century explorers and travelers to Africa. There are also some early printed works by such authors as Francisco Alvares and Guillaume Delisle. About 100 titles under the heading 'Missions, Africa' comprise a miscellaneous group of missionaries' accounts and reports of societies.

The Library's Rare Book Department contains a few manuscripts of African interest, such as a group of manuscripts from the papers of Admiral Sir William Sidney Smith (1764–1840) relating to his efforts toward the liberation of Christian slaves from the Barbary pirates.

BOSTON UNIVERSITY

The African Studies Center at Boston University, Boston, Massachusetts, was established in September 1953. Its library collections reflect the main emphasis on the social sciences by the teaching staff. In addition, consideration has been given to the library facilities of nearby institutions and to the needs of students, organizations, and individuals in the Boston area which were not being met. Therefore, all publications on the social sciences that cover Africa are purchased. Linguistic, legal, and technical sciences materials are limited whenever covered by institutions in the area. Purchases of North Africa material have been light because of the accessibility of Harvard University's Middle East Center.

The library collections are located in two places. Monographs and back issues of periodicals are in the African Alcove of the Central Library, where their value and usefulness can be made available to graduate students in sociology, economics, political science, religion, anthropology, history, archaeology, etc. All pamphlets, African government documents, newspapers, recent volumes of periodicals, maps, recordings, and the newspaper clipping files constituting much of the primary source material are deposited in the Documents Library of the African Center, which moved into larger quarters in the fall of 1964.

Materials on African prehistory are excellent, but primary emphasis has always been placed on the acquisition of recent African and colonial government documentation, and Boston University has one of the largest university collections in this field in the United States. Holdings of the former British areas are exceptional, with an almost complete collection of publications issued since 1953 and with reports dating back to the late nineteenth century in South African material. Selected early-twentieth-century material is available for Nigeria and Kenya. Scattered statistics, laws, annual messages of the President, treasury reports, etc., are available for Liberia for the first half of the twentieth century. The French-speaking area collections have been developed and greatly improved in the past two years. Debates from the 1940's are available from former French Equatorial Africa, and current material from all of French-speaking Africa is being acquired, with statistical information particularly strong from 1940 to date. A collection on the Sudan has been developed and continued. Gazettes are received for all countries, either in printed form or on microfilm. Coverage of North Africa is intensive particularly in materials in European languages published since 1800, but work has begun cooperatively with the Middle East Center at Harvard to strengthen this part of the collection.

Not only is there interest in newly published reports, but out-of-print catalogues are checked for titles, and professors and students are alerted to collect specific material while traveling in Europe and Africa. Acquisitions have not been limited as to subject except in the case of statutory laws—because of the cost of these and because they are readily accessible at law schools in the Boston area. Therefore, all departmental annual reports, Hansards, commission reports, white papers, and speeches are automatically included in the collection. All African material available from the U.S. National Archives, especially consular reports from Africa, are held at the Documents Library on microfilm. If possible, only English and European languages are acquired. Forty-five hundred titles are held at the Documents Library, with an addition of 600 new titles per year. Since many documents are of a serial nature, this total does not reveal the actual size of the collection, which measures 550 linear feet. All government documents are catalogued and arranged by country (using the Library of Congress classification 'J') and subdivided alphabetically by issuing department. For example, Nigerian documents are J 745, annual reports of the Ministry of Education are J 745.*E3*, the Police Force reports are J 745.*P6*. There are both author and subject catalogues available. A *Catalog of African Government Documents and African Area Index* was published in 1960, and a new edition, revised and enlarged, in 1964. New acquisitions are listed in the *Joint Acquisitions List of Africana* compiled by Northwestern University.

The Library is currently receiving 186 periodicals covering the whole of the African continent. They include economics, history, linguistics, political science, education, literature, archaeology, and anthropology. Thirty newspapers are received from countries in Africa, mostly in English, French, and Portuguese. At the end of the year six of these are replaced by microfilm copies, and the others are placed in bindings. In order to have the latest information available, the Library clips three U.S. and two British newspapers. These are filed by area, subject, and chronology. A pamphlet collection is kept of reprints, political party manifestoes, unpublished reports, governmental information service material, etc. These are catalogued and arranged by country and broad subject approach.

Thus far, only small holdings of special materials have been acquired. These include 76 recordings, produced largely by Ethnic Folkways and the African Music Society. In addition, a number of tapes dealing with music and folklore are in the collection, along with black-and-white photographs provided by the embassies of various African and colonial governments. The year 1964 saw rapid growth in the map collection and its facilities, providing all major atlases and 600 individual maps. With an increased effort in 1965, this number should be doubled within a year. Of particular usefulness is a card file of doctoral and master's theses on Africa received in American, British, and French universities since the mid-nineteenth century. These are arranged by country covered and alphabetically by author and include all subjects and all African countries. Some have been acquired on microfilm, and information is available as to their accessibility. The file for American dissertations has been published cooperatively with the Library of Congress, and the file of French dissertations will be published shortly.

Although emphasis has been placed on government documents, it should be stressed that the book collection has reached close to 11,000 titles and is growing at a rate of over 1,000 to 1,500 titles per year, half of which are out of print. New titles covering all of Africa in the social sciences are acquired automatically. Out-of-print items are selected by faculty and graduate students of the Center. The out-of-print collection is strong on primary sources in English, German, and French in the nineteenth century and early twentieth century, including North Africa, and a good beginning has been made in a collection from the eighteenth century. The Library also possesses many Scandinavian items on Africa. There are manuscripts on Africa in the Bortman Collection of Americana originating largely from the purchase of the Lord North papers.

A card catalogue including all material except pamphlets is kept at the Central Library. Duplicate records are also held at the Documents Library,* except for books, which are here given only an author card. The Central Library's stacks are open to graduate students. Hours are from 8:30 A.M. to 10 P.M. Monday through Friday, 9 A.M. to 5 P.M. Saturday, and 2 P.M. to 10 P.M. Sunday during the school year. The Documents Library is open from 9 A.M. to 5 P.M. daily except Saturday, on which it is open from 9 A.M. to 1 P.M. Interlibrary loan requests are placed through the Central Library's Reference Department. The loan of documents is restricted to libraries outside the Boston area, for no more than two weeks, and no renewals are possible. Microfilm, newspapers, newspaper clippings, maps, and unbound periodicals do not circulate. The Documents Library has a full-time staff of three and part-time student help. Several members of the Central Library staff share in the ordering and processing of the books. The Library participates actively in the African Studies Association Libraries-Archives Committee, supporting their cooperative projects for microfilming, preparing of bibliographies, etc. The librarian of the Documents Library submits an annual report to the director of libraries and the director of the African Program each July.

MARION DINSTEL MACDONALD

---

* For additional information on the organization of the collection see Mary D. Herrick, 'African Government Documentation at Boston University,' *College and Research Libraries*, XVIII (May 1957), 206–209, and Mary D. Herrick and Adelaide C. Hill, 'Problems of Bibliographical Control for an Area Research Program,' *ibid.*, XVI (July 1955), 271–295.

BUFFALO AND ERIE COUNTY HISTORICAL SOCIETY

The Buffalo and Erie County Historical Society, Buffalo, New York, has a considerable file of the papers of Samuel Wilkeson (1781–1848), president of the American Colonization Society, 1838–1841, and editor of its organ, the *African Repository*.

UNIVERSITY OF CALIFORNIA, BERKELEY

From its very beginnings over a hundred years ago, the Library has actively collected books about Africa. Because the Library's Africana is scattered throughout the main library and several special branches, it is difficult to assess completely the quantity, but there is little doubt that in quality it is now one of the most important collections in the western United States. The basic and important 'classical' African studies monographs are particularly well represented.

Chronologically and geographically, the materials reflect the great range of the curriculum and of the outstanding faculty at Berkeley. Prehistory, colonial and modern history, anthropology, art, political science, early voyages and travels, geology, botany, zoology, and agriculture—in fact, most subjects, except religion and vernacular languages—are adequately represented, but there is little in the way of manuscript or archival materials. (The General Library does have the papers—about 25,000 items—of David Prescott Barrows, 1873–1954, political scientist, archaeologist, and university president, who wrote *Berbers and Blacks* [1927] on the basis of an extensive journey through West Africa and the Sudan.) An excellent general reference collection contains many useful African items. Although the collection contains books on all the countries and areas of Africa, there is greater concentration on the former English colonial areas of West Africa, East African territories, and the former German colonies. A current special project is the building of a collection of writings by African novelists and poets in all but the African vernacular languages.

The greatest strength of Berkeley's collections, however, is in its serials and documents. Through purchase, gifts, and a large number of exchanges, there are available complete or nearly complete runs of the publications of such organizations as IFAN, the Rhodes-Livingstone Institute, the International African Institute, the Académie Royale des Sciences d'Outre-Mer (Brussels), the Hakluyt Society, Afrika Verein (Hamburg), the Société des Africanistes (Paris), and the South African Institute of Race Relations. The Library subscribes to most of the standard Africana periodicals as well as many unusual ones from India, Eastern Europe, and Africa.

In addition to being an official depository of United States and United Nations publications, the Library's fine collection of documents includes the Great Britain Colonial Office Papers and many publications of the French, German, Belgian, Portuguese, and Spanish colonial ministries. Documents from the newly independent African countries are being added on a selective basis either in their original printed form or on microfilm. No particular effort is made to acquire pamphlet or other ephemeral material, but the Library has purchased on microfilm a portion of the British Colonial Office Library's pamphlet collection. Most other pamphlets are bound and catalogued as regular monographs.

Maps and atlases on a continent-wide basis are collected, and the Library holds a good selection of topographic, subject, and topical sheet maps. The Earth Sciences Branch Library has an excellent collection of geological maps. The Library currently subscribes to more than 35 newspapers from 25 African countries as well as several weeklies about Africa published in Europe. The Library has a microfilm of the *Star* (Johannesburg) for 1889–1899, 1902–1930, and 1958–.

Also on the campus, the School of Law Library has a good general collection of monographs, sets, and journals relating to African subjects. The Lowie Museum of Anthropology's collection of masks, sculptures, and other African objects, mostly from West Africa, are in constant demand for research study and campus display.

LEE PETRASEK

UNIVERSITY OF CALIFORNIA, LOS ANGELES

Library augmentation in the field of African studies began on a large scale at UCLA with the appointment, in January 1960, of a full-time bibliographer to study existing resources and inaugurate an active, long-range acquisition program for the development of major research in cooperation with the African Studies Center.

Africa south of the Sahara was the geographical scope, but the Sudan, Ethiopia, and the Horn were included, leaving North Africa proper to the jurisdiction of the Near East Center and the Library's Near East bibliographer. Subject emphasis was originally directed toward anthropology, history, economics, education, geography, sociology, political science and government, and languages and linguistics; later art, music, and English as a second language were brought into the collecting scope. The sciences were and are included only as they apply to these areas. No limitation was placed on the time period to be covered.

There is no separate African collection as such, the material being dispersed throughout the Library of Congress classification system the Library uses. Further dispersal occurs in the case of such branch libraries as Education, Business Administration, and Biomedical, which keep the majority of titles in their own subject fields.

Exclusive of official documents and serials, the collection at present numbers more than 14,000 volumes of books and pamphlets. There are approximately 550 African serial titles represented, in whole or in part, in the Library's collection, of which over 400 are currently received. Recently purchased was a complete file through 1959 of *Europe France Outremer*, complementing holdings since that date. Of the 147 newspaper titles represented, 42 are wholly or partly on microfilm and 22 are in vernacular languages. The Library is currently receiving 83 titles from 36 countries.

A not inconsiderable amount of current material, both official and nonoffical, is obtained through exchanges with government offices and scholarly and scientific organizations in Africa.

No attempt has ever been made to keep a count of African documents, but bound and unbound volumes at present run well into the thousands. Emphasis in the past was placed on British Africa, and the collection is therefore strongest for countries in those areas; current deposit accounts with the government printers in English-speaking countries assure the Library of continued strength. But research and study demand a wider field, and an endeavor is made to obtain current debates, gazettes, blue books, and other reports from all countries and at the same time fill in the considerable gaps in retrospective files with original material or microfilm. Much of this is of course selective, without an effort toward complete coverage.

The collecting of rare or unusual items is not part of a planned program at UCLA. Nevertheless, the Department of Special Collections has a number of titles which fall into these categories, including John Ogilby's *Africa* (1670), Joseph Hawkins' *History of a Voyage to the Coast of Africa* (1797), and the beautiful *Monumenta cartographica Africae et Aegypti* (5 vols. in 16, 1926–1951).

In the field of African languages and linguistics the collection is rather impressive, particularly in the South African vernaculars. A group of 177 Bibles contributes to its significance, as does a good selection of fiction.

Portuguese Africa has recently received emphasis, and the purchase in 1963 of a sizable collection strong in history, travel, and government publications did much to strengthen steadily increasing holdings.

Because politics and government have long held an important place in the interests of the African Studies Center, the Library has gradually accumulated a choice collection of ephemera in these subjects. Ghana and Nigeria, in particular, have been favored areas, with government propaganda, party publications, and speeches of national and local leaders making up the bulk of the material. The Nigerian Action Party, National Council of Nigeria and the Cameroons (NCNC), and National Youth Congress are well represented.

The entire continent of Africa is one of the three major areas of acquisition in UCLA's Map Library, and the collection now numbers in excess of 10,000 items. The majority are topographical maps, with subject or topical maps running a close second. A complete set of issues from the Institut Géographique National is included; there are many gazetteers and city plans, guides, and directories.

An especially interesting section of the collection is that dealing with the music of the various African nations. The books themselves—several hundred volumes—are housed in the Music Library, and the Archive of the Institute of Ethnomusicology contains related materials. There are 1,026 phonograph recordings, including the 'Music of Africa' and 'Sound of Africa' series, and 42 taped field recordings from Ghana, Nigeria, and the Sudan. In addition, the Archive has a large group of instruments from Ghana and Nigeria: drums of assorted kinds and sizes, bells, gongs, calabash rattles, and xylophones.

The University's Ethnic Collection has been growing steadily over the past few years, and its African Art and Ethnology Section now contains some 4,300 items representing, among others, the Batutsi, Sebei, Bambara, Dogon, Mossi, Mende, Ashanti, Yoruba, Bini, and Bakota. In 1963 a splendid Congo collection was purchased from M. Jean Hallet—approximately 3,000 pieces covering 38 tribes—consisting of musical instruments, artifacts, ceremonial sculptures, fetishes, instruments of war, and other objects. The Balega group, numbering 768 items, is one of the most comprehensive in existence and is rich in artistically outstanding carvings in wood, bone, and ivory.

DOROTHY J. HARMON

CALIFORNIA INSTITUTE OF TECHNOLOGY

A unique private African collection is held by Professor Edwin S. Munger of the California Institute of Technology, Pasadena, California 91109. This private library consists of 12,000 books and documents limited to Africa south of the Sahara. It is strong in accounts of West Africa in the seventeenth century and South Africa in the eighteenth century. The Nigerian section of 800 books is concentrated on the eastern and western regions. Beginning with *Liberia; or, The Early History and Signal Preservation of the American Colony of Free Negroes on the Coast of Africa* by Innes in 1833, the coverage on Liberia is fairly comprehensive.

The South African section is particularly strong on early Afrikaner movements and the National Party (in Nederlands, Afrikaans, and English); on Communist material in books, pamphlets, and newspapers such as *The Bolshevist* (1919); and in biographies of political figures.

Although the collection has books in more than forty languages, most materials are in English. Other random topics of more than average strength are Uganda, Bechuanaland, South-West Africa, Jews in South Africa, Dutch Reformed Churches, Mount Kilimanjaro, and transportation. Coverage of government documentation is uneven and not current. There are unpublished manuscripts.

CALIFORNIA STATE LIBRARY, SUTRO BRANCH

The collections of the Sutro Branch, California State Library, Golden Gate Avenue and Temescal Terrace, San Francisco, California, include copies of the papers of Sir Joseph Banks (1743–1820), president of the Royal Philosophical Society and one of the founders of the Association for Promoting the Discovery of the Interior Parts of Africa (founded in 1788). Approximately 500 items are concerned, directly or indirectly, with Africa. The African papers cover the period from 1788 to 1817. Although a large number of these items are receipts, routine memoranda, etc., the collection includes much that is of interest to the student of African exploration. There are papers, for example, dealing with explorers like John Ledyard, Simon Lucas, and Daniel Houghton; there are payments to and correspondence with the botanists Francis Masson and Adam Azelius. There are lists showing the membership of the Association at various times, as well as correspondence indicative of Sir Joseph's interest in the Sierra Leone project and all efforts to increase current information about Africa. Among the correspondents whose letters are included in the collection are well-known persons such as Josiah Wedgwood, Erasmus Darwin, and Lord Rawdon and many others of a lesser degree of

…e. The collection reflects Sir Joseph Banks's concern with Africa and his continuous efforts to promote African exploration for some thirty years.

THE CENTER FOR RESEARCH LIBRARIES

The Cooperative African Microfilm Project (CAMP) is a project administered by the Center for Research Libraries (the former Midwest Inter-Library Center), 5721 Cottage Grove Avenue, Chicago, Illinois 60637, with the cooperation of the Libraries-Archives Committee of the African Studies Association.

Participants share the cost of acquiring microform copies of scarce materials on Africa, including archival materials, pamphlets, locally distributed political ephemera, newspapers, periodicals, and government documents. This cooperative project allows the participants to make available to their faculty and students many more important source materials for African studies than they could otherwise afford.

The Center acquires when possible a negative microfilm and also maintains a positive copy for loan to the participants. If the Center has the negative film, participants may also purchase a positive copy for their own use, if they so wish.

Libraries of the following are participants in CAMP:

Boston University
University of California, Berkeley
University of California, Los Angeles
Center for Research Libraries
University of Chicago
Duke University
Hoover Institution

Indiana University
Michigan State University
Northwestern University
University of Toronto
University of Wisconsin
Yale University

Special foreign member: Padmore Research Library, Ghana

Nonparticipating libraries may not borrow positive copies of microfilm. But if CAMP owns the negative, nonparticipants may purchase a positive copy by paying the cost of the positive plus a portion of the cost of the negative.

Libraries outside the United States are not allowed to borrow material, but they are eligible to become participants in CAMP on a special basis that entitles them to buy positive prints from CAMP for the cost of the positive only (i.e., without paying a share of the negative cost on such purchases).

The Center welcomes any inquiries from libraries interested in participating in CAMP.

The list of holdings now in CAMP follows. Inventories are held for some of the material, as indicated by an asterisk (*); inventories are being prepared for other collections.

Adams, F., defendant. Crown vs. F. Adams and twenty-nine others; trial for treason in the Supreme Court of South Africa, Special Criminal Court, Pretoria. Documents introduced in evidence, from 1959. 28 reels, negative and positive.

---

* An inventory is held for any item marked with an asterisk.

Collection of all documents introduced by the government during the treason trial (not just the partial document collection filmed by the Treason Trial Defense Committee).

Bot, S. Pierre Njock. 'Studies on Basa Customs: What I Have Heard and What I Have Seen.' Typescript copy of the history of Basa customs by Chief Njock of Makok, Cameroun. 1935. 1 reel, negative and positive.

*Cameroun political ephemera. 'Miscellaneous Short Publications Issued in Cameroun, 1952–1961. Collected by David Gardinier and Victor Le Vine. 1964.' 2 reels, negative and positive.

Lambert, H. E. 'The Social and Political Institutions of the Tribes of the Kikuyu Group.' Unpublished manuscript. 400 pp. 1 reel, negative and positive.

Northern Rhodesia political party material. 1 reel, positive.

Herbert J. Weiss Collection on the Belgian Congo. 1964. 13 reels, negative and positive.

British material on the Belgian Congo:

*Papers relating to the history of the Congo conserved at the School of Oriental and African Studies of the University of London and the British Museum. 4 reels, positive.

> These papers were taken from the correspondence of the Mackinnon Papers, Gladstone Papers, and Dilke Papers.

*Documents relating to the history of Belgium and the Congo conserved in the Public Record Office, London. 1866–1903. 58 reels, positive.

> These documents in the majority are from the British Foreign Office and are composed of the diplomatic correspondence relating to the Congo (1879–1903) between the Foreign Office and diplomatic representatives abroad.

*Papers relating to the history of the Congo conserved at the British Library of Political and Economic Science, London School of Economics and Political Science. 32 reels, positive.

> These papers are composed of books, pamphlets, and articles of E. D. Morel.

The following titles are not in CAMP but are owned by the Center. Libraries can purchase a positive print for the cost of the positive plus one-third of the negative cost.

Church Missionary Society. Archives. 230 reels, negative.

> These records comprise all the papers of the Society, letters, journals, and mission books for the years 1799–1920, relating to Africa.

Great Britain. Colonial Office. African pamphlets. 24 reels, negative.

> These pamphlets collected by the Colonial Office are arranged in chronological order and concern the following areas and countries: Africa; Africa, Central; Africa, West; Congo; Gambia; Gold Coast; Lagos; Mauritius; Nigeria; Rhodesia; Sierra Leone.

Zang-Atangana, Joseph. 'Les partis politique camerounais.' Thesis, Institut Etudes Politiques, Université de Paris, 1963. 824 pp. 1 reel, negative and positive.

CAMP has purchased the following newspapers from the British Museum Newspaper Library.

United Kingdom newspapers on Africa:

African Times. London, 1860–1902. Monthly.
West Africa. London, May 1900–December 1906. Weekly.
West African Mail (African Mail). Liverpool, April 1903–January 1917. Weekly.

African newspapers:

African Interpreter & Advocate. Freetown, 1867–1869. Weekly. (Very imperfect.)
The Anglo-African. Lagos, June–December 1863, July 1864–December 1865. Weekly. (Imperfect.)
The Eagle and Lagos Critic. Lagos, March 1883–October 1888. Monthly.
Gold Coast Aborigine. Cape Coast, January 1898–June 1902. Weekly.
Gold Coast Assize. Cape Coast, November 1883–February 1884. Monthly.
Gold Coast Chronicle. Accra, June 1894–December 1901. Fortnightly.
Gold Coast Express. Accra, July–December 1897, September 1899–May 1900. Weekly.
Gold Coast Independent. Accra, December 1895, June 1896–February, September 1898. Weekly. (Imperfect.)
Gold Coast Leader. Cape Coast, 1902–1929. Weekly.
Gold Coast Methodist. Cape Coast, December 1896. Monthly.
Gold Coast News. Cape Coast, March–August 1885. Weekly.
Gold Coast Times. Cape Coast, March 1874–September 1875, November 1877–January 1878, February 1881–February 1885 (imperfect); January 1930–May 1936, November 1936–July 1940. Weekly.
The Independent. Freetown, December 1874–May 1878. Fortnightly.
Lagos Observer. March 1882–December 1888. Fortnightly.
Lagos Standard. February 1895–January 1920. Weekly.
Lagos Times. November 1880–October 1883. Fortnightly.
Lagos Weekly Record. August 1891–December 1913, May 1914–December 1921. Weekly. (Imperfect.)
The Mirror. Lagos, December 1887–November 1888. Irregular. (Very imperfect.)
Nigerian Chronicle. Lagos. November 1908–March 1915. Weekly.
Nigerian Pioneer. Lagos, February 1914–July 1934. Weekly.
Nigerian Times (Times of Nigeria). Lagos, April 1910–October 1911, January 1914–June 1915, November 1915–November 1920. Irregular.
Rand Daily Mail. Johannesburg, October 1905, November 1906–December 1925. Daily.

Rhodesia Herald. Salisbury, 1921–1926. Daily.

Times of Nigeria. 1914–1920. See *Nigerian Times.*

West African Reporter. Freetown, July 1876–December 1884. Weekly. (Imperfect.)

Western Echo. Cape Coast, November 1885–December 1887. Irregular.

Another newspaper being filmed by CAMP is the *East African Standard,* Nairobi, 1903–.

CAMP has acquired on negative microfilm the titles of the African serials that follow. Files will be as complete as possible.

African Studies. (Formerly *Bantu Studies.*) Johannesburg, Witwatersrand University Press, 1942–.

Afrika und Übersee: Sprachen, Kulturen. Berlin, 1910–.

Etudes Malgaches. Paris, Institut des Hautes Etudes de Tananarive, 1960–.

Historical Society of Ghana. *Transactions.* Achimoto, 1952–.

Institut d'Etudes Centrafricaines. *Bulletin.* Brazzaville, 1945– n.s. 1950–.

Présence Africaine: Revue Culturelle du Monde Noir. Paris, 1947–.

Recherches Africaines. (Superseded *Etudes Guinéennes,* IFAN, 1947–1959.) Conakry, Institut National de Recherche et de Documentation, 1960–.

Rhodes-Livingstone Journal. Manchester, Manchester University Press, 1944–.

Sierra Leone Studies. Freetown, 1918–.

Sudan Notes and Records. Khartoum, Sudan Philosophical Society, 1921–.

Tanganyika Notes and Records. (Journal of the Tanganyika Society.) Dar es Salaam, 1936–.

Uganda Journal. (Journal of the Uganda Society.) Kampala, 1934–.

West African Review. Liverpool. 1922–.

Zaïre: Revue Congolaise; Congolees Tijdschrift. Bruxelles, Editions Universitaires, 1947–.

CAMP will also film the publications of the Institut Français d'Afrique Noire (IFAN), Dakar—*Bulletin* and *Notes Africaines*—as well as allied publications as follows:

Etudes Dahoméennes	*Etudes Sénégalaises*
Etudes Mauritaniennes	*Etudes Soudanaises*
Etudes Nigériennes	*Etudes Voltaïques*

ARL FOREIGN NEWSPAPER MICROFILM PROJECT

The Association of Research Libraries (ARL) Foreign Newspaper Microfilm Project is a cooperative project begun in 1956 for the purpose of acquiring on microfilm important foreign newspapers.

It was evident that research libraries increasingly required access to the current foreign newspapers of many parts of the world. It was also evident that such broad coverage was expensive since many of the titles were subject to very limited use in any one library. As an answer to this problem the Association of Research Libraries proposed to create and maintain a national pool of current foreign newspapers on microfilm. The Center for Research Libraries was selected to house the film because of its strategic location and machinery to handle nation-wide loans fast.

Participants in the ARL Foreign Newspaper Microfilm Project pay a yearly subscription fee. This entitles them to borrow positive film of the holdings or purchase positive copies at cost (i.e., the cost of making a positive film). Nonsubscribers cannot borrow film, but they can purchase a positive copy for one-third the cost of the negative plus the cost of the positive.

The following African newspapers are held by the project. (The program is being expanded and will eventually include many newspapers held in England and Senegal.)

Algeria. *Echo d'Alger*. Algiers, January 1956–April 25, 1961 (ceased publication).
Congo (Brazzaville). *France-Equateur l'Avenir*. Brazzaville, January 1956–March 1960 (ceased publication).
——*Homme Nouveau*. Brazzaville, March 1960–.
Congo (Leopoldville). *Courrier d'Afrique*. Leopoldville, January 1956–.
Egypt. *Al-Ahram*. Cairo, January 1956–.
——*Egyptian Gazette*. Cairo, January 1952–.
Ethiopia. *Ethiopian Herald*. Addis Ababa, June 23, 1956–.
Ghana. *Daily Graphic*. Accra, January 1956–.
Kenya. *Daily Chronicle*. Nairobi, January 1956–May 1962 (ceased publication).
——*Daily Nation*. Nairobi, June 1962–.
Liberia. *Liberian Age*. Monrovia, January 1956–.
Morocco. *Maroc-Presse*. Casablanca, January–April 1956 (ceased publication).
——*Vigie Marocaine*. Casablanca, January 1957–.
Mozambique. *Noticias*. Lourenço Marques, January 1956–.
Nigeria. *Daily Times*. Lagos, January 1956–.
Rhodesia, Southern. *Rhodesia Herald*. Salisbury, January 1956–.
South Africa, Republic of. *Cape Times*. Cape Town, July 1938–.
——*Transvaler*. Johannesburg, January 1956–.
Sudan. *Morning News*. Khartoum, January 1960–.

ARL FOREIGN OFFICIAL GAZETTE PROJECT

The ARL Foreign Official Gazette Project, which began in 1958 with 13 Latin American gazettes, has now grown to include 100 gazettes from all over the world. At present there are 35 subscribers to the project, and each participant pays a yearly subscription fee. This entitles subscribers to borrow positive microfilm of the gazettes whenever needed. Nonsubscribers are not permitted to borrow film, but the Center will welcome any inquiries about joining the project.

The Center has only the positive film of the gazettes. Any institution wishing a positive microfilm for their own library should write to the New York Public Library.

Following are the African gazettes included in the ARL project:

Algeria. *Journal Officiel de l'Algérie*. 1960–.
——*Recueil des Actes Administratifs de la Délégation Générale du Gouvernment*. 1960–.

Angola. *Boletim Oficial.* 1960–.
Camerouns. *Journal Officiel.* 1960–.
Chad. *Journal Officiel.* 1959–.
Congo Republic. *Journal Officiel de la République du Congo.* 1960–.
French West Africa. *Journal Officiel.* 1960–.
Ghana. *Ghana Gazette.* 1960–.
——*Subsidiary Legislation—Supplement.* 1960–.
Guinea (Republic). *Journal Officiel de la République de Guinée.* October 1958–.
Ivory Coast. *Journal Officiel de la République de Côte d'Ivoire.* December 6, 1958–.
Kenya Colony and Protectorate. *Official Gazette* and legislative supplement. 1960–.
Malagasy Republic. *Journal Officiel.* October 18, 1958–.
Mali, Federation of. *Journal Officiel.* 1959–.
Nigeria. *Federation of Nigeria Official Gazette* and supplements. 1960–.
Nigeria, Eastern Region of. *Gazette* and supplements. 1960–.
Nigeria, Northern Region of. *Gazette* and supplements. 1960–.
Nigeria, Western Region of. *Gazette* and supplements. 1960–.
Nyasaland. *Government Gazette* and supplements. 1960–.
Rhodesia, Northern. *Northern Rhodesia Gazette* and supplements. 1960–.
Rhodesia, Southern. *Government Gazette* and supplements. 1960–.
Rhodesia and Nyasaland, Federation of. *Federal Government Gazette, Acts, &c.* 1960–.
Senegal. *Journal Officiel de la République du Sénégal.* 1960–.
Sierra Leone. *Sierra Leone Royal Gazette.* 1960–.
Somalia. [Official Gazette.] 1960–.
South Africa, Republic of. *Government Gazette.* 1960–.
Sudan. *Republic of the Sudan Gazette* and supplements. 1960–.
Tanganyika. *Tanganyika Gazette* and supplements. 1960–.
Togoland. *Journal Officiel de la République Autonome du Togo.* 1960–.
Uganda. *Official Gazette.* 1960–.
Zanzibar. *Official Gazette* and supplements. 1960–.

DISSERTATIONS

The dissertation collection at the Center consists of approximately 500,000 titles and includes both member deposits and the European universities collection formerly in the Library of Congress. The collection has only foreign dissertations, mostly German, French, and Dutch. No United States dissertations are held.

Since 1952, the Center has been receiving all printed dissertations of all the universities in France in all subject fields except medicine. Printed dissertations are also being received currently from universities and other higher education institutions in the following countries: Denmark, Germany, Hungary, the Netherlands, Sweden, and Switzerland.

Although the majority of the dissertations are on scientific and technical subjects, many are in the humanities and social sciences. Undoubtedly there is important source material relating to Africa in the collection. At present, the dissertation collection is shelved by author, and any subject approach to the collection would have to be by dissertation bibliographies.

THE UNIVERSITY OF CHICAGO

The Africa collection of the University of Chicago Library, Chicago 37, Illinois, consists of 5,000 titles and 53 serial publications. The collection concentrates upon a few geographical areas of the continent: Egypt, former British East Africa, the Republic of South Africa, and Northwest Africa. In the social sciences the strongest subject field is history, with over 3,000 titles, followed by ethnology, sociology, political science, religion, law, and education; the collection of philology in the Oriental Institute consists of 4,530 monographs and 120 serial publications of and about languages and literatures of Ancient Egypt and Arab Africa. The majority of publications in the collections date from the second half of the nineteenth century and from the twentieth century. In connection with the new research program at the University of Chicago, library collections will be expanded to include West African material. There will also be subject expansion to include more publications in economics and statistical materials, and the Law Library will intensify its acquisition of law publications and parliamentary debates.

The Library contains the papers of Orator F. Cook (1867–1949), a distinguished botanist who served most of his professional career with the United States Department of Agriculture. From 1891 to 1898, he was employed as special agent of the New York State Colonization Society and spent much of his time in Liberia. He was charged with the establishment of an industrial department as part of the College of Liberia. In 1896, Cook was elected president of Liberia College, a position he held until 1898. In addition to his teaching duties, he continued his botanical studies, collecting plant specimens, and he made a study of the problems of Negro colonization in Liberia.

The collection is made up of 2 manuscript boxes and deals principally with Cook's activities in Liberia. Most of the material falls into the period from 1891 to 1898. The papers include correspondence to Cook concerning the College of Liberia, mainly from the Board of Trustees of Donations for Education in Liberia, the various colonization societies, and missionaries in Liberia, as well as miscellaneous business materials, such as order sheets for provisions, invoices, bills and drafts, miscellaneous copies of West African newspapers, reports, articles, and photographs of Liberia. Also included in the collection is a group of letters on botanical topics from the noted American botanist Lucien M. Underwood (1853–1907), with whom Cook studied and worked at Syracuse. In connection with these letters, Dr. Helen Cook Newman, Dr. Cook's daughter and the donor of the papers, has available to scholars letters of a more personal nature from Underwood. There is, in addition, a group of letters concerning collections and specimens which Cook donated to various institutions.

Other African manuscripts include those of Louis de Curt (Manuscrits prévenant de Louis de Curt, Commissaire de la Marine, Vol. 1, 'Mémoires sur les colonies, sur le commerce,' and Vol. 2, 'Etablissements au de la du Cap de Bonne

Esperance,' 1771–1792). There are also interview notes and drafts by John Gunther for his book *Inside Africa* (1955), as well as proofs.

CHICAGO HISTORICAL SOCIETY

The Chicago Historical Society, North Avenue and Clark Street, Chicago, Illinois 60614, has a collection on the American Colonization Society, 1820–1858, of about 110 items. The collection contains correspondence and other papers, among them account sheets, the constitution of the Society, instructions to its agents, letters of introduction from the Board of Managers, and material on the formation of auxiliary societies, on the importance of suppressing the slave trade, on the African settlements, and on fund-raising measures. Correspondents include Eli Ayres, E. Bacon, Elias B. Caldwell, Henry Clay, Ralph Randolph Gurley, Harry D. Hunter, Joseph King, T. Kirkman, J. Macaulay, William McLain, John Mason, Joseph J. Roberts, Smith Thompson, and Thomas Tyson.

The Society also has South African items in their collection on William Layton Sammons (1801–1882): six letters and notes from Cape Town, 1867–1882, genealogical data, newspaper clippings, etc.—approximately 20 items, acquired in 1943 and 1953.

COLUMBIA UNIVERSITY

The African collections at Columbia University, New York, New York 10027, are divided among the University Libraries. The African collection in Butler Library, the main library on campus, numbers about 7,500 separate titles (there are approximately 4,300 books, serials, and monographs dealing with African history, travel, description, etc., approximately 1,200 items dealing with such varied topics as railroads and anthropology). There are scattered African holdings in the Science, Engineering, Botany-Zoology, Mathematics, Business (about 250 separate titles listed under economic conditions, commerce, public finance, etc.), and Fine Arts (about 150 separate titles concerned with African subjects, a third of which are about Ancient Egypt) Libraries.

In the Avery Architectural Library, the collection devoted to Africa consists of an approximate total of 350 separate titles or 500 volumes. Included in this figure are books on Ancient Egypt and Ancient Africa, which compose the greatest percentage of the above count (225 separate titles or 375 volumes). Planning reports from various African countries are beginning to reach the planning section of the Library. The only periodical currently received is the *South African Architectural Record*. Among the valuable items in this collection are the 12 volumes of Richard Lepsius' *Denkmäler aus Ägypten und Äthiopien nach den Zeichnungen der von Seiner Majestät dem Könige von Preussen Friedrich Wilhelm IV nach diesen Ländern Gesendeten und in den Jahren 1842–1845 ausgeführten wissenschaftlichen Expedition auf Befehl Seiner Majestät* (Berlin, Nicolaische Buchhandlung, 1849–1856) and various editions, including the original, of the Commission des Monuments d'Egypte study, *Description de l'Egypte; ou, Recueil des observations et des recherches qui ont été faites en Egypte pendant l'expédition de l'armée française, publié par les ordres de Sa Majesté l'Empereur Napoléon le Grand* (Paris, Imprimerie Impériale, 1809–1822).

The Music Library has approximately 30 books about African music. In the record collection, the number of recordings is considerable, including the Ethnic Folkways Series and the African Music Transcription Library of Gramophone Records, which is comprised of 30–40 recordings made in African villages of various tribes and presents a wide cross-section of African music.

Columbia University has acquired one of the largest and most comprehensive collections of ethnic music recordings in the world—'The Laura Boulton Collection of Traditional and Liturgical Music.' It consists of some 15,000 items of music and was acquired through a recent bequest to the University.

The collection of traditional music includes examples from many cultures in all parts of the world and is particularly strong in the music of Africa and the North American Indians. Mrs. Boulton collected the music in a series of 25 expeditions throughout the world, 7 of them in Africa. Some of the early African recordings were made on cylinders, some on discs, but all the more recent material is on tape.

In addition to recorded music, the collection includes musical instruments from many lands. Among the African musical instruments are drums from several regions, sansas, musical bows, etc. There are also many photographs pertaining to music and the dance.

Special Collections is comprised of rare items selected from the University Libraries (early printed books, rare editions, special copies, early manuscripts, etc.). For example, it includes a papyrus collection (700 papyri and 17 parchments), which dates from the third century B.C. to the sixth century A.D.; in large part, they are Greek papyri of the documentary type, although there are a few Latin pieces, along with a considerable number of Coptic items. In the Historical Map Collection, there are a few old maps of the African continent, including *Africa es magna orbis terrae descriptione Gerardi Mercatores desumpta, studio et industria* (G. M. Iuniores, 1609; 18½ × 15 in.). There are approximately 200 books on Africa in Special Collections, especially in the Phoenix Collection. Among the early printed books in Special Collections are Leo Africanus' *De totius Africae descriptione libri IX* (Tiguri per Andream Gesnerum. F. anno M.D.LIX; 14 p. l., 517 [i.e., 523], 21 p.; 16½ cm.); Sir Thomas Herbert's *Some Years Travels into Divers Parts of Africa and Asia the Great* (London, R. Everingham, for R. Scot, 1677), and Jodocus Crull's (?) *An Introduction to the History of the Kingdoms and States of Asia, Africa and America Both Ancient and Modern, According to the Method of Samuel Puffendorf* (London . . . printed by R. J. for T. Newborough, J. Knapton, and R. Burrough, 1705).

The Geology Library has one of the best collections of African geological materials in the country, although no serious effort has been made to specialize in this field. Under the regional geology (African) heading, the holdings number 350 separate titles or 600 volumes approximately, particularly geological surveys. In other areas, such as soils, petrology, and economic geology, the Library has about

200 volumes. It receives a number of African periodicals, for example, the *Journal of Geology of the UAR* and *African Soils*, as well as the Scientific Council for Africa South of the Sahara's proceedings of regional scientific meetings, published by the Commission for Technical Co-operation in Africa South of the Sahara. It also has an almost complete collection of the publications of the International Geological Congress of 1952, which was held at Algiers. The Library possesses little on physical geography in Africa. In the Map Collection, there are 15 drawers filled with geological and physical geography maps (topographic, climatic, etc.) and a vertical file collection consisting mostly of explanations of geological maps issued by various African governments.

The Law Library of Columbia University began collecting African materials on a greatly intensified scale about two years ago. The African legal material now numbers approximately 1,000 items. These fall primarily into the following categories: treatises and texts, periodicals, laws, codes, constitutions, and court decisions. Aside from the treatises and texts which comprise the greatest percentage, the breakdown is as follows: periodicals, 15; laws, 175; codes, 25; constitutions, 50; court decisions, 50. In addition, the Library is receiving gazettes of 12–15 newly independent countries, previous French, Italian, Dutch, and English territories, such as Somalia, Dahomey, Nigeria, Mali, Sierra Leone, etc.

The International Law section of the Law Library contains about 250 additional international law documents and treatises concerning Africa. It is also a depository for UN publications; for example, there are over 500 separate mimeographed items for the United Nations Economic Commission for Africa.

Manuscript Collections

The Slavery Collection, A.D. 1200–1833, in the Columbia University Libraries has letters and papers, 118 items, relating to slavery and the slave trade in England and the Americas.

Also held are papers, 1880–1903, of Frederick William Holls (1857–1903), lawyer and publicist, 26 volumes and 3 boxes. Included are correspondence and miscellaneous papers, relating in part to such matters as the South African War. Some 245 items are held for Sir Henry Rider Haggard (1856–1925), novelist and British imperial official in South Africa in the late 1800's.

Luther Evans

CORNELL UNIVERSITY

In the libraries of Cornell University, Ithaca, New York 14850, there are more than 18,000 volumes directly relating to Africa, of which over 15,000 are about sub-Saharan Africa. In addition, Cornell receives more than 150 serials and almost 300 annual government reports. Anthropological works on Africa total over 1,000 books. The main strength, however, consists in works of early travel and exploration and in political studies, both during and after the colonial period.

Acquistitions are being rapidly accelerated. As recently as nine years ago there was only a single index-card tray of African holdings under the Library of Congress index code DT, whereas now there are six such trays, i.e., more than 12,000 entries.

Recently several rare collections were purchased. One of these is a collection of confidential reports, at the post and province level, by officers of the administration of the former Belgian Congo, covering more than the last decade of Belgian rule.

Manuscript material includes the papers (about 4,000 items) of Bayard Taylor (1825–1878), traveler and author. Taylor wrote *A Journey to Central Africa* (1854) and a later work on Egypt (1874).

DARTMOUTH COLLEGE

The Library of Dartmouth College, Hanover, New Hampshire, has 100 pieces of material on Levi Woodbury (1789–1851), New Hampshire Senator and Secretary of the Navy, who was one of the prime movers in the establishment of official relations between the United States and Zanzibar in the 1830's. (See also Dartmouth College Museum under Art and Ethnographic Collections below.)

UNIVERSITY OF DELAWARE

The Library of the University of Delaware, Newark, Delaware, contains papers of Peter Strickland, manufacturers' agent and consul at Gorée, Senegal, 1883–1906, 1 linear foot.

DEPARTMENT OF STATE LIBRARY

The Library of the Department of State, located in the new State Department Building, C Street at 22d, N.W., Washington 25, D.C., is the oldest and one of the largest federal libraries. Founded in 1789, it has collected materials pertinent to the interests of the Department on all countries of the world and their peoples.

In the area of African studies, the collection is estimated at 30,000 volumes. This collection consists of monographic studies, serials, and official government documents of African states both in colonial and in independent status. While emphasis has been placed on publications produced in the countries themselves, much has also been acquired on a world-wide basis and in languages not in common use on the continent, including Slavic. Approximately 1,200 serial titles are received, and special effort has been made to acquire the official publications of each country, including official gazettes.

The subject coverage reflects the official interests of the Department. History and current political and economic conditions are well represented; subjects of less extensive coverage are law, cultural anthropology, and sociology.

DETROIT PUBLIC LIBRARY

The Burton Historical Collection of the Detroit Public Library, Detroit, Michigan, includes about 15,000 pieces on Etienne Dutilh and Company, Philadelphia export-import house. The name may be merely a variant of the contemporaneous Dutilh and Wachsmuth.

DICKINSON COLLEGE

The Dickinson College Library, Carlisle, Pennsylvania, contains typewritten diaries and reports of Martin Johnson (1884–1937) concerning his African expeditions, 1923–1925, through British East Africa.

DREW UNIVERSITY

The Drew University Library, Madison, New Jersey, contains journals, letters, and diaries of Methodist missionaries in Liberia, particularly those of S. M. E. Goheen ('Journal of a Voyage from Philadelphia to Monrovia 1837 as a Physician with Methodist Missionaries'), John Syes (papers and letters, 1835–1855), and Walter P. Jayne (journal, 1834–1841). The Library also possesses the papers (journals, correspondence, scrapbooks, etc.) of Joseph Crane Hartzell (1842–1928), who was the missionary bishop in Africa of the Methodist Episcopal Church from 1896 to 1916. Numerous periodicals, conference reports, and annuals of the Methodist and Methodist Episcopal Churches dealing with Africa are also held.

DUKE UNIVERSITY

Among the 1,648,774 volumes in the Duke University libraries, Durham, North Carolina, are an estimated 20,000 monographs, official and nonofficial serials, learned and professional journals, documents, etc., on various phases of African life—political, economic, social, and historical. This figure does not include a large collection on American Negro slavery and the slave trade.

Part of the Duke collection supports the University's work in the Divinity School and undergraduate and graduate religion departments. Among areas covered are the archaeology and history of Egypt and North Africa as Biblical lands; the history of Christian missions; African religions; Islam as a religion and culture; and Coptic liturgy, language, and church history.

The acquisition of library materials dealing with the British Commonwealth has been an objective of the Duke Commonwealth-Studies Center since the inception of its program in 1955. Emphasis has been placed on primary source materials, particularly public documents including parliamentary debates and papers, legal materials, reports of government departments, fiscal accounts, census materials, and economic and statistical reports. South Africa, Ghana, Nigeria, and the Rhodesias have been the African countries covered in this project.

In 1959 the Commonwealth-Studies Center compiled *A List of Selected Official Publications and Serials of the British Commonwealth in the Duke University Library*, which was distributed among libraries and interested individuals throughout the world. Approximately 115 African titles appear in this work. In addition, the Library has holdings of about ten African newspapers.

The Manuscript Department of Duke University contains valuable material pertaining to African slavery and its abolition and dating from the late eighteenth century to the American Civil War. Among manuscripts from the United States are those of John Richardson Kilby (1819–1878). Alexander Robinson Boteler (1815–1892), and Charles Wesley Andrews (1807–1875). Kilby was a Virginia lawyer active from 1840 to 1878. Andrews was an Episcopal rector representing Bishop Meade and the Page family. Their collections include letters from former slaves reporting conditions in Liberia. Both Kilby and Andrews were interested in the American Colonization Society, as was Congressman Boteler, whose papers refer to the beginnings of the American Colonization Society. The Library also holds the original journal kept by Dr. John Moore McCalla, Jr., on a voyage aboard the *Star of the Union*, June–December 1860, as special agent for the U.S. government and physician appointed by the American Colonization Society; the ship was chartered by the Society for the transportation of 'recaptured Africans' to Liberia. There is a large collection of Navy papers, 1804–1944, 10 volumes and some 500 items, and material can be found on Elie A. La Vallette (ca. 1790–1862), commander of the African Squadron,* 1851–1853. British manuscript material includes about 160 letters, mostly for the years 1814–1815, of William Wilberforce (1759–1833), M.P. and long-time leader of the British abolitionist movement, active also in the anti-slave trade movement; there are as well 34 letters written to William's son, Samuel Wilberforce (1809–1873), bishop of Winchester, about missionary activities of the Church of England in East Africa and various British colonies.

In addition, the Library has such items as the papers (164 items) of Matthew Fontaine Maury (1806–1873), noted oceanographer and astronomer who conducted oceanographic studies of the Indian Ocean and the South Atlantic. It also has letters (53 items, 1873–1913) of Garnet Joseph Wolseley (1833–1913), British army officer and viscount, which include a number relating to trouble with Africans in the Gold Coast in 1873 and events in the Sudan in the late 1880's.

DUQUESNE UNIVERSITY

The holdings of the Duquesne University Library, Pittsburgh, Pennsylvania, and the University's Institute of African Affairs specialize in missionary activities and linguistics. General materials include about 4,500 volumes, 217 periodicals, about 1,000 pamphlets, and 74 reels of microfilm. Archival materials include a complete collection of the *Bulletin, La Congregation du Saint-Esprit et du Saint Cœur de Marie*, Paris, bimonthly from 1857 to the present. This contains documents covering the missionary activities of the Holy Ghost Fathers in Africa from 1857. There are 37 records and tapes of music and language instruction in Swahili and Gio. Manuscripts include Phillip Bermel, CSSp., 'Idoma Grammar,' 7 chapters, typewritten; Robert Laessig, 'Nomen und Verbum in afrikanischen Sprachen: Eine Struktur-studie; Okpa Iho' (Bible history), 32 pp., typewritten, in Idoma; John M. Schreier,

---

* The African Squadron was engaged in suppressing the slave trade along the African coast. Matthew C. Perry became its first commander in 1843.

CSSp., 'English-Idoma Dictionary,' containing 4 notebooks totaling 267 pages and about 1,500 cards, all handwritten, dated 1942–1943. Hwa-Wei Lee, 'Africana at Duquesne University Library,' *African Studies Bulletin*, VI (October 1963), 25–27, gives more detailed information on this collection.

EMORY UNIVERSITY

The Library of Emory University, Atlanta, Georgia, holds the papers of Frederic E. Davis, seaman and soldier, for the period 1860–1863, 73 items. Two items, 'Journal of a Cruise to the East Coast of Africa and Arabia' (August 19, 1860–March 4, 1861) and a letter from Davis to his parents written September 30, 1860, from Zanzibar, are related to his experiences in Africa.

The Library also holds the following: Africa Provisional Central Conference Minutes (Methodist), 1943, 1952, 1956; Congo Mission Conference Minutes (Methodist), 1897, 1899, 1915, 1928–1933; Liberia Conference Minutes, 1893, 1897, 1899, 1901, 1903, 1910; Rhodesia Conference Minutes (Methodist), 1932–1938, 1940–1941, 1943, 1945, 1955, 1958; Southeast Africa Conference Minutes (Methodist), 1928–1929, 1932–1933, 1938–1939, 1940; Africa Provisional Central Conference Minutes, 1943, 1952, 1956 (handwritten).

FISK UNIVERSITY

The Negro Collection in the Fisk University Library, Nashville, Tennessee, contains nearly 1,000 books about African history. Other Africa-related materials include the Baldridge Collection and several hundred African museum pieces. The Baldridge Collection, which is on exhibit in the lobby and third-floor halls of the Library, consists of 68 African drawings by Cyrus Leroy Baldridge. Because of the broad scope of their subject matter and their authentic portraiture, they form one of the most complete records in America of native life and native types. The drawings were a gift from Samuel Insull of Chicago. The museum pieces (housed and exhibited in the Social Science Division Library) include such items as coiled basketry from the Mende of Sierra Leone, gourd rattles, ivory tusks, and African brasswork.

The American Missionary Association Archives, 1839–1879, contain more than 250,000 manuscripts. Materials relating to Africa include reports from missionaries in Sierra Leone and correspondence, pamphlets, and various other papers bearing on African slavery and the colonization of Africa, as well as the journal kept by H. M. Ladd while exploring in Africa for a mission station. The Archives are fully catalogued and may be used by bona fide scholars.

GIRARD COLLEGE

The papers of Stephen Girard, a Philadelphia merchant who was active in the East India trade, are held in the Library of Girard College, Corinthian and Girard Avenues, Philadelphia, Pennsylvania. Letters to Girard's agent, Martin Bickham, on the Ile de France (Mauritius), cover the period 1789–1824 and deal primarily with the Oriental trade and affairs of Mauritius.

HAMPTON INSTITUTE

The African holdings of the Huntington Memorial Library at Hampton Institute, Hampton, Virginia 23368, are primarily in the George Foster Peabody Collection on the Negro. There are an estimated 1,200 volumes on Africa, approximately 800 of which were published before 1940. The subject matter of these earlier volumes concentrates on discovery, geography, history, ethnography, biographies and literature, race relations, colonization, and missionary activity. (See also Hampton Institute College Museum under Art and Ethnographic Collections below.)

HARVARD UNIVERSITY

The Faculty of Arts and Sciences of Harvard University, Cambridge, Massachusetts, currently offers a variety of undergraduate and graduate courses and seminars that concern themselves exclusively with the history, government, and social organization of the peoples of northern and sub-Saharan Africa. The Department of Tropical Public Health in the School of Public Health, the Law School, and the School of Business Administration also find a place for Africa in their respective curricula. The Center for International Affairs has for a number of years sponsored an interdisciplinary faculty seminar on Africa. It has also supported research in the fields of African history and government and maintains a continuing interest through its Development Advisory Service in the economic problems of Africa.

The resources of the Harvard University library system serve these varied teaching and research needs. Of the more than 7 million volumes housed in the various constituent libraries of the University, approximately 34,000 form the core of the African collection. Much of this collection is scattered throughout the component libraries and, within each, shelved among a number of subject classifications. The largest single centralized Africana grouping is found, appropriately enough, under 'Africa,' in the Harry Elkins Widener Memorial Library. It contains about 14,000 books and periodicals. A total of about 6,000 additional volumes is classified according to language or under the categories 'folklore,' 'archaeology,' 'economics,' 'education,' 'sociology,' 'geography,' 'South America,' and 'Asia.' (Early printed titles are often housed, however, in the Houghton Library.) The Law School Library holds about 5,500 volumes pertaining to Africa; nearly half of its collection relates to the Republic of South Africa. The Library of the Peabody Museum of Archaeology and Ethnology contains about 2,400 volumes of monographs, 1,600 volumes of serials, and several hundred pamphlets, all of which, together with an index of periodical articles by author and subject, appear in the 53-volume printed catalogue of the Library (Boston, G. K. Hall and Co., 1963; plus 1-volume index to subject headings). The Andover-Harvard Theological Library of the Harvard Divinity School has about 700 volumes that deal with the churches of the Republic of South Africa and some 1,500 volumes on Protestant missions in tropical Africa. The libraries of the Harvard Schools of Medicine and Public Health, the Graduate School of Business Administration, the Graduate School of Public Administration, and the Museum of Comparative Zoology each contain several hundred books and serials directly relevant to the study of Africa. The Library of the Center for International Affairs also maintains a select collection of books and periodicals dealing with contemporary Africa.

For research purposes, the printed book resources of the Widener, Houghton, and Peabody Libraries are, despite the absence of any recent concerted acquisitions program, excellent. Nevertheless, no brief survey can do justice to such a vast collection. Of Africana published before 1800, the three libraries together hold numerous important and a variety of less significant titles. For the nineteenth century, their holdings are equally full. The Widener Library boasts a more than usually complete collection of travel literature, including the various compendia of Hakluyt and the Hakluyt Society, Pinkerton, and the Churchills and the books written or compiled on the basis of visits by a number of individual Europeans. It possesses a large array of slave-trade tracts, pamphlets, and contemporary disquisitions on the slave trade. Victorian and Edwardian authors are well represented, as are their French, Portuguese, German, Italian, and Spanish contemporaries. For the modern period, the Widener Library also possesses numerous publications in Afrikaans, and both the Peabody and the Widener Libraries hold nearly all of the most important ethnographical monographs published in English and French. Geological and zoological materials are housed in the Library of the Museum of Comparative Zoology. The Medical Library has largely acquired books pertaining to Africa in the fields of general public health, demography, nutrition, population control, and tropical medicine.

Government publications and other documents of exclusively African provenance are found in the Widener Documents Division. The debates of the colonial legislative councils and parliaments of many of the independent countries, nonself-governing territories, and federal organizations of Africa form a substantial part of this comparatively small collection. Widener Library possesses a full set of Ghanaian (formerly Gold Coast) *Debates* from 1926, an incomplete set of Nigerian *Debates* from 1924, the *Official Gazette* of the High Commissioner for Basutoland, Bechuanaland, and Swaziland from 1926 to 1963, and the complete *Proceedings* of the African Representative Council (not to be confused with the Legislative Council) of Northern Rhodesia (now Zambia) from 1946 to 1958. Additional Nigerian documents appear to be comparatively abundant. Widener Library also holds a typescript catalogue of the Archives of Basutoland, a number of assorted British and French doctoral dissertations pertaining to Africa, and the numerous graduate and undergraduate theses on Africa written by students in the Harvard Faculty of Arts and Sciences. In addition, the Law School Library acquires the official gazettes of many of the same countries and dependencies. It also collects law reports and other government publications relating to legal matters and holds a few proceedings of the nonelected legislatures of former African colonies. It is particularly strong in South African legal documents, for which it remains the principal Farmington Plan library. The Medical Library holds the pertinent publications of the World

Health and Food and Agriculture Organizations of the United Nations and reports from various parts of the British Commonwealth.

The Corporation Records Division of the Baker Library of the Graduate School of Business Administration maintains extensive files of company reports. It receives the annual reports of about 100 companies incorporated in Africa (mainly in Zambia and the Republic of South Africa). Many of these files represent substantial long runs. Among the more important Zambian concerns represented in the Baker Library collection are Nchanga Consolidated Copper Mines Ltd. (1938–1964), Rhodesian Anglo-American Ltd. (1930–1962), Rhodesian Selection Trust Ltd. (1929–1963), Rhokana Corp. Ltd. (1924–1963), and Roan Antelope Copper Mines Ltd. (1928–1961). The only Rhodesian firm represented by a long run is the Wankie Colliery Co. Ltd. (1945–1963). South African companies are African Explosives & Chemicals Industries Ltd. (1938–1963), Anglo-Aldha Cement Ltd. (1935–1963), Anglo-American Corp. of S.A. Ltd. (1927–1963), De Beers Consolidated Mines Ltd. (1890–1891, 1911–1962), Anglo-Transvaal Consolidated Investment Co. Ltd. (1934–1963), Brakpan Mines Ltd. (1923–1963), Modderfontein Deep Levels Ltd. (1915–1952), Natal Navigation Collieries & Estate Co. Ltd. (1925–1962), Rand Leases (Vogelstruisfontein) Gold Mining Co. Ltd. (1933–1964), Rand Mines Ltd. (1917–1964), Simmer and Jack Mines Ltd. (1924–1963), Union Corp. Ltd. (1902–1963), Vlakfontein Gold Mining Co. Ltd. (1935–1963), and Vogelstruisbult Gold Mining Areas Ltd. (1933–1963). In addition, the Library also holds the annual reports of several important railways and airlines: Benguella Railway Co. (1919–1937), Central African Airways Corp. (1951–1962), East African Airways (1950–1962), Mashonaland Railway Co. Ltd. (1905–1936), Rhodesian Railways Ltd. (1903–1949), and West African Airways Corp. (1947–1961). Of the many European industrial companies operating in Africa, the Library also maintains numerous files: British South Africa Co. (1896–1963), Tanganyika Concessions Ltd. (1910–1963), Compagnie du Congo pour le Commerce et l'Industrie (1953–1962), Compagnie du Katanga (1951–1963), Société des Mines d'Or de Kilo-Moto S.C.R.L. (1930–1963), and Union Minière du Haut-Katanga (1908–1963).

The Harvard University libraries possess complete runs of nearly all the major periodicals that, from 1800 to the present, have included material pertaining to Africa. In addition to the standard journals of European and American origin, the Widener collection includes the *Journal of the African Society* (now *African Affairs;* 1901 to date), *Bulletin du Comité de l'Afrique Française* (1891 to date), *Bantu Studies* (now *African Studies;* 1921 to date), *Revue Africaine* (1856 to date), *Bulletin de la Société de Géographie et d'Archéologie de la Provence d'Oran* (1882 to date), *Archives Marocaines* (1904–1927), *Bulletin de la Société de Géographie de l'Alger* (1896–1935), *Recueil de la Société Archéologique, Historique et Géographique du Départment de Constantine* (1853–1957), *Revue Tunisienne* (1894–1939), *Sudan Notes and Records* (1918 to date), *Egypte Contemporaine* (1910 to date), *Bulletin de Comité d'Etudes Historiques et Scientifiques d'Afrique Occidentale Française* (1919–1938), *African Observer* (Bulawayo, 1934–1937), *Congo: Revue Générale de la Colonie Belge* (1920–1940), *African News* (1889–1894), *Annuaire de Madagascar* (1898–1903), *Friend of Africa* (1841–1843), *Portugal em Africa* (1894–1910), *Reports of the Directors of the*

African Institution (1807–1827), and the proceedings and journals of the Royal Geographical Society (London), the Bombay Geographical Society, and the Geographical Society of India.

The Library of the Peabody Museum is particularly rich in journals published in or about the Congo, Egypt, the Sudan, Rhodesia and Zambia, Uganda, Kenya, and South Africa and holds the relevant publications of the Belgian Académie Royale des Sciences Coloniales, a complete collection of the bulletins and *mémoires* of the Institut Française d'Afrique Noire (Dakar), and numbers of the journals and monographs published by the former branches of the Institut in Dahomey, Cameroun, the Ivory Coast, and the Congo (Brazzaville). (See also Harvard University, Peabody Museum, under Art and Ethnographic Collections below.) The publications of the historical societies of individual African countries are fully represented by long runs. It is noticeably weak only in Ghanaian, Malagasy, Ethiopic, and Malawian material, portions of which are covered by periodicals in the Widener and Comparative Zoology Libraries. The Andover-Harvard Theological Library holds a number of mission-oriented periodicals, including a complete set of *Echoes of Service* (originally the *Missionary Echo*), which from 1881 printed letters from Plymouth Brethren missionaries in northern and central Africa. It remains a primary source for the activities in Africa of the Christian Missions in Many Lands. Other, more specialized, periodicals are housed in the Medical Library.

The Center for International Affairs has, since 1959, received a number of African newspapers and periodicals. It now takes the *Jeune Afrique* (formerly *Afrique Action*), *Afrique Nouvelle*, *Central African Examiner*, *Contact*, and several of the other standard sources of current information about Africa. Widener Library also subscribes to most of the same periodicals.

MANUSCRIPT AND ARCHIVE COLLECTIONS

The American Board of Commissioners for Foreign Missions has deposited 107 volumes of records pertaining to its African missions in Houghton Library. Nearly all the volumes, which are indexed, contain in-letters from the American Board's Missions to Zululand, Rhodesia, and West Africa. They cover the period from 1834 to 1949 and may be consulted only with the permission of the United Church Board for World Ministries, 14 Beacon Street, Boston.

The Houghton Library also houses 5 boxes of the African papers of the Presbyterian Board of Missions for the years 1857–1911. The papers themselves are in a poor state of preservation, and the Presbyterian Commission on Ecumenical Mission and Relations (475 Riverside Drive, New York) prefers that the microfilm copies—which it retains—should be consulted rather than the originals. In any case, only the Commission can authorize persons to use the papers.

The papers of the late Professor Raymond L. Buell, author of the two-volume pioneer study, *The Native Problem in Africa* (New York, 1928), and shorter studies of Liberia, have been given to the Houghton Library. In the Library's Kipling Collection, some of his writings appear in the form of clippings from African newspapers. The Houghton Library has as well papers (about 1,100 items) of

Bayard Taylor (1825–1878), traveler and author who wrote *A Journey to Central Africa* (1854) and a later work on Egypt (1874).

The Medical School Library has a diary kept by Simeon Burt Wolbach (1880–1954), Harvard Medical School pathologist, on an expedition to the Gambia in 1911.

The Baker Library of the Harvard School of Business Administration contains the following manuscript collections:

Melatiah Bourn, Silvanus Bourn, Timothy Bourn, Nathaniel Holmes, and Samuel Sturgis, eighteenth-century Boston merchants engaged in fishing and whaling expeditions off Africa, accounts, current bills, references to whaling ships and merchant vessels, 2 linear feet.

James DeWolf (1764–1837), slave trader of Bristol, Rhode Island, papers, 3 volumes, 1 box.

Ephraim Emerton (1791–1877) and James Emerton (1789–1835), Salem merchant and sea captain, business records, 1816–1835—correspondence, logbooks, account books, invoices, including records of business at Majunga (Madagascar), Mozambique, and other places, 5 volumes, 1 box.

Aaron Lopez (1731–1782), merchant and slave trader of Newport, Rhode Island, papers, 4 volumes.

B. S. Pray & Co., Boston export-import firm engaged in South African trade, business records, 1868–1926 (total of 120 linear feet of records includes other business interests).

William Rotch (1734–1828), major Nantucket and New Bedford whaling merchant, papers.

ROBERT I. ROTBERG and YEN-TSAI FENG

HAVERFORD COLLEGE

The Library of Haverford College, Haverford, Pennsylvania, contains about 500 volumes on Africa. There is a small amount of material in the Quaker collection on slavery and the Friends' stand against it. Rare items include the following: John Ogilby, *Africa: Being an Accurate Description of the Regions of Aegypt . . . Billedulgerid [Numidia], the Land of Negroes, Guinee, Aethiopia, and the Abyssines* (London, 1670); Anthony Benezet, *A Short Account of That Part of Africa Inhabited by the Negroes* (Philadelphia, 1762), and a German edition (1763); and James Cropper, *American Colonization Society* (from the *Tourist*, London, 1833), broadsheet, disapproving of the Society.

The Quaker collection also has papers relating to Negroes, between 1676 and 1937, about 200 items, in part photocopies—letters, journals, articles, essays, manumissions, minutes, testimonies, accounts, pictures, and printed items relating to the slave trade, slavery, abolition, freedmen's activities, and discrimination, primarily in the Americas. The bulk of the material is from the period 1775–1875 and includes an account entitled 'The History of the Rise, Progress and the Accomplishment of the Abolition of the African Slave Trade,' written (partly in his hand) in 1840 by Thomas Clarkson (1760–1846).

HOWARD UNIVERSITY

Africana at Howard University, Washington, D.C., developed as records on the African background of the American Negro were required to supplement the Library's collection of works written by and about persons of African descent.

Among the first books acquired by the Library soon after Howard University was incorporated on March 2, 1867, were titles on Africa. Some of the founders of the University interested in foreign missions donated to the Library their files on periodicals, books of travel and description, histories of Africa, and biographies of missionaries. Among these was the first edition of Churchill's *Collection of Voyages and Travels* issued in four volumes in 1704; seven editions of the works of Hiob Ludolf, the Elder (. . . *Historia Aethiopica*, 1681; . . . *Aethiopicam . . . commentarius*, 1691; . . . *Lexicon Amharico*, 1698; . . . *Grammatica Aethiopica*, 1702; *A New History of Ethiopia*, 1682 and 1684); Barbot's *Description of the Coasts of North and South Guinea* (1732); the 1639 reissue of the 1632 edtion of *Africae descriptio* of Leo Africanus; and works of travel by Bosman, Proyart, Kolbe, Bruce, Smith, Vaillant, and Sparrman. Some of the serial files presented were the *Missionary Herald* (1821–1882), *Africa's Luminary* (1839–1840), *African Repository* (1825–1900), *Mouvement Antiesclavagiste* (1889–1906), *Liberia* (1892–1908), *Journal of the Royal Geographical Society* (1833–1849), *Afrique Explorée et Civilisée* (1879–1882), and *Bulletin du Comité de l'Afrique Française* (1891–1919).

In 1873, the University Library received the extensive antislavery collection of Lewis Tappan comprising about 2,000 printed and nonprinted items on the American Colonization Society, on the African slave trade and its suppression, and on the abolition of slavery.

In gifts from the private Negro collection of Jesse Edward Moorland, a former member of Howard's Trustee Board, received by the Library in 1914 and 1940 were a number of books on Africa, as well as manuscript letters written by African students who in the 1920's while enrolled in leading universities corresponded with Dr. Moorland, the then adviser to the African Student Union. Among these were Simbini Mamba Nkomo of Southern Rhodesia, S. B. Mfoafo, and Charles G. Blooah, who later enabled George Herzog to publish *Jabo Proverbs from Liberia* (1936). Other African writers were James Emman Aggrey and M. Q. Cele.

By 1923, three courses relating to the culture and civilization of the Negro people in Africa were being offered in the Department of History. Today, at least thirty courses on Africa are offered along with a number of courses which include the African background.

In 1930, publications on the Negro in the main University Library were withdrawn from the shelves and brought together with the Tappan, Moorland, and smaller gift collections on the Negro and organized into a collection calculated to meet the needs of the inquiring student or scholar interested in Negro history and of educational agencies and institutions requiring such information as might be present in Howard's unique African library. There followed a rapid expansion of the collection as books, pamphlets, serials, and newspapers on Africa were acquired, together with writings which reflected the American Negro's interest in Africa.

With the purchase in 1946 of the Arthur B. Spingarn Collection of Negro authors many titles of African authorship were added. Some of the rarest titles received were those written by sixteenth-, seventeenth-, and eighteenth-century Africans who were transplanted to Europe and in whom advantages of education wrought a scholarship the equal of any in their day.

Juan Latino, one of the most interesting Africans of the Spanish renaissance, published two volumes. One, *The Austriados*, published in 1573 at Granada, is an epic poem on the battle of Lepanto. The second work, published in 1576, is a collection of poems and epigrams in honor of the tombs and sarcophagi of the kings and queens of Spain, in the Escorial, cathedrals, and palaces. No other copy of the latter volume has been located. Also rare are two volumes written by Jacobus Eliza Capitein and published in Leiden in 1742 and 1744. On March 10, 1742, Capitein delivered an oration in Latin on the question 'Is slavery contrary to Christian freedom or not?' This discourse was later published under the title *Dissertatio politico theologica, qua disquiritur*. . . . His other volume in the collection contains sermons which he preached in Leiden.

References to Africa may be found in many of the early printed sermons, narratives, speeches, and poetry produced by the first generation of Africans imported to America and also in later published slave narratives and fictional works written to promote the abolition of slavery.

Mr. Spingarn has continued yearly to donate approximately 1,000 recently published works, out-of-print books and pamphlets, creative writings by contemporary Africans, vernacular materials, and serials, as well as many ephemeral items which seem of increasing interest to the Africanists. Publications of the small printers in the Eastern Region of Nigeria, in particular the novels from Port Harcourt and Onitsha, the vernacular pamphlets issued by the Eagle Press (Nairobi), and the Yoruba language texts printed by Longmans of Nigeria and the African Universities Press are examples of the material now in demand. The up-to-dateness of Nigerian publications is illustrated by recent acquisitions such as *Twilight out of the Night* (Ibadan, 1964, 139 pp.), a collection of poems written by Dr. E. Latunde Odeku, a brilliant, American-educated psychiatrist; *The Constitution of the Federal Republic of Nigeria* (1963); and *The Report of the Commission on the Review of Wages, Salary and Conditions of Service of the Junior Employees of the Governments of the Federation and in Private Establishments, 1963–64*, known as the Morgan Report.

Relationships between Africa and Brazil, Haiti, Cuba, and the English- and French-speaking West Indies where African survivals were strong can readily be followed in works by Latin American scholars who have long been interested in African studies. The Afro-Brazilian collection of about 800 titles is significant and has been purchased over the past twenty years largely from Brazil. Among the Brazilian authors represented in the collection whose works are important are Renato Mendonça, Nelson de Senna, Evaristo de Moraes, Manoel Querino, Edison Carneiro, Camara Cascudo, Gilberto Freyre, Braz Hermenegildo Armaral, Gonçalves Fernandes, Vicente Lima, and Nino Rodriques.

Important for the Africanist is the collection of African artifacts housed in the art gallery of the new Fine Arts Building. This rapidly growing collection, consisting primarily of the Alain LeRoy Locke Collection of African Sculpture, contains 400 objects representing some of the major art-producing centers of West African culture. Many of the objects are of wood, ivory, or brass, but the largest number consists of a diversified group of gold weights from Ghana and the Ivory Coast. Other items of less importance, such as handicrafts and musical instruments, illustrate in a limited way decorative and industrial art as practiced today among the Vai, Temne, and Mende tribal groups in Liberia and Sierra Leone. During the past four years numerous examples of the high tribal arts of West Africa and the handicrafts of both East and West Africa have been added by gift, purchase, or loan. Also of interest are the Art Department's collection of 500 photographs of African art and architecture given by the Museum of Modern Art of New York and the Carnegie Art Teaching set of photographic reproductions of representative artifacts and historical monuments of ancient Egyptian and Arabic civilizations. There are several hundred slides devoted to African art. The Department of Art now offers a course on the art and architecture of Black Africa and a course on Negro art which includes the related African-American experience in painting and sculpture.

Today, the Negro collection has about 95,000 catalogued and indexed items of which about 10,000 are specifically on Africa. There are nearly 500 serial titles relating to Africa and 164 African newspaper titles. Some of the antislavery serials directly concerned with Africa, such as the *Anti-Slavery Monthly Reporter* (later the *Anti-Slavery Reporter and Aborigines' Friend;* 1825 to date), supplement titles on the African slave trade and African colonization. Also in the collection are shorter runs of useful periodicals—*Sudan Notes and Records* (1918–1955), *Uganda Journal* (1934–1956), *Tanganyika Notes and Records* (1936–1957), *Bulletin de Recherches Soudanaises* (No. 1, 1936–No. 8, 1937), and *Revue des Colonies* (1834–1841), edited by Cyrille Charles Auguste Bissette. The *Revue*, the first French Negro periodical, protested conditions in French overseas posseessions. African newspapers are being microfilmed as funds become available. Some of these, printed by the Zik Press, were donated over a period of years by the President of the Federal Republic of Nigeria, Dr. Nnamdi Azikiwe, who was once a student at Howard University.

Manuscript holdings are few, but items of interest are coming to light as collections are processed. One of the important manuscript volumes is John Clarkson's diary (August 6, 1791—March 18, 1792) entitled 'Clarkson's Mission to America.' It contains the memorial and petition of Thomas Peters and information on the efforts of the Sierra Leone Company to establish a settlement of free Negroes on the African coast. John's brother Thomas Clarkson, the English philanthropist and abolitionist, is represented in the collection by about 50 items. Another manuscript item is the diary of Charles Brown, who describes his trip to Africa in 1921 and 1922. Brown, as a representative of the Lott Carey Mission, had gone to Monrovia and Sierra Leone, where he conferred with missionaries concerning needs and work of the missions. These he describes in this diary. The

Thomas Narven Lewis Papers, 1898–1934, contain about 80 items. Lewis, a Liberian, studied medicine in the United States and upon his return to Grand Bassa, Liberia, in 1907 attempted to reduce the Bassa language to a written one. The first work he printed in Bassa was the Lord's Prayer. His letters, chiefly to Frank Clawson, tell of his efforts to build a school and hospital.

The collection possesses a unique letter written by Gustavus Vassa and dated London, September 30, 1794, as well as an autographed presentation copy of the 1794 London edition of his narrative which contains a page and a half presentation statement.

The Library contains all the Folkways Library Records, the Laura C. Boulton records on the Straus West African Expedition, the Tribal and Folk Music of West Africa by Arthur S. Alberts, and several tapes made in Monrovia of Liberian songs, drum music, and addresses of President William V. S. Tubman. A pamphlet file of a dozen drawers arranged by country frequently yields needed information, as do the numerous mounted newspaper clippings which have been retained over the years. Among the clippings may be found more than 240 mounted pages on the Italo-Ethiopian War. There is also a large scrapbook of clippings on the South African tour of Orpheus McAdoo and his Jubilee Singers who toured South Africa for three years.

Unpublished card indexes and typed lists serve as finding aids to some of the materials in the collection, such as the 10,000-card index to music by Negro composers and compositions based on an African or Negro idiom. These aids supplement the dictionary card catalogue, which also includes references to articles in periodicals not covered by the periodical indexes, as well as author and subject entries for reprints and abstracts. The identification of authors as African or Negro writers has been included on the main-entry catalogue card when known.

In 1958, *A Catalogue of the African Collection* was published which lists 4,865 books and pamphlets, 250 periodical titles, and 64 newspaper titles. This catalogue is now out of date. A bibliography of works of authors of African descent is in preparation, and a compilation of African newspaper and periodical holdings was scheduled for distribution in the very near future. An index to the *Journal of Negro Education* (1930–1962) has recently been published. Other aids published by the staff of the Negro collection to help locate information of African interest are 'Early American Negro Writings: A Bibliographical Study,' *Papers of the Bibliographical Society of America*, XXXIX (Third Quarter, 1945), 192–268; 'Library Resources for the Study of Negro Life and History,' *Journal of Negro Education*, V (April 1936), 232–244; 'A Bibliographical Checklist of American Negro Writers about Africa,' *Africa Seen by American Negroes* (Paris, Présence Africaine, 1958), pp. 379–399; 'The African Collection at Howard University,' *African Studies Bulletin*, II (January 1959), 17–21; 'Research Centers and Sources for the Study of African History,' *Journal of Human Relations*, VIII (1960), 54–63; 'Notes on Some African Writers,' in U.S. National Commission for UNESCO, *Africa and the United States: Images and Realities*, Background Book (1961), pp. 165–173; 'Fiction by African Authors: A Preliminary Checklist,' *African Studies Bulletin*, V (May 1962), 54–66.

In the light of the increasing demand on the resources and services of the collection, it will be necessary to keep adding material. Funds are being sought in order that this may be done on a continuing basis.

The reading room, named for Jesse Edward Moorland, is open to readers between the hours of 9:00 A.M. and 5:30 P.M. Monday through Friday and from 9:00 A.M. to 1:00 P.M. Saturday.

DOROTHY PORTER

HUNTINGTON LIBRARY AND ART GALLERY

The Henry E. Huntington Library and Art Gallery, San Marino, California, contains the following manuscript materials:

James Brydges, 1st duke of Chandos, two large folio volumes, one containing papers, ca. 1725, that relate to African affairs and include a voyage up the Gambia, notes on fortifications, etc., transcribed for the duke, and the other comprising a collection of remarkable papers, ca. 1735, transcribed for the duke on various topics, among them the Royal African Company.

Sir Richard Francis Burton (1821–1890), British explorer and consul in Africa, about 120 items.

Thomas Clarkson (1760–1846), leading British abolitionist associated with the establishment of Sierra Leone, 210 items.

Sir Henry Rider Haggard (1856–1925), novelist and British imperial official in South Africa in the late 1800's, about 215 items.

Zachary Macaulay (1768–1838), prominent British abolitionist, about 1,000 items, including a journal while Governor of Sierra Leone, 1793–1799, and some letters about slavery in West Africa.

Matthew Fontaine Maury (1806–1873), noted oceanographer and astronomer, who conducted oceanographic studies of the Indian Ocean and the South Atlantic, 165 items.

William Collins Mosher, notebook, 1814–1906, including letters of Laura and Silas Johnson, Presbyterian missionaries in Africa, 1904–1906.

Bayard Taylor (1825–1878), traveler and author who wrote *A Journey to Central Africa* (1854) and a later work on Egypt (1874), 460 items.

INDIANA UNIVERSITY

Indiana University, Bloomington, Indiana, has had an African Studies Program since 1960. Although the Program has progressed at a phenomenal rate in terms of total faculty and student involvement and number and range of courses offered, the library collection of Africana does not yet reflect the caliber of the other aspects of the Program. It will take several more years' work before the current investment in time and effort will show a visible dividend and Indiana will have the first-rate collection it intends to have.

The African collection is primarily devoted to the social sciences and the humanities, though material on the social aspects of law and medicine is also included. The natural sciences do not fall within the purview of the African collection—these are the responsibility of the branch libraries serving the scientific departments. A generous grant from the Ford Foundation for African acquisitions provided the stimulus for the Library to recruit a bibliographer in mid-1963 to direct the growth of the collection, which by the end of 1964 comprised some 7,000 volumes of books and bound periodicals.

Prior to 1960 the bulk of the material in the collection was essentially academic in nature. Publications in languages other than English were poorly represented. Hence the collection is strongest in English-language publications on anthropology, linguistics, and folklore. Folklore has been a long-standing interest at Indiana, and there is a Folklore Library located in a separate room in the Main Library. Recent acquisition work on out-of-print material has tended to concentrate on standard accounts by missionaries, travelers, administrators, and the like, in order to satisfy the needs of students in government and history who have had particular difficulty in finding material to complete assignments.

The present aim is to build a collection concerning sub-Saharan Africa which will contain every significant work in the major European languages published since 1959 and the most important material issued before that date. Special emphasis has been given to West Africa, and it is intended to build additional strength around current research interests in Sierra Leone.

The Seminar on Contemporary Africa held in the second semester each year is devoted to 'The Humanities in Sub-Saharan Africa,' and this never fails to generate considerable interest among students in the literature, music, and arts of Africa. In response to the demands thus created the Library is paying particular attention to these topics and is attempting to build a comprehensive collection of neo-African literature.

Although 160 serial titles are currently taken, 90 of which are African imprints, subscriptions to the majority were initiated only a year or two ago, and even the most important titles are not represented by lengthy runs. An effort is being made to remedy the situation by purchase of back files in original paper or reprint or, failing this, in microform. Only two African newspapers—*Afrique Nouvelle* and *Moniteur Africaine*—are currently received in paper form. The Library is looking to microfilm for the back files and semicurrent holdings in this space-consuming category.

Little attention has been given to the problem of African government documents. Documents published by the colonial offices of the colonial powers are not well represented at Indiana. As a depository library Indiana has excellent holdings of U.S. documents and those of the United Nations and its agencies, but the collection of foreign documents is weak in comparison. In response to pressing demands the Library is paying particular attention to development plans, census reports, and other statistical publications relating to economic development in Africa, and the scope of the collection will be broadened to take in additional interests in the near future.

While the acquisition of pamphlets, party political material, and other kinds of ephemera has not so far been tackled in a dynamic fashion, the Library nevertheless has a small collection of about 400 items which is slowly growing. This collection is not catalogued but is filed in pamphlet boxes by subject in the office of the bibliographer where it may be consulted by students. African nationalist parties of Mozambique, Basutoland, Rhodesia, and South Africa have, or have had, organizations in Cairo publishing political pamphlets and newsletters. This material comes to Indiana by virtue of its participation in the Public Law 480 program for the United Arab Republic.

Most of the African collection is housed in the University Main Library, but it is scattered throughout the stacks according to the Library of Congress classification. In the new library building, now planned for occupation in the fall of 1969, the collection will be brought together near a separate reading area.

In addition to the holdings of the Main Library, there are small collections of useful material in some of the other libraries on the Bloomington campus. The Law Library possesses recent textbooks, periodicals, decisions, and statute law of some of the African countries, notably the English-speaking ones. The Library of the Institute for Sex Research includes a small collection of anthropological material relating to Africa. The Department of Fine Arts has a good basic collection of books on African art, most of which, with the exception of certain rare and expensive items like Kjersmeier's *Centres de style de la sculpture nègre africaine* (4 vols., Paris and Copenhagen, 1935–1938), are duplicated in the Main Library. Books and periodicals on African music are held in the Main Library and not in the Music Library, but the latter has a few older titles not in the Main Library's collection.

The University's collection of rare, valuable, and antiquarian books and manuscripts is established in the Lilly Library. There the recently acquired Mendel Collection is outstanding for its holdings of general material concerning the great age of geographical discovery and European expansion. The Lilly Library has only a few of the seventeenth- and eighteenth-century works relating to Africa, and those that it has are largely concerned with the slave trade. There are no manuscript collections of African interest.

Indiana has two collections of material at least one of which is currently of greater significance than its book collection. The lesser known of the two is the collection of art objects numbering some 500 pieces (western Sudan, Guinea coast, Congo, South Africa) and held in the Museum of the Department of Fine Arts.

The other collection is in the Archives of Traditional Music, better known by its old name, Archives of Folk and Primitive Music—a repository of recordings of folk music, tribal music, cultivated music of the Orient, and certain types of popular music as well as recordings of verbal folklore (tales, proverbs, etc.). The collection numbers more than 5,000 cylinders, 1,300 original tapes, 3,000 field discs and 400 commercially published discs, and 300 albums; the Archives' own collection of copy tapes numbers over 3,000. The total collection amounts to more than 100,000 individual pieces (i.e., songs, instrumental recitals, and oral folklore recitations). Approximately a fifth of the total relates to Africa, and significant items are the 234 cylinders cut in Dahomey and West Africa by Melville Herskovits and the bulk of the 'Sound of Africa' series issued by the International Library of African Music.

There are also musical instruments and photographs and manuscripts relating to the recordings on deposit.

Within the restrictions imposed by the depositors tape copies of recordings and Verifax copies of the accompanying documentation are furnished at stated fees to anyone interested. The Archives support collecting by faculty members and students of the University through the loan of recording tape and equipment and, under appropriate circumstance, field collecting by individuals not connected with the University.

As a further service the Archives publish in association with the Indiana University Folklore Archives the *Folklore and Folk Music Archivist*. This periodical is devoted to the collection, documentation, indexing, and cataloguing of folklore and folk music; it also includes articles based primarily on unpublished manuscripts or recordings of traditional materials which are on deposit in archives and similar institutions and which are accessible to other scholars. With three issues per year, the annual subscription cost is $2.00. The Archives also issue a series of commercial disc albums, through Folkways Records, Inc., of selected recordings on deposit.

ALAN TAYLOR

IOWA STATE DEPARTMENT OF HISTORY AND ARCHIVES

The Iowa State Department of History and Archives, Historical Building, Des Moines, Iowa, has 6 volumes of correspondence and 7 volumes of other papers of John A. Kasson (1822–1910, politician and diplomat) for the period 1844–1910. Kasson was head of the American delegation to the Berlin Conference (1884–1885), which dealt primarily with Congo Basin problems. From the Fred W. Wead Collection there are several letters to Kasson by correspondents who include H. S. Sanford, Alphonso Taft, and Josiah Leeds.

UNIVERSITY OF KENTUCKY

The correspondence of the Gordon family (1771–1924) and the Shelby family in the University of Kentucky Library, Lexington, Kentucky, contains material dealing with the colonization of Negroes in Liberia.

LIBRARY COMPANY OF PHILADELPHIA

The Library Company of Philadelphia, Pennsylvania, holds extracts from the De Vries voyages: *Korte historiael ende journal Aenteyckeninge van verscheyden Voyagiens in de vier Deelen des Wereldts Ronde, als Europa, Africa, Asia ende America*, by David Pietersz de Vries, 1655, relating to his first voyage in 1630 and a third one in 1644, 35 pp.

THE LIBRARY OF CONGRESS

The Library of Congress holdings of works from or relating to Africa were described in the *African Studies Bulletin* of January 1959. The present article is a very necessary revision and updating of that report.* The changed situation regarding Africa in the

---

* It should be emphasized that this account, based on information available in published form, is in no sense official. It has been prepared by Miss Helen F. Conover; the section on the Manuscript Division is contributed by Peter Duignan.

Library of Congress is striking. Developments of the past five years have occasioned an outburst of world interest, expressed in a flood of writing, that is amply reflected not only in collections but also in the organization of the library staff.

In 1960, in recognition of the vigorously growing interest in, and literature on, Africa, an African Section was established in the General Reference and Bibliography Division of the Reference Department, under a Carnegie Corporation grant. This section, which has been headed since its beginning by Dr. Conrad C. Reining and now has a staff of six, provides bibliographical and reference services, advises and collaborates in the Library's acquisitions program, and acts as liaison with other bodies concerned with Africa. In the latter connections frequent trips are made to Africa and Europe, as well as to centers for African studies in this country, giving strong impetus to progress in acquisitions of Africana. Even before the establishment of the African Section, the shift of African countries from colonial status to independence began to overburden the European Section in the Exchange and Gift Division of the Processing Department, which had had charge of matters within its purview relating to British and French colonies; responsibility for exchange relations with Africa was therefore gradually shifted to the Orientalia Section, and in 1962 was definitely lodged in that office, now called the Asian and African Section. A similar situation in the Library's control of current official publications led to the appointment in 1962 of a special reference librarian for Africa in the Government Publications Reading Room. In 1964 there was added to the Section for Near East and North African Law, already set up as a single unit in the Law Library, a specialist for the law of sub-Saharan Africa. Likewise in the Legislative Reference Service, the increased Congressional interest in Africa has led to the allocation of one or more political scientists, as well as an economist, to specific concern with African affairs.

It is impossible to give even an approximate estimate of the amount of material relating to Africa held by the Library of Congress. Africana are not kept in any single block or under any separate unifying control but are merged in the general collections of the Library. The collections in 1963 were estimated to number well over 43,000,000 pieces, of which about 12,800,000 are books and pamphlets. As these collections have traditionally represented a broad selection of world literature, it may be presumed that the holdings relating to the second largest continent are very substantial. Scholars working in the African field usually find a visit to the Library of Congress richly rewarding.*

The Library acquires Africana as it does its materials in general, by copyright, purchase, gift, exchange, and transfer. An informal card record of new books and pamphlets in the African field maintained in the African Section shows that about 1,500 titles are being added each year to the library collections. Practically all American works and many from European publishers are received on copyright. As to purchase, in Africa as in Western Europe, the Library has standing 'blanket

---

* Here a word of warning is in order. All too often visitors from outside the city come to the Library late Friday afternoon, hoping to find research treasures during a two-day stay, and are sharply disappointed. The size and scattered nature of the collections make it difficult if not impossible for much of the less obvious material to be supplied quickly or without the aid of members of the staff directly concerned with its control. Most of these staff members are not on duty during weekends.

order' arrangements with commercial booksellers wherever available for the selection and transmission of currently published material of significance. The publication survey trips of the African Section have notably advanced these arrangements. The African posts of the Department of State are authorized to obtain for the Library important materials, official and nonofficial, published in the countries in which they are located. Many slighter documents are received by transfer from the Department of State and other government agencies. The Order Division, in collaboration with the African Section, checks national bibliographies and catalogues, lists, and other offers of new and retrospective literature received from numerous dealers throughout the world on the placing of individual orders. Receipts by purchase in 1963/64 were well over 10,000 pieces; this figure, it must be understood, is not of separate titles but includes individual issues of serials.

Official documents and publications of learned societies and institutions are acquired in large part through exchange and gift. Great attention is given to the arrangement of exchanges with agencies of foreign governments for the acquisition of official documents. The Library's intent is to collect and maintain on a comprehensive basis the publications of all governments on national levels, with a generous selection on lower government levels. As the new African nations have come into existence, an intensified effort has been made to ensure receipt of their official documents, as well as the publications of the steadily growing number of scientific and learned institutions in Africa and those in Europe whose interests concern or include Africa. In 1959 nearly a thousand exchange agreements with African organizations were in force; the figure has now risen to about 1,500, including European institutions involved in Africa. In the single fiscal year ending in June 1964 the Orientalia Exchange Section established 253 new exchanges with African agencies and institutions, and the number of items received by exchange from countries in Africa rose to 14,841, compared with 8,069 for the previous fiscal year.

The increase is particularly evident in the collection of serials, both official and unofficial. In the past it has happened too often that both government agencies and institutions have sent an early issue of a new serial as a gift to the Library, after the acknowledgment of which no further issues have been received. The Exchange and Gift Division, the African Section, and the Government Publications Reading Room, which maintains as yet uncatalogued African documents, work together to ensure that exchanges—or, if necessary, purchase orders—have been arranged to bring to the Library complete files of the needed publications. The growth in the field of African periodicals indeed warrants attention. In a bibliography prepared by the African Section in 1961, *Serials for African Studies*, there were cited 2,082 titles (exclusive of government reports), most of which are held, in part at least, by the Library. During the succeeding years between 700 and 800 new serial titles have been added to the card file of the African Section; the majority of these are cited in the monthly issues and cumulative annual volumes of *New Serial Titles*. The Library's collection of current and retrospective African newspapers now numbers about 450 titles in bound and unbound form and on microfilm. This is an increase of more than 125 over the number reported as held by the Library in *African Newspapers in Selected American Libraries* (1962).

The Library's acquisition of Africana began with the Library itself, when in 1800 the first shipment of books from England to form the nucleus of the newly authorized library for the use of members of Congress included 'Adanson's Voyage to Senegal, 8vo. large paper (£2/16/0).' The Jefferson Library, purchased in 1815, contained 10 histories of North Africa and Ethiopia and 13 volumes of travels in Africa, among which were such classics as Thomas Shaw, William Bosman, and James Bruce. These are typical of the early acquisitions. Throughout the nineteenth century and for perhaps the first three decades of the twentieth century, African materials incorporated in the collections did not in general go much beyond works of notable scholarship or books of the best-seller class, along with the most important serials and documents. Since World War II, and especially since 1952, when the first formal bibliography, *Introduction to Africa*, was published (earlier lists had been of the title list or catalogue nature), the policy of acquisitions of Africana has been steadily expanded, as to both current and retrospective materials—this in spite of an increasingly rigid standard of selection in general, necessitated by the acceleration of world publication. In the Africana collections works in English naturally predominate, but since Jefferson's time there has been a generous proportion of French publications, and increasing numbers are being obtained in Spanish, Italian, Portuguese, Afrikaans, and other European and non-European languages; recently texts aside from grammars, dictionaries, and religious writings are being acquired in African languages. Russian Africana began to reach the Library after 1948. In 1957 and 1958 the Library was receiving half a dozen books or pamphlets on Africa each year from the Soviet Union, with a conspicuous increase in periodical references entered in the *Monthly Index of Russian Accessions*. In 1963 at least a hundred books and pamphlets in Russian were received, as well as a trickle from other East European countries, notably East Germany and Poland.

Probably the largest single block of works on the subject of Africa is the collection of general surveys, history, description, and travel. This is represented in the shelf list by about 20,000 titles; recently reshelved to allow room for expansion, it now is allotted over 2,500 feet of shelving, fully two-thirds of which is solidly filled.

Of equal importance is the collection of official legislative documents of African governments. (Departmental reports, unless issued and bound as sessional papers, are in classes by subject fields—agriculture, commerce, finance, etc.). Retrospectively, the representation for British Africa is outstanding. Through the vigorous effort of Mr. James B. Childs in the 1920's the Library secured sets of governmental blue books, official gazettes, and debates, minutes, votes and proceedings, etc., of the legislative councils or assemblies of the several British colonies almost from their foundation. The library collection of British Colonial Office records is good, in frequent cases including material from the mid-nineteenth century. The holdings for South Africa are of unique importance, containing debates and proceedings of both houses from 1910/11, with some in both English and Afrikaans editions; documents of the Cape of Good Hope, Natal, and other states date from the 1860's.

From 1946 to the late 1950's the Library's efforts to acquire complete files of documents on the national level were reasonably successful, and, as noted above, the holdings have been greatly increased in the concerted drive since 1960. The African Section is publishing a series of bibliographies recording official publications of the governments of sub-Saharan Africa, with indication of those available in the Library; these compilations have aided substantially in identification of missing items in the collections and consequent efforts to fill the gaps. The results are encouraging. For instance, in the first of these lists, *Nigerian Official Publications, 1869–1959* (Washington, 1959, 153 pp.), there were recorded 1,204 entries; a revision of this bibliography covering the period 1861–1963 now in preparation will include approximately 2,000 entries, a large proportion of which are in the Library's collections. Holdings of official material from Ghana, Kenya, Southern Rhodesia, South Africa, Tanganyika, and Uganda are also excellent.

Since 1960 the Library's collections of both current and retrospective documents on French-speaking Africa have more than doubled in size. In the retrospective picture, there are *journaux officiels* for a few states of former French West Africa, as well as of AOF and AEF, continuously from before World War I or from the mid-1920's; other material is scattered. French government publications relating to Africa and published in Paris are well represented, but the record for documents issued in tropical Africa (and not only French Africa) is fragmentary. Apparently the local government printing offices issued their processed publications in limited quantity, and the documents were not available through commercial channels, so that even the colonial offices of the governing powers did not hold complete files. However, through correspondence and contacts made on publication survey trips, the Library has recently acquired several thousand documents of the federal and territorial governments of former French West Africa and French Equatorial Africa and is developing useful collections of documents for most independent French-speaking states.

The chief publications of Belgian official and government-sponsored institutions concerned with the Congo but published in Belgium have for many years been received with impressive near-completeness. The reports of the Administering Powers to the United Nations on administration of the former trust territories, Cameroons, Togoland, and Ruanda-Urundi, are in unbroken rows on the shelves. The Library's significant collection of material on Liberia has recently been augmented by a number of official economic and statistical studies, and there has been a steady increase in holdings of documents relating to Portuguese Africa. Among interesting documents in the noncurrent holdings is an almost complete file of the official journal *Lumière et Paix* of Ethiopia, with text in Amharic, published from 1925 to 1936.

Since many of the official documents received from all governments are serials, and many others small sessional papers and the like, which can be conveniently bound in groups, much of the material for several years back is still to be found in the Government Publications Reading Room, where, with the aid of recent reshelving, the reference librarian for Africa holds it under efficient control until ready for binding.

The exception to the dispersement of Africana in the general collections is the literature of North and Northeast Africa in Arabic, Amharic, and other Ethiopian languages, all of which—documents, books (except legal works), newspapers, etc.—is in the custody of the Orientalia Division of the Reference Department. The heads of the Near East and Hebraic Sections have both made acquisitions trips to the field within the past few years, resulting in significant increases in the holdings, especially as regards official publications of Egypt, North Africa, and Ethiopia. The Arabic scholars of the Near East staff declare their material now adequate to satisfy practically all research needs. The Ethiopic collection, held by the Hebraic Section, whose staff has language competence, comprises about 500 items in Amharic, many of them speeches and decrees of the Emperor, with bilingual text. Some date from the years before the Italian conquest. There are also some older texts, chiefly Coptic religious works, and a few items in Tigriniya.

The Map Division is rich in regard to Africa, its collection of separate African maps, exclusive of hydrographic charts, maps in general atlases, etc., numbering well over 18,000. Through the cooperation of the Department of State, the Library since 1946 has participated in an interagency program for the procurement of foreign maps. A geographic attaché covers the African continent at least every two years, and at present the Library is receiving almost 3,000 maps a year of Africa and its subdivisions. The Map Division holds also about 200 atlases for Africa.

The collection of pictures relating to Africa in the Prints and Photographs Division may be roughly guessed to number between 6,000 and 7,000. More than half of these are in 66 groups which include reproductions of photographs of the Italian campaign in Ethiopia, World War II pictures, reproductions from the British Office of Information, pictures resulting from American expeditions and safaris, etc. A collection of some 600 photographs in two big albums, with brief handwritten captions, by the geographer-photographer Frank G. Carpenter forms the largest catalogued group. Five hundred-odd pictures of the American Colonization Society collection, described rather fully by Paul Vanderbilt in his *Guide to the Special Collections of Prints and Photographs in the Library of Congress* (Washington, 1955, p. 3) and very popular with readers, are now catalogued. About 1,200 uncatalogued pictures are stereographic views, many of them relating to the Boer War.

The Motion Picture Collection, which in 1959 was reported as having about 13 African titles, now has more nearly a hundred. These include 15 or 20 feature films of the sort that have abounded during recent years, e.g., *Something of Value;* the rest are documentaries showing African scenery, life, and customs. An interesting group of very early films by Thomas A. Edison dates from 1900 and was purportedly taken during the Boer War—a Boer commissionary supply train on trek, the capture of a Boer battery, etc. It is suspected, however, that these were faked, filmed in New Jersey. Six reels of Paul J. Rainey's African Hunt, taken in 1912, are considered genuine, as is also a film of African sea birds taken on an island off the tip of South Africa by Edison in 1913. Audio-visual educational film strips, now being widely produced, are beginning to come into the collection, which is selecting only those on the adult educational level, and very few are concerned with Africa.

Of microfilms of African interest available in the Microfilm Reading Room, most are American doctoral theses which, like other writing on Africa, grow in number from year to year. The index of *Dissertation Abstracts* for 1962/63 includes 20-odd titles for Africa; the reels for all covered in the abstracts are received by the Library of Congress. An important holding of the Microfilm Reading Room is the series of the world-wide Foreign Radio Broadcasts. Such documents as come on microfilm are usually extra copies from the fuller files of the National Archives. Some of the African newspapers currently received are being preserved on microfilm; these, which are detailed in the latest issue of *Newspapers on Microfilm* (Library of Congress, 1963, 305 pp.), are held in the Newspaper Reading Room.

In the Music Division the catalogue of single songs and song collections contains over 900 African items, 750 of them in a special subdivision for the music of South Africa, both African and European, the rest from Africa south of the Sahara, written down or collected by Western or Western-trained musicians. There are also some 45 to 50 books on African music. A particular treasure is the original manuscript of the Ravel composition *Chansons madécasses*, a setting to music of three French verse translations of folksong texts from Madagascar. The Archive of Folksong has several quite important collections of records of African music from Africa south of the Sahara. One good-sized collection, compiled by a USIS officer, consists of folk and café music of Madagascar and of the French colonies. (There is also a valuable 60-hour tape recording of the variegated musical traditions of Morocco, made by Paul F. Bowles in 1959.) Besides music and records, the Music Division has in its collection of flutes about a dozen instruments from Africa. A specialist in African music on its staff has prepared an authoritative bibliography, published by the Library of Congress in 1964.

The chief finding aids for the Library's collections of Africana are the general instruments of control—the dictionary catalogues* in the Main Reading Room and the Jefferson Reading Room (the latter complete only from 1939) and, for periodical material, the usual library indexes. There are also card files in the above-mentioned special divisions and sections, relating to their own holdings. The working card files for books and pamphlets and that for serials used in the African Section, readily made available to visitors engaged in research, are notable in that they include not only titles of works catalogued but also those of material received but not yet passed through the processes of cataloguing and binding necessary before they are put in place on the shelves. Because much of the foreign literature comes in pamphlet form or with soft covers and requires a trip to the bindery in addition to the usual cataloguing steps, a good many of the tempting items in the African Section's files must for some time remain titles only, to be seen, if anywhere in America, in more specialized libraries. The African Section receives and

---

* These include the Library of Congress catalogue *Books: Subjects*, the *National Union Catalog*, 1956–, which replaces the printed author catalogues of the Library of Congress, and the monthly and cumulated *New Serial Titles*.

holds for display and working use current issues of about a hundred periodicals of importance for African studies; reviews and notices of new books in these often are helpful in assessment of as yet inaccessible works. The bibliographies prepared by this section and other units of the Library usually include catalogued collections, the uncatalogued titles, and works not yet received by the Library of Congress.

Reference service for African research in the general collections is provided, as above indicated, in the African Section and the Government Publications Reading Room and, for Congress, in the Legislative Reference Service. Many books can be made accessible to scholars outside Washington through interlibrary loan, and the Photoduplication Service is equipped to provide photostats or microfilms of needed material not subject to copyright restrictions.

Bibliographies for Africa and independent African countries were prepared from time to time in the General Reference and Bibliography Division and its predecessor before World War II, the Division of Bibliography. These were either catalogues or unannotated lists of books, pamphlets, and articles based almost entirely on the Library's catalogued collections. A dozen lists of several hundred items each for the various European possessions in Africa and for Liberia were issued during World War II; most of these are now out of print. Several lists were devoted to Ethiopia, before and after the Italo-Abyssinian conflict, the latest in 1947. In 1952 a more formal survey of literature for the layman was presented in the annotated *Introduction to Africa: A Selective Guide to Background Reading*, prepared by Miss Helen Conover, then in the European Affairs Division. This was followed by *Research and Information on Africa: Continuing Sources* (1954 and revised edition, 1957). The *Introduction to Africa* was brought up to date and extended to include more scholarly material in two compilations published by the General Reference and Bibliography Division in 1957, *Africa South of the Sahara* and *North and Northeast Africa*, now superseded by the 1963 volume, *Africa South of the Sahara*. A survey of periodicals and organizations throughout the world that publish serially about Africa, *Research and Information on Africa*, was superseded by the *Serials for African Studies* published by the African Section in 1961. Much of the bibliographical effort of late years has been directed to lists of official publications of African governments.

The following are recent Library of Congress publications on Africa:

Africa South of the Sahara: A Selected, Annotated List of Writings, compiled by Helen F. Conover. 1963. 360 pp.*
    This list replaces earlier compilations of 1952 and 1957 and includes almost 3,000 entries.
African Libraries, Book Production, and Archives: A List of References, compiled by Helen F. Conover. 1962. 64 pp.†
African Music: A Briefly Annotated Bibliography, compiled by Darius L. Thieme. 1964. 55 pp.*

---

* Available from the Superintendent of Documents, Government Printing Office, Washington, D.C. 20402.

† Available from the Card Division, Library of Congress, Washington, D.C. 20540.

Agricultural Development Schemes in Sub-Saharan Africa: A Bibliography, compiled by Ruth S. Freitag. 1963. 189 pp.*

A List of American Doctoral Dissertations on Africa. 1962. 69 pp.*

Madagascar and Adjacent Islands: A Guide to Official Publications, compiled by Julian W. Witherell. 1965. 58 pp.*

Official Publications of British East Africa:†
> Part I. *The East Africa High Commission and Other Regional Documents*, compiled by Helen F. Conover. 1960, reprinted 1961. 67 pp.
> Part II. *Tanganyika*, compiled by Audrey A. Walker. 1962, 134 pp.
> Part III. *Kenya and Zanzibar*, compiled by Audrey A. Walker. 1962. 162 pp.
> Part IV. *Uganda*, compiled by Audrey A. Walker. 1963. 100 pp.

Official Publications of French Equatorial Africa, French Cameroons and Togo, 1946–1958: A Guide, compiled by Julian W. Witherell. 1963. 78 pp.*

Official Publications of French West Africa, 1946–1958: A Guide, compiled by Helen F. Conover. 1960, reprinted 1961. 88 pp.†

Official Publications of Sierra Leone and Gambia, compiled by Audrey A. Walker. 1963. 92 pp.*

The Rhodesias and Nyasaland: A Guide to Official Publications, compiled by Audrey A. Walker. 1965. 285 pp.*

Serials for African Studies, compiled by Helen F. Conover. 1961. 163 pp.*

United States and Canadian Publications on Africa in 1960. 1962. 98 pp.*

Following are publications which are out of print:

Nigerian Official Publications, 1869–1959, compiled by Helen F. Conover.

North and Northeast Africa, 1951–1957, compiled by Helen F. Conover.‡

Official Publications of Somaliland, 1941–1959, compiled by Helen F. Conover.‡

MANUSCRIPT COLLECTIONS

As holdings of the Manuscript Division are essentially of material relating to America, the African items are not significant compared with those of Great Britain and European countries, whose connections with Africa were longer and wider. The most conspicuous collection is that of the American Colonization Society concerning Liberia. Other African items are not easily identified, as they must be sought out among the papers of Presidents, diplomats, army and naval officers, travelers, missionaries, and other prominent Americans who have been associated with Africa. However, a survey of the published catalogues and an article by Morris Rieger in the *African Studies Bulletin* (VIII, No. 3, December 1965, 1–11) reveal that the Manuscript Division has in its collections the following:

Papers of Cleveland Abbe (1838–1916), astronomer and meteorologist, about 9,500 items for the period 1850–1916, among them correspondence concerning Abbe's participation in the West African Eclipse Expedition in the 1880's.

---

* Available from the Superintendent of Documents, Government Printing Office, Washington, D.C. 20402.

† Available from the Card Division, Library of Congress, Washington, D.C. 20540.

‡ Positive microfilm available from Photoduplication Service, Library of Congress.

Archives of the American Colonization Society, 1816–1908, 689 volumes, 55
folders, 18 cartons, 14 boxes, and 1 portfolio, including materials on Liberia.

Papers of George Ferdinand Becker (1847–1919), geologist, geophysicist, mathe-
matician, and engineer, including correspondence, diaries, notebooks, reports,
and articles, about 15 linear feet. Of chief interest are his professional papers
from long service as geologist in charge, U.S. Geological Survey; he conducted
significant studies of the Witwatersrand gold fields in the 1890's.

Papers of James Gillespie Birney (1792–1857), antislavery leader, for the period
1830–1850, 14 items, 4 volumes, and 1 reel of negative microfilm. Materials
include diaries (1830, 1834, 1840–1850), notebook, and correspondence (1834–
1835) mainly from Birney to Theodore D. Weld and Gerrit Smith, relating to
slavery, abolition, African colonization, emancipation, and politics of the
period. The microfilm consists of letters from Birney to Ralph Randolph
Gurley, Gerrit Smith, Theodore D. Weld, Elizur Wright, and others.

Diary of Carrie Chapman Catt (1859–1947), lecturer, author, and women's suffrage
leader, for the period 1911–1912; typescript with photographs of trip around
world, including South and East Africa.

Papers of Charles Chaillé-Long, soldier, explorer, author, and U.S. consular
official, for the period 1865–1915, 3 boxes. Chaillé-Long was an Egyptian
government official in the Sudan under Gordon and was one of the earliest
European visitors to Buganda.

The Reverend Daniel Coker, agent of the American Colonization Society, 'Journal
Kept in the West Coast of Africa at Fourah Bay, April 21–September 21, 1821.'

Papers of William Augustus Croffut (1835–1915), author, editor, and poet, 7,500
items covering the period 1774–1933. In the correspondence (chiefly 1880–
1915) are letters on Croffut's activities with the Anti-Imperialist League, and
drafts of articles among League papers include advocacy of the cause of the
Boers in South Africa.

Papers of John Chandler Bancroft Davis (1822–1907), Assistant Secretary of State,
82 volumes, 7 boxes. On behalf of President Grant, Davis arbitrated an Anglo-
Portuguese dispute over Bulama Island (an area now part of Portuguese
Guinea), 1869–1870.

Papers of Stephen Decatur, U.S. naval officer, among those of the Decatur House
and the Beale family.

Papers of Dutilh and Wachsmuth, Philadelphia merchants, 1784–1797, 2 boxes
and 1 portfolio, including material on the African slave trade.

Papers of Admiral Andrew Hull Foote, 1822–1868, 30 volumes, including the
journals he kept during the cruise of the U.S. brig *Perry* to the African coast.

Papers of Moneton Frewen (1853–1924), Anglo-Irish reformer, economist, and
author, for the period 1871–1924, 20 feet, including printed materials on his
business ventures or government service in Kenya.

Papers of William Crawford Gorgas (1854–1920), U.S. Army Surgeon General
and pioneer in tropical medicine, 18 linear feet. In 1913–1914 he visited South
Africa as consultant to the Transvaal Chamber of Mines to advise on measures
for improving the health of the African miners.

Great Britain, Colonial Office, Act registers for the West Coast of Africa and St. Helena, 1782–1892, 18 reels of microfilm.

Papers of Matthew Fontaine Maury (1806–1873), noted oceanographer and astronomer, who conducted oceanographic studies of the Indian Ocean and the South Atlantic, 64 volumes, 26 boxes.

Papers of Edgar Alexander Mearns, U.S. army officer and naturalist, including material on the African expedition of Theodore Roosevelt in 1909–1910.

Papers of John Tyler Morgan (1824–1907), Alabama Senator and chairman of the Senate Foreign Relations Committee in the 1880's, about 9,000 items. Morgan played a major role in American diplomatic recognition of Leopold II's International Congo Association and in the origins of the Congo Free State.

Papers of Simon Newcomb (1835–1909), world-famous astronomer, 95 volumes, 246 boxes. He headed two astronomical expeditions to Southern Africa, 1882 and 1889.

Papers of Matthew C. Perry (1794–1858), early participant in the establishment of Liberia and first commander of the African Squadron, 1843–1845, 3 boxes.

Papers of Edmund Roberts, New England merchant who opened trade to Zanzibar in 1828 and was sent as diplomatic agent of the U.S. government in 1832 to negotiate trade treaties with powers bordering on the Indian Ocean, for the period 1804–1842, 10 volumes and 5 boxes.

Voluminous papers of Theodore Roosevelt include some chronicling of his African expedition in 1909–1910.

Papers of the Royal African Company, British slave-trading consortium, 1735–1744, 2 volumes.

Papers of Thomas Oliver Selfridge (1836–1924), naval officer on duty with the African Squadron, 1858, 16 boxes.

Papers of Mary French Sheldon, writer, 1885–1936, mainly related to Belgium, the Congo, and Africa in general, 9 boxes. Important correspondents are Henry Morton Stanley, Albert I, King of the Belgians, and several of Albert's cabinet ministers.

Papers of Robert W. Shufeldt, U.S. naval officer, 1864–1884, 22 boxes, in the Naval Historical Foundation Collection on deposit in the Library of Congress. Shufeldt sailed to Africa and Asia in 1878 under instructions to extend American influence along the coasts of these continents and among the islands of the Indian Ocean, to investigate changes in Zanzibar and their effect on the United States, and to determine if improvements could be made in the 1867 treaty with Madagascar.

Papers of Nicholas Philip Trist (and family), consul at Havana and special agent in Mexico, for the period 1783–1873, 44 volumes and 11 boxes; valuable for information on the slave trade.

The Reverend M. Wakefield of the Methodist Mission, compilation of vocabulary of the Kavirondo language, 1882.

Papers of Booker T. Washington (1859–1915), including approximately 25 items (letters, speeches, reports, and documents) that deal with African affairs. Correspondence with J. C. Clarkson, Frederick Douglass, W. E. B. Du Bois, and Anson Phelps Stokes records interests in African business and education, Liberia, and Pan-Africanism. There is also a copy of a manuscript by Emmett J. Scott, 'Tuskegee in Africa and Africa at Tuskegee.'

Papers of Levi Woodbury (1789–1851), New Hampshire Senator and Secretary of the Navy, who was one of the prime movers in the establishment of official relations between the United States and Zanzibar in the 1830's, 60 volumes, 29 boxes.

Papers of George Wunderlich (1897–1951), professor of law, international lawyer, and consultant to the U.S. Department of State, including his activities for clients in West Africa.

LINCOLN UNIVERSITY

The Vail Memorial Library of Lincoln University, P.O. Lincoln University, Chester County, Pennsylvania, has about 2,100 separate items (books and pamphlets), exclusive of unbound periodicals and newspapers, language tapes, and a small manuscript collection relating to Africa south of the Sahara.

Of more than 1,300 fully classed and catalogued volumes, about 50 percent are in the allied fields of history, exploration, travel, and description and another 10 percent in anthropology and ethnology. Of the remainder, the older titles comprise chiefly missionary literature, and the newer titles are principally in the fields of socioeconomic and constitutional problems, politics, linguistics, and art. Although the great bulk of the collection is in English, there are an appreciable number of monographs, and a number of periodical titles, in French.

There are 115 bound volumes of periodicals, including near-complete series of *Africa* and *Nigeria*, and a somewhat larger collection of incomplete volumes, unbound. About 20 periodicals are currently received.

The collection has more than doubled in the past five years, the current rate of growth being about 175 (catalogued) volumes per year, apart from pamphlets and periodicals. Although the great majority of titles are recent and contemporary publications, there are almost 200 nineteenth-century imprints, including 25 volumes of *African Repository* (incomplete series from 1828 to 1873).

Government documents comprise several series of legislative debates and about 400 miscellaneous items from the three West African governments of Nigeria, Ghana (ex-Gold Coast), and Sierra Leone.

Unclassed pamphlets in vertical files, topically arranged under subject entries but not individually catalogued, number between 300 and 400 pieces. The bibliographical collections are supplemented by a large and growing collection of African art and artifacts.

The Library has manuscripts of Robert Hamill Nassau, a Presbyterian missionary to West Africa; the minutes of the Pennsylvania Colonization Society, 1838–1849, 1856–1913; a composite volume of minutes and colonization records to be described below; and an archive of early missionary correspondence. Robert Hamill Nassau (1835–1921) was a pioneer in African linguistics and founder of mission stations on the Ogowe River. Typescripts, with manuscript additions and emendations, of the following works by him are held by the Library: 'Corisco Days, the First Thirty Years of the West Africa Mission' (undated typescript of book published under same title, Philadelphia, 1910); 'Where Animals Talk' (first and second typescript drafts, dated 1911, of book published at Boston, 1912); and 'Two Women, the Lives of Two Native African Christians' (typescript, dated Philadelphia, 1911, of chapters originally intended for inclusion in *Tales out of School*, Philadelphia, 1911, but suppressed at the instance of the American Tract Society).

The minutes of the Pennsylvania Colonization Society run from January 2, 1838, to December 11, 1849, and from July 15, 1856, to January 28, 1913, 6 volumes. The Society's constitution and bylaws, together with rosters of officers and managers from 1837 to 1866 and a roster of life members, 1882, 1 volume, are also held. These are supplemented by a single manuscript volume captioned 'Minutes of the Executive Committee of the Young Men's Colonization Society of Pennsylvania' but actually a composite of the minutes of the named committee, superseded at some date not later than 1837 by the minutes of the Executive Committee of the parent Pennsylvania Colonization Society. The minutes cover the period 1834–1840, with a few perfunctory entries for 1841 and 1843. Later pages of the book include lists of local colonization societies in Pennsylvania and neighboring states organized during the years 1835–1839; copies of invoices for supplies shipped to Bassa Cove and lists of donations during the years 1834–1837; registers of emigrants for the years 1834–1864; and record of applicants for passage to Liberia during the years 1835–1838.

Among institutional archives the letter files of the Reverend Edward Webb, financial secretary of Lincoln University from 1872 until his death in 1898, include letters to and from the Reverend Epaminondas J. Pierce, sometime missionary to the Gabon, as well as letters from Lincoln alumni in the Liberian mission field. A liberal selection from this correspondence exists in mimeographed form, as an appendix to a statement on African missions prepared in 1949 by President Honorarius Horace M. Bond, under the title 'God Be Glorified in Africa.'

LOUISIANA STATE UNIVERSITY

Louisiana State University, Baton Rouge, Louisiana, has in the Department of Archives of its Library papers totaling 488 items, 1 volume, for Joseph Crane Hartzell (1842–1928), Methodist Episcopal missionary bishop for Africa.

MARINE HISTORICAL ASSOCIATION

The Marine Historical Association, Mystic, Connecticut, has extensive material on Aaron Lopez (1731–1782), who was a merchant and slave trader of Newport, Rhode Island. It also has the papers, 1870–1879, 234 items, of Anthony Smalley, shipmaster of Nantucket, Massachusetts. Among them are letters and telegrams sent to him as agent for Francis C. Butman (a Boston shipping and commission merchant) in St. Vincent, Cape Verde Islands, and Gorée, near Dakar.

MARYLAND HISTORICAL SOCIETY

The Maryland Historical Society, 201 West Monument Street, Baltimore, Maryland, holds records of the Maryland State Colonization Society to Liberia, 1827–1902, 84 volumes, 5 boxes. Also held are papers of John H. B. Latrobe (1803–1891), long-prominent figure in the American Colonization Society, 52 volumes, 11 boxes.

MASSACHUSETTS HISTORICAL SOCIETY

The Massachusetts Historical Society, 1154 Boylston Street, Boston 15, Massachusetts, contains a 'Liberia College' collection which includes some materials from the Massachusetts Colonization Society. The collection covers the years 1842–1927 and is arranged chronologically in about a dozen boxes. There are also 4 boxes labeled 'miscellaneous,' 19 boxes of letters, letter books, manuscripts, and receipts, and a small collection of pamphlets.

Other manuscripts are filed under the name of the collection rather than the subject. The Edward Everett Collection contains 7 letters (1840's); the J. C. Warren Collection, 2 letters (1850's); the A. A. Lawrence Collection, 4 letters (1850's); and the Edes Collection, 1 letter (1880). There are also papers of William Rotch (1734–1828), major Nantucket and New Bedford whaling merchant.

MEDFORD HISTORICAL SOCIETY

The Medford Historical Society, 10 Governor's Avenue, Medford, Massachusetts, has a few letters and business papers relating to the slave trade, 1759–1769.

UNIVERSITY OF MICHIGAN

The Manuscript Division of the William L. Clements Library of the University of Michigan, Ann Arbor, Michigan, contains the papers (about 1,700 items) of James Gillespie Birney (1792–1857). Birney was active in the American Colonization Society and the American Anti-Slavery Society and in the publication of the *Philanthropist*, an antislavery journal.

The Division also contains manuscript items on Africa from the Shelburne Papers as follows:

Shelburne Papers, Volume 80, labeled 'Minutes of African Affairs,' includes a report entitled 'State of the British Settlements on the Coast of Africa' [ca. 1767], 20 pp.; extracts of reports relative to the African trade, etc., 1708–1712, 15 pp.; abstract of letters from Africa from Mr. Barnes and Governor O'Hara, 1766–1767, 27 pp; minute for the Province of Senegambia, 24 pp.; abstract of a letter from Mr. Hippisley, chief of Cape Coast Castle, to the African Committee, July 1766, 2 pp.; and eleven returns giving the state of the forts on the coast of Guinea for the year 1765.

Shelburne Papers, Volume 81, labeled 'Africa' and 'Senegal Affairs,' covering the period 1757–1767, contains copies of papers and dispatches relative to Senegal affairs and includes a paper relative to the trade of Senegal by Mr. Townshend [1766], 3 pp.; a letter to Mr. [Thomas] Cummings presuming to endeavor to procure him an exclusive right to trade to Senegal, February 9, 1757, 2 pp.; draft in Lord Shelburne's hand as regards Col. [Charles] O'Hara's information respecting the coast of Africa [1766], 3 pp.; John Barnes, observations on Fort Lewis at Senegal, with a description of that country, etc. [1764?], 17 pp.; Charles O'Hara on the subject of French encroachments on the coast of Africa, September 1, 1766, 3 pp.; memorial from Charles O'Hara to Lord Shelburne containing a proposal for the more safely navigating the River Senegal, August 3, 1767, 10 pp.; and [Thomas Cumming's] petition to the King concerning Senegal, February 9, 1757, 3 pp.

Shelburne Papers, Volume 84, has copies of official correspondence relative to the coast of Africa, 1767–1768, with an original letter from Joseph Debat, Lieutenant Governor of Senegal, August 13, 1767.

Other University of Michigan Africana are in the Museum of Anthropology—100 Kenya pieces.

MICHIGAN STATE UNIVERSITY

The area of international programs, as part of a rapidly developing university, has become increasingly important to Michigan State University, East Lansing, Michigan, in the last two decades. Faculty research abroad has been a primary factor in the growth of private and federal agency-sponsored technical assistance programs in educational activities overseas. Projects in Turkey, Pakistan, India, Thailand, Vietnam, Taiwan, Okinawa, Guatemala, Colombia, Brazil, and Nigeria have been and are being conducted in the fields of business administration, public administration, agriculture, community development, education, and general university development. Continued outside financial assistance has enabled further enlargement of such programs on the campus as a whole.

The initiation of the African Studies Center at Michigan State University in 1960 owes much to an offer from the U.S. Office of Education to support the teaching of West African languages on campus. By coincidence, this occurred at the same time that the University was engaged in two closely related projects: the ICA (AID) contract of establishing and developing the University of Nigeria at Nsukka and the initiation of a Ford Foundation-supported research program for African studies.

New courses and additional teaching staff now allow for specialized courses in the departments of linguistics and Oriental and African languages, political science, history, anthropology, and geography. Much research is emerging from the Center's activity. In 1963–1964, for example, field research was under way in education, fisheries and wildlife, political science, economics, history, and geography, and there were four projects in the area of languages and linguistics.

Developments such as these have demanded simultaneous growth of the resources of the University Library. Increased acquisitions and expansion of library services in anticipation of future needs became essential, and the last few years marked, indeed, a substantial growth of library resources related to the study of Africa. Moreover, in 1963 a separate unit, the International Division, was formed to coordinate a systematic expansion of library resources and the University's international programs of teaching and research. This new division has been responsible for the Library's acquisition of materials relevant to the study of the three geographical areas Africa, Asia, and Latin America, as well as development of a collection of documents, pamphlets, and maps and introduction of a bibliographic advisory service for faculty and graduate students engaged in foreign area research.

In the fall of 1965 Michigan State University Library held about 13,000 volumes of Africana materials. Of the 14,200 serial titles that the Library currently receives, 1,200 titles are relevant to the study of Africa and some 480 of these concern African matters exclusively. The University Library's holdings of African newspapers consist of subscriptions to 17 titles from 11 countries, in addition to the titles on microfilm held by the Center for Research Libraries (formerly the Midwest Inter-Library Center), of which MSU is a founding member. MSU also participates in the Center's Cooperative African Microfilm Project (CAMP). African government documents number more than 700 items, supplemented by several subscriptions to official yearbooks, current parliamentary debates, and such other sources as a complete file of the British sessional papers.

The geographical scope of the collecting policy of Africana at Michigan State includes the entire continent and the islands, with special stress on the sub-Saharan region. Within the sub-Saharan area and in line with faculty and course interests, the Library has emphasized West, South, and then East Africa in its holdings. Although no limitation was placed on the time period to be covered, new acquisitions give priority to nineteenth- and twentieth-century Africa along with the so-called literature of development of the post-World War II period. Current acquisition emphasis is in the social, economic, and cultural areas, especially in anthropology, languages and linguistics, history, political science, and economics. Education, music, and art were brought into the collecting scope of the Library in the last year or two. Older collected books form a large section of early exploration and travel accounts and of historical works concerning Africa. Before 1960 library acquisitions showed considerable attention to the biological and agricultural sciences, and holdings on these subjects are substantial, particularly in periodical literature, with about 235 serial titles specifically related to these topics. While maintaining this strength, periodical acquisitions have currently been emphasizing the newer areas of teaching and research, namely, the social sciences and the humanities.

Of the 1965 total of about 13,000 Africana books, the subject fields can be ranked as follows: history, description, and travel, 5,300; agriculture, forestry, and animal sciences, 1,450; anthropology, folklore, religion, and sociology, 1,400 volumes; political science, government, and law, 1,300; language and literature, 1,100; economics and labor, 900; education, 450; geography and geology, 350; music and fine arts, 300; science and technology, 300; bibliographical materials, 150. The acquisition of Africana materials in recent years has varied between 1,500 and 2,000 volumes per year. Excluding periodical subscriptions and standing orders, the book budget encompasses about $12,000 annually.

There is no separate Africa library at Michigan State University—except for a collection of pamphlets housed in the International Division of the Library. The Africana materials are spread throughout the Central Library according to the Library of Congress classification scheme. The increasing importance of the Africana library program is noticeable in the number of personnel assigned to it. In 1960–1961 the Africana field was still handled by the Acquisitions Department, but in 1965 a half-time bibliographer and a half-time clerk, one graduate assistant, and some 30 hours a week of student help were concerned with the material. Plans call for employment of a full-time Africana bibliographer.

The Library's special features are quite diverse. Among them is the pamphlet collection in the International Division (mentioned above) which consists of 2,900 pieces of political ephemera. Many of these originated in the newly independent West African countries and contain such items as speeches and statements of African leaders, party literature, general information about the countries and their governments, and other fugitive-type materials. Writings and speeches of prominent African leaders like Padmore, Azikiwe, and Nkrumah are in the collection. The pamphlets are catalogued and classified in a special classification system allowing for quick reference and self-service through an author-subject card index.

A U.S. Office of Education depository status was granted to MSU for the NDEA-sponsored Title VI studies—research projects in the area of languages and linguistics, of which a substantial number are concerned with African studies. Currently taught on campus are Bambara, Bemba, Hausa, Igbo, Swahili, Yoruba, and West African pidgin. It might be added that French, German, Spanish, Portuguese, Dutch, and Afrikaans sources on African languages have increased owing to graduate and faculty research demands. The *Journal of African Languages* (3 parts yearly, 1962–), which is virtually the international house organ for all African linguists, is published in England but has its main editorial office at MSU and is sponsored by this university.

Holdings related to language instruction consist of about 170 literary pamphlets in the vernacular or translated items and 468 text- and handbooks related to different language families, with the largest concentration on West and East African languages. Of the 468, the Niger-Congo languages have the largest number—155 titles with such authors as Ida Ward (Efik, Ibo, Yoruba, Twi); Roy C. Abraham (Tiv, Yoruba); D. Westermann (Ewe, Guang, West African languages); M. Delafosse (Bambara, Mande); H. Labouret, A. Klingenheben, and F. W. Taylor (Fulani); J. De Gaye and Hans Wolff (Yoruba); Ernst Henrici (Ewe); and Jack Berry, formerly of the MSU faculty (Twi, Fanti, Ewe, Ga). Bantu and Khoisan have about 125 titles. Among them can be found works by Bleek, De Boeck, C. M. Doke, M. Guthrie, H. H. Johnston, R. Roberts, C. Meinhof, A. Tucker, M. Bryan, J. Torrend, Dirk Ziervogel (Swazi), Ashton (Swahili), Sa Nogueira (Thonga), and Irvine Richardson of the MSU African Studies Center (Northwestern Bantu, Bemba, Sukuma). The Hamito-Semitic family numbers about 80 items, with strongest holdings for Hausa—31 titles by R. C. Abraham, Robinson, Migeod, Kraft (MSU faculty), and others. A different classification of these sources breaks down the holdings as follows: manuals, grammars, lessons on pronunciation, etc., about 170; general sketches of individual languages, 50; tonal, phonetic, and morphological studies, about 40, and sources describing the classification of the languages, about 15; dictionaries and vocabularies, 130; and about 60 works discussing the nature of African linguistics as a whole. Representative scarce books concerning African linguistics are Samuel A. Crowther, *A Vocabulary of the Yoruba Language* (1852); William H. Bleek, *A Comparative Grammar of South African Languages* (1862–1869); Joris van Geel, *Le plus ancien dictionnaire bantu* (1928 ed. of 1652 original); Sigismund Koelle, *Grammar of the Bornu or Kanuri Language* (1854); Friedrich Müller, *Die Sprache der Bari* (1864); James F. Schön, *Vocabulary of the Hausa Language* (1843); Ernst Henrici, *Lehrbuch der Ephe-Sprache, Anlo, Anecho- und Dahome Mundart mit Glossar und einer Karte der Sklavenküste* (1891); and Arthur Madan, *Lenji Handbook* (1908). Fiction, drama, and poetry by African writers are also collected, and their number is about 200 books by such authors as Achebe, Ekwensi, La Guma, Dei-Anang, Soyinka, Césaire, Damas, Senghor, Viderot, Abrahams, Rabemananjara, David and Birago Diop, Oyono, Djebar, and others.

Michigan State is a depository of all FAO and UNESCO publications and maintains standing orders with UN and other international agencies (e.g., the European Common Market; ORSTOM, Paris; etc.). An exchange program evolved over the past several years has augmented the currently received Africana serials with some 68 additional titles from 17 different African countries; the subject fields of these publications is about equally divided between biological and agricultural sciences and social sciences.

Among rare periodicals in the Michigan State University Library are those listed below. (*Research Sources for African Studies: A Checklist of Relevant Serial Publications in the Michigan State University Library* [1966] lists the 1,200 serial titles that are concerned with Africa.)

Antananarivo Annual and Madagascar Magazine. London Missionary Society, 1875–1900 (on film).

Bibliothèque Coloniale Internationale. Ser. 1–11, 1895–1914.

Revue Belge de Géographie. Bruxelles, Société Royale Belge de Géographie, 1877–1952, 1957–.

Sociedade de Geographia de Lisboa. *Boletim.* 1880–1928, 1960–.

Società Geografica Italiana. *Bollettino.* Rome, August 1868–1936.

Société de Pathologie Exotique et de Sa Filiale de l'Ouest-Africain. *Bulletins.* 1908–1916, 1918–1919, 1923–.

Société Royale de Géographie d'Anvers. *Bulletin.* 1876–1949, 1956–.

The field of missionary literature is fairly well represented at MSU. There is also an excellent research source concerning Africa in the French Monarchy Collection of more than 10,000 volumes, which the University Library acquired several years ago. A substantial recent donation of books, multivolume sets, and periodical subscriptions by the Lisbon-based Calouste-Gulbenkian Foundation contributed to the strengthening of MSU's holdings on Portuguese Africa. Moreover, Michigan State assumed a Farmington Plan assignment in July 1963 for Togo and Dahomey.*

With regard to Nigeria, the Library's resources are impressive. These are the result of Michigan State's general university development project at the University of Nigeria at Nsukka. Nigerian archival holdings, for example, contain the records of initial surveys as well as the planning and organizing reports of the university teams from 1958 and the records of conferences on higher education in Nigeria.

Other archival material includes the unbound writings (held in the International Division of the Library) of Major Arthur Victor Langton, a British officer who was connected in a semiofficial advisory capacity with the Royal African Society and whose correspondence from this body has been collected. With these are clippings he retained from the London *Times* dealing with 18 British Commonwealth nations, Africa in general, and the High Commission Territories. The correspondence and clippings, ranging from the early 1940's to about 1957, contain interesting information about the Society and British Africa's relations with Britain.

The Library's phono-record collection holds the 210-piece LP series 'Sound of Africa,' and there are several smaller phono-record sets.

In addition to library holdings, the University Museum has in its custody over 400 items of jewelry, weapons, musical instruments, pottery, sculpture, masks, and other art objects. Most of these are from West Africa, chiefly Nigeria and Liberia. The Kresge Art Center has additional items, such as old Egyptian-Coptic sculpture and Benin bronzes.

EUGENE DE BENKO and MARGO A. WELLS

MISSIONARY RESEARCH LIBRARY

The Missionary Research Library, 3041 Broadway, New York, New York 10027, has a small but wide-ranging collection of manuscript materials, including typed manuscripts dealing with missions and language problems, with bibliographies for the African countries, and with statistics, written in the early part of the century; a 'Diary of a Trip to Interior Abyssinia, Nov. 20, 1919, to Jan. 6, 1920,' by Tom Lambie; the letters of R. H. Nassau concerning mission work in the Cameroun from 1868 to 1906; and the diary of E. H. Richard, a missionary in Natal from 1881 to 1908. The collection also contains a typewritten survey of the actions of the General Conference of the Methodist Episcopal Church concerning missions from 1872 to 1902; copious reports from missionaries in Africa for use by the World Missionary Conference, Edinburgh, in 1910; and a statement concerning Christian educational policy in Tanganyika, 1932.

The Library's extensive holdings in published works on Africa are outlined in two of its own bibliographies: *Africa South of the Sahara* (1959; with supplement, 1961) and *Books about Africa South of the Sahara: A Reading List* (1963).

---

* As this book was in press, MSU acquired the library of M. M. De Ryck (former governor of the Equator province) containing much materal published in or about the Belgian Congo.

MOUNT HOLYOKE COLLEGE

The Library of Mount Holyoke College, South Hadley, Massachusetts, holds the correspondence with alumnae who have served as missionaries in Africa (Angola, Congo, Gabon, South Africa, etc.) during the past century.

NANTUCKET HISTORICAL ASSOCIATION WHALING MUSEUM

The Nantucket Historical Association Whaling Museum, Broad Street, Nantucket, Massachusetts, holds shipping papers, account books, assurance policies, and records of the whaling industry in Nantucket (which had many contacts with southern and eastern Africa), 1810–1860, and the logs of whaling vessels, 1790–1864, totaling 115 volumes.

NASSAU COUNTY HISTORICAL
AND GENEALOGICAL SOCIETY

The Nassau County Historical and Genealogical Society, Nassau County Historical Museum, Nassau County Park, Salisbury, East Meadow, New York, contains the letters written to William H. Onderdonk, of New York, by William H. Bull from Gambia, 1836–1841, concerning the difficulties of commerce off the African coast.

THE NATIONAL ARCHIVES*

The holdings of the National Archives consist of noncurrent records of the Federal Government considered to have permanent value for the government itself, for individuals in connection with their rights as citizens, and for scholars. Although the bulk of the records originated in the various agencies, past and present, of the Executive Branch, the Legislative and Judicial Branches are also well represented.

Organization of the records in Archives custody is by 'record group,' the typical record group consisting of the files of an independent agency or those of a bureau or comparable organizational unit within an executive department. Often the files of the head of an executive department, together with central and other records relating to the department as a whole, are designated the 'General Records' of the department and the covering record group is so entitled. In some cases 'collective' record groups that have been established are made up of the files of a number of small and short-lived agencies having a functional or administrative relationship. There are also other variations on the constitution of record groups.

For custodial and other archival purposes record groups are distributed between the following records branches in the National Archives: Legislative Branch; Diplomatic, Legal, and Fiscal Branch; Social and Economic Branch; Army and Air Corps Branch; and Navy and Military Service Branch. The title of each roughly indicates its area of responsibility. As a rule the records within each record group

* Revision of the author's article in *African Studies Bulletin*, Vol. II, No. 2 (April 1959). Mr. Rieger is currently Director, National African Guide Project, National Historical Publications Commission, National Archives and Records Service.

are maintained in their original order, no attempt being made to rearrange them by subject, by function, or otherwise.

Several types of finding aids are prepared and published in either printed or processed form by the Archives to facilitate reference to its holdings.* These include general finding aids which describe records held in several or all records branches and not restricted to a particular subject;† subject-matter guides such as reference information papers which describe materials throughout the Archives pertaining to specific fields of interest; and finding aids relating to individual record groups—registration statements, preliminary inventories, preliminary checklists, and special lists. Most general of these is the registration statement, essentially a brief one- or two-page summary description of the content of the record group. The preliminary inventory and the now-discarded preliminary checklist provide a detailed description of the record group in terms of the individual 'series' of which it is composed. (A series generally consists of a body of records filed together by the agency that accumulated them in accordance with some integrating scheme: alphabetical, numerical, chronological, geographical, subject-classification, etc.) The special list, often prepared as an appendix to a preliminary inventory or checklist but also issued separately, is most detailed of all since the individual item (the document, the dossier, the file folder) is its unit of description. The Archives does not ordinarily prepare card indexes to its holdings, although many useful indexes created by the agencies of origin have been received with the records to which they relate.

Records in Archives custody may neither circulate nor go out on interlibrary loan; they can be used only in the search rooms of the National Archives Building. Records branch search rooms are open daily from 8:45 A.M. to 5:15 P.M., weekends and federal holidays excepted. The Central Search Room, to which branches will send records on request, is open between 8:45 A.M. and 10 P.M. weekdays and from 9 A.M. to 5. P.M. Saturday, again federal holidays excepted. Though records may not be borrowed, electrostatic, photostatic, or microfilm copies of them may be purchased at standard rates; the exact price in each case will be quoted when the order is placed. Many series of records have been reproduced in full or in part as National Archives microfilm publications;‡ the cost of these prints is substantially less than that of specially ordered microcopies.

---

* A complete current list, *Publications of the National Archives and Records Service*, is available on request from the Exhibits and Publications Division of the Service.

† (1) *Guide to the Records in the National Archives* (1948, 684 pp.); (2) *National Archives Accessions*, issued quarterly, 1948–1952, and irregularly thereafter; (3) *Your Government's Records in the National Archives* (1950, 102 pp.); (4) *Guide to Federal Archives Relating to the Civil War* (1962, 721 pp., $3.00); (5) *Handbook of Federal World War Agencies and Their Records, 1917–1921* (1943, 666 pp.); (6) *Federal Records of World War II:* Vol. I, *Civilian Agencies* (1950, 1073 pp.), Vol. II, *Military Agencies* (1951, 1061 pp.). (1) is out of print but widely available in research and university libraries. (2), (3), (5), and (6) may be obtained without charge, as long as the limited supply lasts, from the Exhibits and Publications Division, National Archives and Records Service, Washington, D.C. 20408. (4) may be purchased from the Superintendent of Documents, Government Printing Office, Washington, D.C. 20402.

‡ A complete *List of National Archives Microfilm Publications, 1965*, which contains detailed descriptive and price information, is available on request from the Exhibits and Publications Division.

Access to records in the Archives is largely unrestricted. However, in the case of specific series or categories of records, restrictions on use may have been imposed for various reasons by action of the Congress, the President, the agency of origin, or the Archivist of the United States. In addition, many documents, of the post-1939 period especially, relating to matters of national security are security-classified and therefore unavailable except by permission of the appropriate authorities.

As is clear from the foregoing, there is in the National Archives no separate collection of materials relating to Africa; rather such materials are located in each of the many record groups of agencies concerned to any degree—greater or lesser— with Africa. Because of this wide distribution it is impracticable to attempt any estimate of volume; but it is considerable, particularly in the record groups of agencies responsible for aspects of foreign relations.

For the most part the Africa-related records are in written or typed manuscript form but also include maps, photographs, and motion picture films. As a rule there are no published materials except for occasional government documents, pamphlets, and newspaper clippings attached to correspondence. In the descriptions that follow it should be assumed that the records covered are in manuscript form unless otherwise noted.

A preliminary survey of the Archives' Africa holdings, the results of which are reported below,* indicates clearly the variety and the wide geographical and disciplinary scope of these materials. The survey report is organized by the individual record groups in which pertinent materials are located, the record group entries being assembled under the following main headings: Department of State; Information Agencies; Department of the Treasury; War Department; Navy Department; Intelligence Agencies; Department of Justice; Department of the Interior; Department of Agriculture; Department of Commerce; Independent Economic Agencies; Department of Health, Education, and Welfare; United States Congress; Federal Courts; and Axis Powers. The entry for each record group consists of a summary description or characterization of records, a list of Archives finding aids and microfilm publications, and a statement of reference restrictions as these have relevance for students of Africa.† Out-of-print finding aids are so designated.

---

* See also the following Reference Information Papers concerning Africa-related records which were issued by the Archives early in World War II: No. 13, *Materials in the National Archives Relating to French Possessions in Africa* (December 1942, 8 pp., $1.60); No. 14, *Materials in the National Archives Relating to Spanish Possessions in Africa* (December 1942, 5 pp., $1.00); No. 18, *Materials in the National Archives Relating to Portuguese Posessions in Africa* (April 1943, 4 pp., $0.80). These are all out of print, but electrostatic (Xerox) copies can be purchased from the Exhibits and Publications Division for the prices quoted above in each case.

† Except as otherwise specifically indicated, record group finding aids mentioned in the entries which are in print, as well as the registration statements for all record groups, may be obtained without charge from the Exhibits and Publications Division. In the case of out-of-print items, the Division will quote estimates on the cost of electrostatic, photostatic, or microfilm copies upon request.

DEPARTMENT OF STATE

RG 11, U.S. GOVERNMENT DOCUMENTS HAVING GENERAL LEGAL EFFECT: Among the foreign treaty series, 1778–1962, are treaties with African states, or with European states in connection with African territories or matters in whole or in part, together with associated formal documents and maps. (Most substantive documentation respecting the negotiation of treaties is filed in RG 59, General Records of the Department of State.) There are several major categories of Africa-related treaties: (i) 'peace and friendship' treaties (nine with the various Barbary States between 1786 and 1836, beginning and ending with Morocco); (ii) commercial treaties (with Muscat and Zanzibar, 1833; Madagascar, 1867 and 1881; Orange Free State, 1871; Egypt, 1884; Congo Free State, 1891; and Ethiopia, 1903 and 1914); (iii) anti-slave trade treaties (two with Great Britain, in 1842—the Webster-Ashburton Treaty—and in 1870; and one in 1890 with the European powers multilaterally, the Statute of Brussels); (iv) treaties of extraterritoriality (with respect to Zanzibar, 1905, and Tripolitania and Cyrenaica, 1912–1913); (v) treaties defining U.S. rights in the post-World War I African mandates (seven between 1923 and 1925 with the mandatory powers: England, France, and Belgium). Other important treaties include that of 1884 recognizing the flag of the International Congo Association, the Algeciras Convention of 1906 regarding Morocco, and the 1919 Versailles multilateral agreement regulating the liquor traffic in Africa.

FINDING AID: *Preliminary Inventory of United States Government Documents Having General Legal Effect.*

RG 59, GENERAL RECORDS OF THE DEPARTMENT OF STATE: The basic head-quarters records of the Department are in this record group and consist of separate series of instructions to and despatches from American diplomatic and consular representatives and special agents abroad, notes to and from foreign missions and consuls in the United States, and miscellaneous outgoing and incoming correspondence, 1789–1906; materials of the same kind organized in two series of subject classified central files, the numerical file, 1906–1910, and the decimal file, 1910–1944; and a separately filed series of consular reports, 1925–1950. Scattered through these records is a great volume and variety of documentation on Africa, in fact the greatest in any single Archives record group except perhaps RG 84 discussed below. This documentation primarily concerns American relations with the various African territories and/or their European metropoles during the past century and a half, but it also contains, particularly for the postpartition period, much information on the emergent patterns of African geography, population, politics, government, finances, resources, infrastructure, and economy. To locate materials relating to specific fields of interest it is necessary for the searcher to consult the guides to its records created by the State Department: the various series of registers covering the pre-1906 correspondence* and the card indexes, the lists of papers, and the 'Classification of Correspondence' filing manual pertaining to the post-1906 central

---

* See also the detailed analysis of the materials in the diplomatic correspondence relating to each country published in Claude H. Van Tyne and Waldo G. Leland, *Guide to the Archives of the Government of the United States in Washington* (2d ed., Washington, 1907), pp. 7–20.

files. Small-scale political and economic maps of Africa and its regions and photographs on miscellaneous African subjects are also included in this record group.

FINDING AIDS: *Preliminary Inventory of the General Records of the Department of State* (includes complete listings in its appendixes of pre-1906 series of diplomatic instructions and despatches, notes to and from foreign missions, and consular despatches for African countries and posts—all of which have been filmed and are tabulated under 'Microfilm Publications' below). *List of Documents Relating to Special Agents of the Department of State, 1789–1906* (includes references of 63 agents whose missions were concerned with African areas, mostly North Africa), out of print.

MICROFILM PUBLICATIONS: In addition to the following publications focused entirely upon Africa, large segments of the pre-1906 central files relating to the metropole countries are also available in microfilm form; for details, see *List of National Archives Microfilm Publications, 1965.*

Country or Post	Period	Microcopy No.	No. of Rolls	Price
DIPLOMATIC INSTRUCTIONS				
Barbary Powers	1834–1906	M–77 (Roll 18)	1	$ 6
Egypt	1875–1886	M–77 (Roll 53)	1	3
Liberia	1863–1906	M–77 (Roll 110)	1	3
DIPLOMATIC DESPATCHES				
Liberia	1863–1906	M–170	14	$65
Morocco	1905–1906	T–725	1	4
CONSULAR DESPATCHES				
Algiers	1785–1906	M–23	19	$63
Bathurst	1857–1889	T–365	2	5
Bissão (included in Santiago below)				
Boma	1888–1895	T–47	1	2
Cairo	1864–1906	T–41	24	105
Cape Town	1800–1906	T–191	22	73
Freetown (included in Sierra Leone)				
Gaboon	1856–1888	T–466	1	5
Gorée-Dakar	1883–1906	T–573	2	7
Grand Bassa	1868–1882	M–171	1	2
Monrovia	1852–1906	M–169	7	19
Mozambique-				
Lourenço Marques	1854–1906	T–171	6	23
Port Said	1870–1896	T–658	1	3
Pretoria	1898–1906	T–660	3	13

Country or Post	Period	Microcopy No.	No. of Rolls	Price
St. Paul (São Paulo) de Loanda	1854–1893	T–430	5	$19
Santiago, Cape Verde Islands	1818–1898	T–434	7	26
São Tomé (included in St. Paul de Loanda)				
Seychelles	1868–1888	T–437	1	6
Sierra Leone	1858–1906	T–438	5	19
Tamatave	1853–1906	T–60	11	56
Tangier	1797–1906	T–61	27	117
Teneriffe	1795–1906	T–690	10	45
Tetuan	1877–1888	T–156	1	1
Tripoli	1796–1885	T–40	11	43
Tunis	1797–1906	T–303	12	54
Zanzibar	1836–1906	T–100	11	34

NOTES TO FOREIGN LEGATIONS

Country or Post	Period	Microcopy No.	No. of Rolls	Price
Liberia	1850–1903	M–99 (Rolls 58, 60)	2	$ 5

NOTES FROM FOREIGN LEGATIONS

Country or Post	Period	Microcopy No.	No. of Rolls	Price
Congo	1894–1901			
Egypt	1906	T–953 (Roll 3)	1	3
Morocco	1889–1903			
Liberia	1862–1898	T–807	1	4
Madagascar	1883–1894	T–806	1	2
South African Republic and Orange Free State	1876–1902	T–953 (Roll 1)	1	3
Tripoli	1876			
Tunis	1865–1876	T–953 (Roll 4)	1	3
West Africa	1877			
Zanzibar	1848–1905			
Tunis	1805–1806	M–67	1	1

DECIMAL FILE, 1910–1929

Country or Post	Period	Microcopy No.	No. of Rolls	Price
Egypt				
Internal Affairs		M–571	31	$197
Political Relations with U.S.		M–572	1	2
Political Relations with Other States		M–573	1	2
Ethiopia				
Internal Affairs		M–411	4	28
Political Relations with U.S.		M–412	1	2
Morocco				
Internal Affairs		M–577	24	115

RESTRICTIONS: Pre-1933 records, except for certain specified categories, are currently open to the general public. (The terminal date of this 'open period' is periodically advanced since it has been fixed by departmental regulation at 10 years prior to the year covered by the latest published volume in the 'Foreign Relations' series.) Later records fall into two classes: 'limited access' (1933–1941) and 'closed' (1942 to date). The former class is available to qualified researchers with the permission of the State Department. The latter class is generally not accessible to nonofficial researchers except that the Department may permit its use for 'broad studies regarded as desirable in the national interest, and studies of more limited scope involving non-sensitive and generally unclassified materials.'

RG 84, FOREIGN SERVICE POSTS OF THE DEPARTMENT OF STATE: The basic field records of the State Department in this record group contain the same wide variety of information relating to Africa and to American relations with Africa as do the headquarters records in RG 59. Such information, scattered among the records of diplomatic posts in European metropole capitals, is to be found in concentrated form in the records of the legations to independent African countries and in those of the consular posts throughout the continent. The Archives now has in custody records from diplomatic posts in the metropoles as follows: Belgium, 1832–1935; France, 1789–1935; Germany, 1835–1913; Great Britain, 1826–1935; Italy, 1839–1939; Portugal, 1824–1935; and Spain, 1801–1935. Also on hand are records of the legations in Egypt, 1873–1935; Ethiopia, 1908–1936; Liberia, 1870–1935; Morocco, 1903–1917; and Union of South Africa, 1921–1935. In addition, there are files of 60 consulates in every part of Africa. The dates of these consulate records range from the early nineteenth century (the Algiers, Zanzibar, and Cape Town materials begin in 1803, 1834, and 1835 respectively) to the mid-1930's.*

FINDING AIDS: *Preliminary Inventory of the Records of Selected Foreign Service Posts* (includes those of the U.S. Embassy in Great Britain, 1826–1935). *List of Foreign Service Post Records in the National Archives* (gives locations of posts and inclusive dates of their records).

MICROFILM PUBLICATION: Papers of R. Dorsey Mohun, 1892–1913 (T–294, 3 rolls, $13).†

RESTRICTIONS: Same as those cited for RG 59 above.

RG 43, UNITED STATES PARTICIPATION IN INTERNATIONAL CONFERENCES, COMMISSIONS, AND EXPOSITIONS: Contains printed copies of the proposals and projects, protocols, reports of commissions, and the General Act of the Berlin

---

* For a detailed description of the West African diplomatic and consular post records in the National Archives, see Supplement I beginning on p. 79 below.

† Mohun's papers consist of correspondence, telegrams, and cablegrams (both incoming and outgoing), reports, diaries, field notebooks, manuscript maps, autobiographical articles, and photographic prints relating to his activities as U.S. commercial agent, Boma, Congo Free State, 1892–1895; U.S. consul, Zanzibar, 1895–1897; chief, Congo Free State Telegraphic Expedition, 1898–1901; chef de Mission de Recherches Minières for Forminière in the Congo, 1907–1909; and agent of the Rubber Exploration Co. of New York in South Africa, Mozambique, and Madagascar, 1910–1911. Of special interest are materials relating to Mohun's service in the Belgian campaign against the Arab slavers in the Eastern Congo during his incumbency as U.S. commercial agent. (The originals of these papers were given to the Belgian government by Mohun's heir in 1959.)

Conference on West African Affairs, 1884–1885, at which the United States was represented. The principal official documentation of the major American role at the Conference is in RG 59 (General Records of the State Department) and RG 84 (Foreign Service Posts of the Department of State), particularly among the records of, or relating to, the Berlin Legation. Also in RG 43 are general records concerning the Capitulations Conference of 1937 at Montreux which dealt with the termination of extraterritorial rights in Egypt.

FINDING AID: *Preliminary Inventory of the Records of United States Participation in International Conferences, Commissions, and Expositions* and *Supplement* thereto.

RESTRICTIONS: Same as those cited for RG 59 above.

RG 76, BOUNDARY AND CLAIMS COMMISSIONS AND ARBITRATIONS: Contains the records, 1868–1870, of an arbitration proceeding in a dispute between Great Britain and Portugal regarding sovereignty over the coastal island of Bulama and adjacent mainland territory in what is now Portuguese Guinea. President Grant, the arbitrator, handed down an award in Portugal's favor.

RG 256, AMERICAN COMMISSION TO NEGOTIATE PEACE: The central files of the U.S. delegation to the Versailles Conference contain—among the minutes and reports of the conference Commissions on Colonies, German Colonies, Colonial Mandates, Morocco, and Revision of the General Acts of Berlin (1885) and Brussels (1890), as well as elsewhere in the series—materials relating to the partition of the German empire in Africa, the rival claims of Britain, France, Italy, and Belgium, and the origins of the mandate system. (Card indexes, lists of papers, a 'Key to Records,' and a classification manual prepared by the State Department serve as guides to the series.) The records of The Inquiry, a predecessor of the American Commission established under Colonel House in 1917 at President Wilson's instigation to make background studies of subjects likely to arise at the conference, include many reports, studies, and other papers pertaining to geographical, demographic, ethnological, religious, diplomatic, political, governmental, military, economic, and social problems of the various regions and territories of Africa. Among them are a couple of lengthy studies by G. L. Beer on international controls in Middle Africa and on Germany's African colonies which were later published posthumously in his *African Questions at the Paris Peace Conference* (New York, 1923). Maps produced or collected by The Inquiry in connection with some of its studies on Africa are also available.

FINDING AIDS: *Preliminary Inventory of the Records of the American Commission to Negotiate Peace* (includes lists of The Inquiry studies). *Preliminary Inventory of the Cartographic Records of the American Commission to Negotiate Peace.*

INFORMATION AGENCIES

RG 208, OFFICE OF WAR INFORMATION: Among the files of the Overseas Operations Branch of this World War II propaganda agency is a 'Mediterranean-Africa Region Informational File' containing OWI outpost, monitoring, intelligence, and research reports from and about the region. Other series contain cabled news stories and bulletins received from OWI outposts in North Africa and miscellaneous newspapers, clippings, photographs, and motion picture films that originated throughout the continent. There is also on file documentation of OWI policies with respect to Africa and copies of news stories and recordings of broadcasts directed there.

FINDING AID: *Preliminary Inventory of the Records of the Office of War Information.*

RESTRICTIONS: Records of several offices may be used only with the permission of the Secretary of State.

RG 306, U.S. INFORMATION AGENCY: The Agency's photographic files contain a wide variety of news pictures of African scenes during the period 1900–1957.

FINDING AID: *List of Titles in the General Photographic Subject File of the International Press Service, 1948–57.*

DEPARTMENT OF THE TREASURY

RG 36, BUREAU OF CUSTOMS: Scattered among the vessel entrance and clearance records of such American ports as New York, Philadelphia, and Baltimore, 1789–1900, are data on individual vessels sailing to and from African ports. The information given includes name of vessel, dates of entrance or clearance, registry, tonnage, and names of ports of destination or embarkation. For the earlier years the nature of the cargo is also indicated. The cargo manifest files for several East and Gulf Coast ports, 1789–1918, contain manifests for vessels engaged in the African trade.

RG 104, BUREAU OF THE MINT: In a series of reports to the Bureau on foreign gold and silver production and consumption, coinage, and other monetary subjects are reports for the Union of South Africa, Portuguese Africa, and French West and Equatorial Africa, 1910–1932.

WAR DEPARTMENT

The War Department record groups listed below contain documentation pertaining to military and supporting operations in the African theaters during World War II. There is also coverage of related political, economic, and public health matters in some of the record groups.

RG 107 Office of the Secretary of War
RG 165 War Department General Staff
*RG 319 Army Staff, 1939–
*RG 336 Army Technical Services
*RG 112 Office of the Surgeon General (Army)
*RG 160 Headquarters Army Service Forces
RG 18   Army Air Forces
*RG 339 Headquarters Army Air Forces
*RG 331 Allied Operational and Occupation Headquarters, World War II

FINDING AIDS: A preliminary inventory is available for each of the above record groups marked by an asterisk(*).

---

* The asterisk here indicates that a preliminary inventory is available for the War Department ecord group listed.

RESTRICTIONS: Reference to these record groups is limited by widespread security classification, provisions of certain laws and Department of Defense and Army regulations, and the requirement that 'papers less than 50 years old that have originated in the Joint (and Combined) Chiefs of Staff' may be used only with the permission of the Adjutant General.

NAVY DEPARTMENT

RG 45, NAVAL RECORDS COLLECTION OF THE OFFICE OF NAVAL RECORDS AND LIBRARY: Among the miscellaneous records of the Secretary's Office herein are letters relating to the Barbary pirates, 1803–1808. There is also considerable correspondence, 1819–1861, between the Secretary of the Navy and commanding officers of the African Squadron (established under the Webster-Ashburton Treaty of 1842 with Britain to help suppress the slave trade), U.S. agents on the Guinea coast, federal executive and judicial officials, the American Colonization Society, and private individuals and firms relating to the seizure of American slaving vessels, their condemnation in U.S. district courts, arrangements for shipment of liberated Africans to reception centers at Sherbro Island and along the Liberian littoral, the establishment, maintenance, and supply of these centers, the role of U.S. naval vessels in combating the traffic in slaves and in facilitiating African and American Negro colonization in Liberia, and the activities of the American Colonization Society and state societies. Separately filed are letter books of the first commander of the African Squadron, Commodore Matthew C. Perry, 1843–1845, and of a successor, Commodore William C. Bolton, 1847–1849.

FINDING AID: *Preliminary Checklist of Naval Records Collection of the Office of Naval Records and Library, 1775–1900* (out of print).

MICROFILM PUBLICATIONS: *Miscellaneous Letters Sent by the Secretary of the Navy ('General Letter Book'), 1798–1886* (M–209, 42 rolls, $325).* *Letters Sent by the Secretary of the Navy to Commandants and Navy Agents, 1808–65* (M–441, 5 rolls, $26). *Letters Sent by the Secretary of the Navy to Officers ('Officers, Ships of War'), 1798–1868* (M–149, 86 rolls, $263).† *Letters Received by the Secretary of the Navy from Commanding Officers of Squadrons ('Squadron Letters'), 1841–86: African Squadron, 1843–61* (M–89, Rolls 101–112,‡ $46). *Letters Received by the*

---

* Includes 'letters to United States agents on the African coast, officials of the American Colonization Society, and others regarding African colonization, 1844–61.'

† Includes 'instructions to commanding officers of squadrons and vessels and to other naval officers of all ranks.'

‡ Following is the content of these rolls:

Roll No.	Inclusive Dates	Name of Commander	Price
101	Apr. 10, 1843—Apr. 29, 1845	Commo. Matthew C. Perry	$6
102	Jan. 14, 1845—Aug. 8, 1846	Commo. Charles W. Skinner	$4
103	May 27, 1846—Oct. 11, 1847	Commo. George C. Read	$3
104	Nov. 22, 1848—Sept. 3, 1849	Commo. Benjamin Cooper	$2
105	Oct. 11, 1849—June 25, 1851	Commo. Francis H. Gregory	$4
106	Jan. 23, 1851—Mar. 30, 1853	Commo. Elie A. F. LaVallette	$3
107	Jan. 4, 1853—June 4, 1855	Commo. Isaac Mayo	$3
108	Jan. 17, 1855—June 2, 1857	Commo. Thomas Crabbe	$3
109	June 9, 1857—Aug. 31, 1859	Flag Officer Thomas A. Conover	$4
110	May 28, 1859—Feb. 13, 1860	Flag Officer William Inman	$4
111	Mar. 28–Sept. 30, 1860	Flag Officer William Inman	$5
112	Oct. 1, 1860—Sept. 28, 1861	Flag Officer William Inman	$5

Secretary of the Navy from Commanders ('Masters Commandant' through 1837, thereafter 'Commanders' Letters'), 1804–86 (M–147, 124 rolls, $758). *Letters Received by the Secretary of the Navy from Officers below the Rank of Commander ('Officers' Letters'), 1802–86* (M–148, 518 rolls, $2,733). *Letters Received by the Secretary of the Navy from Captains ('Captains' Letters'), 1805–61, 1866–85* (M–125, 413 rolls, $1,221). *Correspondence of the Secretary of the Navy Relating to African Colonization, 1819–44* (M–205, 2 rolls, $15). *Letter Books of Commodore Matthew C. Perry, Mar. 10, 1843—Feb. 20, 1845* (M–206, 1 roll, $5).

RG 80, GENERAL RECORDS OF THE DEPARTMENT OF THE NAVY: The general files of the Office of the Secretary, 1885–1940, contain a scattering of correspondence relating to the movements of American naval vessels along the African coasts and to the state of and facilities in various ports there.

RESTRICTIONS: No departmental records dated later than June 30, 1941, may be used except by permission of the Navy Department.

RG 38, OFFICE OF THE CHIEF OF NAVAL OPERATIONS: Contains, in the series of naval intelligence reports, 1882–1922, reports concerning various African—particularly North African—areas. The reports deal primarily with ports, harbors, fueling facilities, and other matters of naval interest but also with economic conditions more generally. Included too are related maps.

FINDING AID: *Preliminary Inventory of the Cartographic Records of the Office of the Chief of Naval Operations.*

RESTRICTIONS: Same as those cited for RG 80 above.

RG 313, NAVAL OPERATING FORCES: Among the records of squadrons and fleets, 1865–1940, are materials relating to visits to African ports by U.S. naval vessels (e.g., to Boma and the estuary of the Congo River during the Berlin African Conference, 1884–1885).

FINDING AID: *Preliminary Inventory of the Records of Naval Operating Forces.*

RESTRICTIONS: Same as those cited for RG 80 above.

RG 181, NAVAL DISTRICTS AND SHORE ESTABLISHMENTS: Contains operational records of Advanced Amphibious Training Bases at Port-Lyautey, Morocco, and Béni-Saf, Cherchel, Mostaganem, Nemours, and Ténès, Algeria, 1943–1944. These bases were used for the training and servicing of amphibious squadrons during the World War II North African and Sicilian campaigns.

FINDING AID: *Preliminary Inventory of the Records of Naval Establishments Created Overseas during World War II* (out of print).

RESTRICTIONS: Same as those cited for RG 80 above.

RG 24, BUREAU OF NAVAL PERSONNEL: The logbook series, 1801–1946, contains information—usually of a technical nature after 1860 but more general before that—on African ports visited by specific naval vessels. Among the Bureau's personnel files are records of officers who served in the African Squadron.

FINDING AID: *Preliminary Inventory of the Records of the Bureau of Naval Personnel.*

MICROFILM PUBLICATION: *Officers' Service Abstracts ('Records of Officers'), 1798–1893* (M–330, 19 rolls, $65).

RESTRICTIONS: Same as those cited for RG 80 above.

RG 37, HYDROGRAPHIC OFFICE: Contains nautical charts of African coast lines, river mouths, ports and harbors, and significant headlands, 1855 to date.

FINDING AID: *Preliminary Inventory of the Records of the Hydrographic Office* (out of print).

RESTRICTIONS: Same as those cited for RG 80 above.

INTELLIGENCE AGENCIES

RG 226, OFFICE OF STRATEGIC SERVICES: Contains correspondence, reports, and other records of the Europe-Africa Division of the Research and Analysis Branch, 1941–1945. Among declassified 'Numbered Reports' of the Branch are two comprehensive ones *West and Equatorial Africa* (2 vols., January 1942) and *Spanish Morocco and the Tangier Zone* (Vol. I only, November 1942).

RESTRICTIONS: These records are closed for 50 years except by permission of the State Department.

RG 262, FOREIGN BROADCAST INTELLIGENCE SERVICE: The files of this World War II monitoring agency contain transcripts (full and partial), summaries, and sound recordings of short-wave broadcasts emanating from African stations (e.g., Leopoldville, Brazzaville), 1941–1945. In addition, in a series of 'Special Reports,' 1942–1944, on topical themes are several pertaining to Africa (e.g., 'Axis Propaganda Preparations for Defeat in Tunisia').

FINDING AID: *Preliminary Inventory of the Records of the Foreign Broadcast Intelligence Service.*

RG 263, CENTRAL INTELLIGENCE AGENCY: The records of the Foreign Broadcast Information Branch, 1947–1948, include transcripts and reports of radio broadcasts from Algiers, Brazzaville, and Cairo.

FINDING AID: *Preliminary Inventory of the Records of the Central Intelligence Agency.*

DEPARTMENT OF JUSTICE

RG 60, GENERAL RECORDS OF THE DEPARTMENT OF JUSTICE: The Attorney General's papers, 1790–1870, contain scattered correspondence relating to the African slave trade, particularly to court cases arising from the trade. Among the Secretary of the Interior's letters of the early 1860's concerning judiciary expenses (later inherited by the Justice Department) is correspondence on the enforcement of the laws prohibiting the slave trade and the return of recaptured Negroes to West Africa.

MICROFILM PUBLICATION: *Letters Sent by the Attorney General's Office, 1817–1858* (T–411, 2 rolls, $7).

RG 118, U.S. ATTORNEYS AND MARSHALS: The records of various U.S. attorneys for the period before 1865, particularly those of the Southern District of New York, contain scattered correspondence concerning the enforcement of legislation prohibiting the import of slaves.

FINDING AID: *Preliminary Inventory of the Records of United States Attorneys and Marshals.*

DEPARTMENT OF THE INTERIOR

RG 48, OFFICE OF THE SECRETARY OF THE INTERIOR: With the transfer from the Navy to the Interior Department in 1861 of responsibility for administering the anti-slave trade laws and those providing for the colonization of free and recaptured Negroes in Liberia and other tropical countries, the Secretary of the Interior accumulated much correspondence on these and related subjects, including letters from the President, Congress, and various executive departments, 1858–1872; from the U.S. agent for liberated Africans in Liberia, 1860–1865; and concerning the proceedings of mixed prize arbitration courts in New York, Cape Town, and Freetown, 1861–1870.

FINDING AID: *Preliminary Inventory of the Cartographic Records of the Secretary of the Interior* (out of print).

MICROFILM PUBLICATION: *Records Relating to the African Slave Trade and Negro Colonization, 1854–72* (M–160, 10 rolls, $37).

RG 70, BUREAU OF MINES: In its collection of foreign mining company reports and associated minutes of company meetings, 1913–1945, the Bureau has such documents in quantity for the Transvaal as well as for French West Africa, Nigeria, Belgian Congo, and Angola. There are also in the Bureau's Point IV program files, 1950–1952, correspondence and some substantial reports on mining conditions and technical assistance requirements in several African countries, particularly Egypt, Ethiopia, Liberia, and Libya.

RG 115, BUREAU OF RECLAMATION: Contains a number of reports and related correspondence on reclamation matters and activities—e.g., water supply, irrigation, colonization of new lands—in the following African territories, 1902–1945: Morocco, Algeria, Egypt, British and French West Africa, Belgian Congo, Angola, Kenya, Uganda, Mozambique, and Madagascar. Included are substantial reports on irrigation in the Nile Valley, 1927, and water problems in Algeria, 1943.

FINDING AID: *Preliminary Inventory of the Records of the Bureau of Reclamation* (out of print).

DEPARTMENT OF AGRICULTURE

RG 166, FOREIGN AGRICULTURAL SERVICE: In the series of foreign agricultural reports, 1903–1954, filed by consular officials, agricultural and commercial attachés, trade commissioners, and special agents, there are many reports concerning African territories throughout the continent. General reports on the agricultural scene as a whole in a particular territory or on a major staple of an area are common; but for the most part the reports are specific in nature, relating to a great variety of subjects of agricultural interest ranging from land, labor, and production to prices, marketing, and consumption. An analogous series of reports on foreign forestry practices, 1901–1954 (originally collected by the Forest Service but now part of this record group), include many of African provenance.

FINDING AID: *Preliminary Checklist of Reports Received by the Office of Foreign Agricultural Relations, Department of Agriculture* (out of print).

RESTRICTIONS: Certain post-1941 reports may be used only by permission of the Agriculture Department.

RG 17, BUREAU OF ANIMAL INDUSTRY: Contains, in the general correspondence files of the Bureau, 1895–1939, consular reports and related correspondence pertaining to the laws and regulations of African territories (primarily in northern and southern Africa) governing the slaughter, inspection, and sale of meat, especially in connection with export and import. There are also reports on economic aspects of stock raising and on animal diseases.

FINDING AID: *Preliminary Inventory of the Records of the Bureau of Animal Industry*.

RG 54, BUREAU OF PLANT INDUSTRY, SOILS, AND AGRICULTURAL ENGINEERING: Contains reports, correspondence, and photographs relating to agricultural field investigations by departmental agents in various parts of Africa (e.g., Spain–North Africa Expedition of 1903, East Africa Expedition of 1927–1928). Among the subjects studied were climate, topography, soils, and individual plants and crops of economic value.

FINDING AID: *Preliminary Inventory of the Records of the Bureau of Plant Industry, Soils, and Agricultural Engineering*.

RG 95, FOREST SERVICE: The 'Research Compilation File,' 1897–1935, contains reports on timber resources, management, production, and marketing in African territories.

FINDING AID: *Preliminary Inventory of the Records of the Forest Service*.

RG 114, SOIL CONSERVATION SERVICE: Contains, in the 'Soil Erosion History File,' 1936–1944, extracts from books, articles, and other published materials relating to soil conditions and problems in many African areas.

DEPARTMENT OF COMMERCE

RG 151, BUREAU OF FOREIGN AND DOMESTIC COMMERCE: Contains correspondence with, and regular and special reports of, U.S. commercial attachés in various African territories concerning the economic, commercial, and financial situation, investment opportunities, and port, transportation, and communications facilities in their respective areas, 1919–1940. Complementing the attaché reports is correspondence among the 'general records' of the Bureau, 1914–1958, pertaining to American commercial relations with African territories and economic and other internal conditions there affecting commerce. There is also an extensive file of photographs covering foreign agricultural, commercial, industrial, and transportation subjects, 1912–1941, including many African items representative of the entire continent.

FINDING AID: *Preliminary Inventory of the Records of the Bureau of Foreign and Domestic Commerce*.

RG 23, COAST AND GEODETIC SURVEY: Among the Survey's scientific records are observations and computations of terrestrial magnetism and determinations of the force of gravity made at several stations on the West Coast of Africa from Freetown to the Cape of Good Hope during the American Solar Eclipse Expedition of 1889–1890.

FINDING AID: *Preliminary Inventory of the Records of the Coast and Geodetic Survey.*

RG 27, WEATHER BUREAU: Data on marine meteorological conditions in areas adjacent to Africa are scattered through the Bureau's series of marine logs, reports, and observations, 1842–1941 (with retrospective data going back to 1784). Among the records of 'international simultaneous observations,' 1874–1892, are several volumes of observations made in Algeria, Egypt, and South Africa.

FINDING AID: *Preliminary Inventory of the Climatological and Hydrological Records of the Weather Bureau. Preliminary Inventory of Operational and Miscellaneous Meteorological Records of the Weather Bureau. List of Climatological Records in the National Archives* (out of print).

MICROFILM PUBLICATION: *Climatological Records, 1819–92* (T–907, 539 rolls, $4,199).

RG 29, BUREAU OF THE CENSUS: Contains statistical tabulations on U.S. exports and imports, 1911–1938, which show, in terms of physical quantity and/or dollar value, the volume of African-American commerce during the period by country and commodity.

RG 41, BUREAU OF MARINE INSPECTION AND NAVIGATION: Data regarding American merchant vessels in the African trade are scattered through the various series of vessel ownership and documentation files, 1789–1952 (usually arranged by home port), and the official merchant marine logbook files, 1916–1940. (The documents for an individual vessel—the 'certificate of registry' being the principal one required for vessels engaged in foreign trade—typically contain detailed information on its owners, masters, home ports, place and date of construction, tonnage, rig, dimensions and other physical characteristics.)

FINDING AID: *Customhouse Marine Documentation: A List by Series Showing Ports for Which Documents Are Available in Record Group 41.*

MICROFILM PUBLICATION: *Certificates of Registry, Enrollment, and License Issued at Edgartown, Mass., 1815–1913* (M–130, 9 rolls, $52). (Edgartown was a famous whaling port on Martha's Vineyard.)

INDEPENDENT ECONOMIC AGENCIES

RG 234, RECONSTRUCTION FINANCE CORPORATION: In connection with the RFC's World War II function of helping to finance the acquisition of strategic and 'critical' commodities, certain of the agency's subsidiaries—the U.S. Commercial Company especially and also the Defense Supplies Corporation, the Defense Plant Corporation, the Metals Reserve Company, the Rubber Reserve Company, and the Rubber Development Corporation—accumulated a substantial volume of records relating (i) to the procurement and stockpiling of a wide range of minerals and forest products from most of the territories of Africa and (ii) to underlying economic and social trends, conditions, and factors in these territories affecting the procurement programs.

RESTRICTIONS: These records may not be used except by permission of the Treasury Department and/or the General Services Administration.

RG 266, SECURITY AND EXCHANGE COMMISSION: Among the files of registration statements submitted to the Commission by corporations proposing to issue securities for sale in interstate commerce, 1933–1943, are statements from corporations doing business in or with Africa (e.g., Firestone Tire and Rubber Co.). The statements and associated documents typically contain summary information on the organization's history, finances, assets, and subsidiaries.

FINDING AID: *Preliminary Inventory of the Records of the Security and Exchange Commission.*

RESTRICTIONS: Only formal documents in the registration dossiers are open to the public.

RG 122, FEDERAL TRADE COMMISSION: Contains a scattering of case files relating to the Commission's investigations of complaints made by South African companies about the trade practices of U.S. exporters and importers, 1921–1929.

FINDING AID: *Preliminary Inventory of the Records of the Federal Trade Commission.*

RESTRICTIONS: These records may not be used except by permission of the Federal Trade Commission.

RG 182, WAR TRADE BOARD: The research and 'country' files of this World War I economic warfare agency contain studies, reports, and statistical tabulations on the contemporary economy of many African territories, with particular emphasis on the principal commodities produced and on the direction of foreign trade. There are especially long narrative reports relating to the Belgian Congo and the Union of South Africa.

FINDING AID: *Preliminary Inventory of the Records of the War Trade Board.*

RG 20, OFFICE OF THE SPECIAL ADVISER TO THE PRESIDENT ON FOREIGN TRADE: Contains reports, analyses, and statistical tabulations on the foreign trade of, and potential markets in, several African territories in the early and mid-1930's, notably the Belgian Congo, South Africa, and British West Africa. Special attention is given to the volume and character of the trade between the territories concerned and the United States.

RG 169, FOREIGN ECONOMIC ADMINISTRATION: There is considerable documentation in this record group on the World War II lend-lease, export control, strategic material procurement, and economic warfare programs and operations of the United States in Africa or affecting Africa. Every major region of the continent was involved. Some of the materials pertaining to Africa are concentrated in the files of the British Colonies Section, the South Africa Section, and the Belgium and Belgian Congo Section and in the papers assembled by the agency historian; but much more is scattered through the record group. Also on file are photographs of African mining and plantation operations during the war.

FINDING AID: *Preliminary Inventory of the Records of the Foreign Economic Administration.*

RESTRICTIONS: For the most part these records may not be used except by permission of the State Department.

RG 188, OFFICE OF PRICE ADMINISTRATION: The records of the Foreign Information Branch, Division of Research, contain correspondence, reports, and publications regarding general economic conditions, foreign trade, transportation and communications facilities, import and production controls, price indexes, price controls, and rationing in the Union of South Africa and, to a lesser extent, in other territories of British Africa during World War II.

RG 179, WAR PRODUCTION BOARD: The Policy Documentation File of the Board and its predecessors, 1939–1945, contains numerous documents—correspondence, minutes, reports, statements—concerning aspects of the African economy, particularly the availability or potential availability from African sources throughout the continent of raw materials, in the main minerals and fibers, required for the war effort. These documents were accumulated from a variety of sources in connection with the WPB's over-all responsibility during World War II for the national industrial procurement and production programs.

FINDING AID: *Preliminary Inventory of the Records of the War Production Board* (out of print).

RESTRICTIONS: Data obtained in confidence from private sources may be made available only in accordance with the protective terms of the Federal Reports Act of 1942.

RG 32, U.S. SHIPPING BOARD: Between 1916 and 1936 the USSB was the federal regulatory agency in the merchant marine field and also owned and operated a substantial percentage of the nation's merchant vessels. Interspersed among its records concerning the state of the shipping market, competition with foreign carriers, shipping route allocations and services, determination of freight rates, port and harbor conditions and facilities abroad, and vessel cargoes and operations is a considerable amount of material relating to various African coastal territories. The USSB maintained at one time or another a number of field offices in African ports, but the files of only one of these (Dakar, 1919–1921) survive.

FINDING AID: *Preliminary Inventory of the Records of the United States Shipping Board.*

RG 178, U.S. MARITIME COMMISSION: This agency was successor to the U.S. Shipping Board between 1936 and 1950, with similar functions and similar records bearing on Africa.

FINDING AID: *Preliminary Inventory of the Records of the U.S. Maritime Commission.*

RG 248, WAR SHIPPING ADMINISTRATION: Contains correspondence concerning plans to develop West African ports, particularly in Liberia, to accommodate wartime traffic, 1942–1943.

FINDING AID: *Preliminary Inventory of the Records of the War Shipping Administration.*

RG 133, FEDERAL COORDINATOR OF TRANSPORTATION: The general files of this New Deal transportation research agency contain, in a series of reports prepared by the FCT on 'Foreign Experience with Transportation Control,' individual reports on the Union of South Africa, Kenya, and Tanganyika, all undated.

RG 237, FEDERAL AVIATION AGENCY: Among the central files of the Agency's predecessor, the Civil Aeronautics Administration, is scattered documentation pertaining to civil air services in southern and central Africa during the 1930's and early 1940's.

FINDING AID: *Preliminary Inventory of the Records of the Civil Aeronautics Administration.*

RG 173, FEDERAL COMMUNICATIONS COMMISSION: The general correspondence files, 1929–1932, of one of the Commission's predecessors, the Radio Division of the Commerce Department, contain reports, regulations, lists, and other documentation relating to wireless and radio station operations, and governmental control thereof, in Egypt, Morocco, Liberia, Ethiopia, Mozambique, and the Union of South Africa.

FINDING AID: *Records of the Federal Communications Commission.*

DEPARTMENT OF HEALTH, EDUCATION, AND WELFARE

RG 90, PUBLIC HEALTH SERVICE: Contains a substantial amount of correspondence and consular and other reports on the general public health situation, sanitation and water supply, disease incidence and control, and medical services in many of the territories of Africa, 1924–1944. Most extensive is the documentation concerning Liberia in which a U.S. medical adviser was stationed since before World War II and to which a Presidential Sanitary Mission was sent during the war.

FINDING AID: *Preliminary Inventory of the Records of the Public Health Service.*

RG 88, FOOD AND DRUG ADMINISTRATION: Contains consular reports, texts of legislation and regulations, and related correspondence concerning food and drug standards and their application in several territories of North, East, and South Africa, 1896–1941.

RG 119, NATIONAL YOUTH ADMINISTRATION: Contains copies of consular reports made during the late 1930's at the NYA's request, on youth conditions, programs, and movements in all of the North African territories (except Libya), Ethiopia, Kenya, Mozambique, Nigeria, Liberia, and the Union of South Africa. The report on the Nigerian Youth Movement, 1940, is particularly substantial.

FINDING AID: *Preliminary Inventory of the Records of the National Youth Administration.*

UNITED STATES CONGRESS

RG 46, U.S. SENATE: The principal unpublished records of the Senate (most of which for the period 1789–1954 are now in Archives custody) consist of journals and minutes of legislative proceedings, bills and resolutions, committee reports and papers, reports and communications from the President and executive agencies (including papers relating to treaties), petitions and memorials from the public, and voting records. These records, separately grouped for each Congress, are rich in Africa-related materials; they reflect to a greater or lesser degree all major and many minor aspects of American diplomatic, military, economic, cultural, and other relations with the various territories of Africa and their metropoles. The subjects documented range from early relations with the Barbary Powers and Zanzibar through the suppression of the ante-bellum slave trade and Liberian colonization to post-World War II economic assistance.

FINDING AID: *Preliminary Inventory of the Records of the United States Senate* (out of print). (Includes an index to subjects and names mentioned in the text.)

RESTRICTIONS: Copies of committee hearings held in executive or closed session may be used only with the permission of the committee chairman or chief counsel. Records of the Committee on Foreign Relations unrelated to legislation may not be used except by authority of the Committee's chief clerk.

RG 233, U.S. HOUSE OF REPRESENTATIVES: House records (most of which for the period 1789–1952 are now in Archives custody) fall into essentially the same categories as those of the Senate and by and large contain similar materials on Africa. However, it should be noted that constitutionally and traditionally the role of the House in foreign affairs has been secondary compared with that of the Senate.

FINDING AID: *Preliminary Inventory of the Records of the United States House of Representatives* (2 vols.).

RESTRICTIONS: Unpublished records less than 50 years old may not be used except by permission of the House.

FEDERAL COURTS

RG 267, SUPREME COURT: The case files of the Court, 1792–1915, include Africa-connected cases relating to the slave trade, as well as to other maritime and foreign commerce matters.

FINDING AIDS: *Preliminary Inventory of the Records of the Supreme Court of the United States* and *Supplement* thereto.

MICROFILM PUBLICATIONS: *Dockets of the Supreme Court, 1791–1950* (M–216, 27 rolls, $183). *Index to the Appellate Case Files of the Supreme Court, 1792–1909* (M–408, 20 rolls, $80). *Appellate Case Files of the Supreme Court, 1792–1831* (M–214, 96 rolls, $669).

RG 21, DISTRICT COURTS OF THE UNITED STATES: Among the pre-1865 case files of district and circuit courts in this record group (e.g., the courts for the Southern District of New York and the Eastern District of Pennsylvania) are admiralty and criminal cases pertaining to the African slave trade. The admiralty cases relate to the seizure, condemnation, and sale of ships engaged in the slave trade, while the criminal cases revolve around charges of outfitting slave ships and service aboard them.

FINDING AIDS: *Preliminary Inventory of the Records of the United States District Court for the Southern District of New York. Preliminary Inventory of the Records of the United States District Court for the Eastern District of Pennsylvania.*

AXIS POWERS

RG 242, WORLD WAR II COLLECTION OF SEIZED ENEMY RECORDS: This collection contains microfilm copies of archives of German and Italian origin, primarily the former. Among the German materials are archives of the Foreign Office, 1867–1945, and, for the period 1920–1945, records of various other government agencies; military offices, commands, and units; the Nazi Party, its formations, affiliated associations, and supervised organizations; and certain private businesses, institutions, and persons. The Italian materials include records, for varying periods between 1922 and 1944, of Benito Mussolini, the Ministries of Foreign Affairs, Italian Africa, and Popular Culture, and various military commands—Armed Forces High Command, Army General Staff, Field Commands, and Territorial Commands. The German archives contain a wealth of documentation on the rise and fall of the German empire in Africa, the post-World War I German ambitions and maneuvers to re-establish that empire, political and economic situations and conditions in various parts of the continent during the interwar and World War II periods, and wartime military operations in North and East Africa. The Italian records are similarly rich in information on Italy's empire in Africa: its administration, its relations with neighboring territories under British, French, and Egyptian control, the conquest of Ethiopia in the mid-1930's and the consolidation of Italian East Africa, and World War II military operations in North and East Africa.

FINDING AIDS: *A Catalog of Files and Microfilms of the German Foreign Ministry Archives, 1867–1920* (American Historical Association Committee for the Study of War Documents, 1959), out of print but available as Microcopy No. T–322 ($5). *A Catalog of Files and Microfilms of the German Foreign Ministry Archives, 1920–1945* (3 vols., Stanford, Calif., Hoover Institution, 1962–1965).* *Index of Microfilmed Records of the German Foreign Ministry and the Reich's Chancellery Covering the Weimar Period* (1958) (out of print). *Guides to German Records Filmed at Alexandria, Va., Nos. 1–42.† Preliminary Inventory of the Seized Enemy Records in the Office of Military Archives* (1965).

MICROFILM PUBLICATIONS: The following are currently available:

Title	Microcopy No.	No. of Rolls
Reich Ministry of Economics	T–71	145
Office of Reich Commissioner for the Strengthening of Germandom	T–74	20
Reich Ministry for Armament and War Production	T–73	193
Reich Air Ministry	T–177	52
Reich Ministry for Public Enlightenment and Propaganda	T–70	118
Reich Office for Soil Exploration	T–401	7
Reich Leader of the SS and Chief of the German Police	T–175	531
Miscellaneous SS Records	T–354	487
Fragmentary Records of Miscellaneous Reich Ministries and Offices	T–178	26
Headquarters, German Armed Forces High Command	T–77	1,041
Headquarters, German Army High Command	T–78	501
German Army Areas	T–79	295
German Field Commands:		
Army Groups	T–311	188

---

* Not available from the National Archives and Records Service but can be purchased from the Hoover Institution, Stanford, Calif.

† A classified list of these guides appears as Supplement II beginning on p. 97 below.

Title	Microcopy No.	No. of Rolls
Armies	T–312	1,119
Panzer Armies	T–313	478
Army Corps	T–314	237
Divisions	T–315	685
Rear Areas, Occupied Territories, and Others	T–501	345
Headquarters, German Air Force High Command	T–321	74
German Air Force Records	T–405	63
Headquarters, German Navy High Command	T–608	3
National Socialist German Labor Party	T–81	680
Nazi Cultural and Research Institutions	T–82	546
Former German and Japanese Embassies and Consulates, 1890–1945	T–179	77
Private German Enterprises	T–83	98
Private Individuals (Captured German Records)	T–253	58
Miscellaneous German Records Collection	T–84	257

RESTRICTIONS: The Italian materials may not be used except by permission of the State Department.

MORRIS RIEGER

SUPPLEMENT I

RECORDS OF THE UNITED STATES DIPLOMATIC AND CONSULAR POSTS IN WEST AFRICA, 1856–1935*

On October 17, 1833, W. M. Haxton was appointed as the first United States consular officer in West Africa, to serve as consul at Bathurst on the River Gambia. His appointment was confirmed on February 10, 1834, and he assumed the duties of his office at Bathurst on May 12, 1834. The post at Bathurst was in turn a consulate, a commercial agency, and a vice-consulate, and when the office was ordered closed on April 14, 1900, its archives were transferred to the consulate at Gorée-Dakar.

The consulate at Gorée-Dakar, Senegal, was the first American post in French West Africa, a consul being appointed to it on September 27, 1883. On January 16, 1890, an agency was created under it at Saint-Louis, Senegal. When the consulate at Gorée was closed in June 1905, both its archives and those of the Saint-Louis and Bathurst offices were taken to the Sierra Leone consulate, British West Africa.

The United States consular post at Freetown, Sierra Leone, was formally established when John E. Taylor was given official recognition as commercial agent on October 15, 1858. It became the only American consulate in West Africa outside Liberia after 1905, keeping custody of the records of the defunct posts at Gorée-Dakar, Bathurst, and Saint-Louis. When the triple city of Dakar (with Gorée and Rufisque) became the headquarters of French West Africa, the consulate at Sierra Leone was removed there. The Sierra Leone office was closed on March 30, 1915.

---

* This inventory, compiled by E. J. Alagoa of the National Archives of Nigeria, is reproduced, with minor deletions and stylistic changes, from the *Journal of the Historical Society of Nigeria*, Vol. II, No. 1 (December 1960), Ibadan University Press.

Thenceforth the Dakar post served American interests in West Africa outside Liberia. On March 29, 1928, the consulate at Lagos, Nigeria, was opened, the consuls at Dakar and Lagos agreeing to the delimitation of consular districts indicated in the introduction to the Lagos records. The Dakar office, however, was closed on September 3, 1931, and its archives, along with those of Bathurst, Gorée, Saint-Louis, and Sierra Leone, were moved to the American Embassy in Paris. From there they were taken to the State Department, Washington, in 1947 and transferred to the National Archives on June 2, 1948.

The United States Foreign Service posts in Liberia were essentially distinct from the other posts in West Africa. A commercial agent was appointed for Monrovia on April 8, 1848, and on March 11, 1863, a commissioner and consul general. An American legation and consulate general was thus established in the only independent Negro republic on the West Coast of Africa. Subordinate agencies were set up at Grand Bassa and Cape Palmas, Liberia. When a consular agent was appointed at Elmina for the Gold Coast (present-day Ghana), British West Africa, on January 2, 1879, he was also put under the Minister Resident and Consul General at Monrovia. The archives of Elmina were accordingly shipped to Monrovia when its office was closed on June 26, 1900.

The general function of the consular representatives was to foster American trade and protect American citizens. They rendered essential services to American trading vessels, seamen, missionaries, and traders residing in West Africa. As all the West African posts were maritime, the consular officers kept records of American vessels arriving and departing and of American import and export trade, and they reported home on any developments believed to affect American commercial interests. The post at Monrovia served these consular duties as well as purely diplomatic functions.

Officers at the more important posts (e.g., Monrovia) were appointed in the United States. In the case of the minor posts, they were either Europeans already serving other powers as consular representatives, Americans doing business or otherwise employed on the Coast, or educated natives of the district concerned. The post officers carried out their duties alone, employed temporary clerks from time to time, or appointed their assistants on the spot.

The records of the various posts are similar in form and character as they result from similar activities.

The records described in this inventory belong to Record Group 84, Records of the Foreign Service Posts of the Department of State. They are both complementary and supplementary to records in Record Group 59, General Records of the Department of State. Both record groups contain communications and other papers transmitted between the Foreign Service posts and the State Department in Washington.

Records of the United States Legation at Monrovia, Liberia

Although American consular posts were established in Liberia as early as 1856, the first diplomatic appointment was not made until March 11, 1863. The diplomatic representative was, however, the same person as the consular representative, and he was known as the United States Minister Resident and Consul General. The

Foreign Service post at Monrovia was itself known as the Legation and Consulate General.

Diplomatic and consular records were kept separate, but some of the books described below contain scattered consular documents. The Legation's records were transferred directly to the National Archives in 1950.

DESPATCHES SENT TO THE STATE DEPARTMENT. 1864–1891, 1903–1910. 5 vols. 1 ft.   *1*

Acknowledgments of circulars and despatches, reports, and requests for instruction. Included are reports on tours of Liberia, commerce, agriculture, the activities of American visiting commissioners, and Liberian wars with native tribes, financial difficulties, and boundary disputes with Britain and France. Also included are a few consular reports on the estates and the effects of deceased Americans, tidal observations, and commodities and goods in trade (ivory, palm oil, piassava, cotton, rice, haberdashery, boots, shoes, and other clothing). Most of the volumes are indexed (alphabetically by subject). Arranged chronologically.

DESPATCHES RECEIVED FROM THE STATE DEPARTMENT. 1871–1910. 5 vols. 1 ft.   *2*

Instructions, acknowledgments, circulars, and inquiries. Included are papers containing information on negotiations, treaties, and international conferences or conventions and correspondence transmitting foreign protests to the Liberian Government or requesting information on Liberian-native wars and the necessity of United States intervention; also included are a few consular despatches dealing with estates of deceased Americans and American seamen, reports on sanitation, and letters from the Treasury and Interior Departments. Indexed alphabetically by subject. Arranged chronologically.

STATE DEPARTMENT CIRCULARS RECEIVED. 1898–1903. 1 vol. 2 in.   *3*

Instructions to consular and/or diplomatic officers relating to the rendering of reports and accounts, customs regulations, the authentication of pensioners' vouchers, and zoological specimens. There are a few death announcements. Indexed alphabetically by subject. Arranged chronologically.

MISCELLANEOUS CORRESPONDENCE SENT. 1856–1885. 1 vol. 2 in.   *4*

Copies of communications to the State and Treasury Departments and commercial agencies at Elmina and Cape Palmas, containing mainly statements of account. Arranged chronologically.

MISCELLANEOUS CORRESPONDENCE RECEIVED. 1862–1910. 11 vols. 2 ft.   *5*

Diplomatic and consular despatches, letters, circulars, and cablegrams from the State Department in Washington, the Liberian Government, foreign legations in Liberia, subordinate American consulates, and American firms. Included are announcements of the deaths of American officials and letters of condolence; statements of consular supplies, and accounts and the estates of deceased Americans; exchanges with the Liberian Government and foreign consuls dealing with boundary disputes; Liberian requests for American assistance in native wars and for loans; Presidential proclamations relating to suppression of the slave trade and the American Civil War; the 'Report of Commissioners of the USA to Liberia' (1909) and an agreement on the basis of the report to maintain Liberian independence, integrity, and financial stability. Contains many returns and correspondence of the consular agency at Elmina, Gold Coast. Indexed alphabetically by subject. Arranged in several groups according to organization from which received and thereunder chronologically.

NOTES TO LIBERIAN OFFICIALS. 1904–1912. 1 vol. 2 in.   6

Copies of notes to President Barclay, the Attorney General, the Statistician of Liberia, the Secretary of State, the Postmaster General, the Chief of Police, the Commissioner of Agriculture, the Secretary of Education, and the General Receiver of Customs. Matters treated include requests for statistics and information, the Liberian boundary with Sierra Leone, and the activities of Liberian frontier officials. There are a few letters addressed to the consuls of Great Britain and France. Indexed alphabetically by subject. Arranged chronologically.

NOTES TO AND FROM THE LIBERIAN GOVERNMENT. 1910–1912. 1 vol. 4 in.   7

Relates to the American commission on the financial stability and territorial integrity of Liberia, the Anglo-Liberian Boundary Commission, the Franco-Liberian dispute on the boundary with Guinea, and Liberian legislation on internal and external loans. Included are copies of a 'Memorandum on the Foreign Relations of Liberia' by F. E. R. Johnson, Liberian Secretary of State; the Liberian Loan Act, 1911; the convention with Britain on the boundary with Sierra Leone, 1911; statistics supplied by the Liberian Treasury Department and Inspector of Customs on appropriations and revenue. There are also cables and letters transmitted to or from the State Department, Washington. Indexed alphabetically by subject. Arranged chronologically.

GENERAL FILES. 1910–1935. 86 vols. 22 ft.   8

Correspondence with U.S. Government agencies in Washington, the Liberian Government, foreign consuls, and American citizens and firms. Included are enclosures, circulars, copies of treaties and agreements, cablegrams (some in code), instructions, and proclamations. The subjects treated are mainly the indebtedness of Liberia and its requests for assistance by the United States, European nations, and the League of Nations; various boundary questions between Liberia and Britain and France, commissions of delimitation and the activities of officials on the frontiers; the organization of the Legation and its relations with other legations; and statistics supplied by Liberian Government departments on navigation, currency, expenditures, trade, and customs revenue. Arranged in two groups: chronologically before August 1, 1912; thereafter, according to the classification scheme summarized in appendix B below. The first group is indexed alphabetically by subject.

INSTRUCTIONS TO CONSULS. 1931. 2 vols. 3 in.   9

Relate mainly to the rendering of accounts and the provision of quarters for consular officers. Arranged chronologically.

PAPERS OF THE DIVISION OF CURRENT AFFAIRS. 1934. 1 vol. 2 in.   10

Contains confidential material.

PAPERS OF THE LEAGUE OF NATIONS COMMITTEE ON THE LIBERIAN REQUEST FOR ASSIST-
    ANCE. 1933. 1 vol. 1 in.   11

Contains the report of the Committee, its proceedings, and the memorandum of the Liberian representative.

INVENTORY OF GOVERNMENT PROPERTY. 1930–1931. 1 vol. 1 in.   *12*

These are forms listing the U.S. Government property at the Legation. Arranged in inverse chronological order.

RECORDS OF CONSULAR POSTS

Records of the United States Consulate General at Monrovia, Liberia

A commercial agent was appointed to Monrovia as early as April 8, 1848, and the post became a legation and consulate general in 1862. The Consul General at Monrovia had oversight of consular agencies in Liberia and of Elmina in the Gold Coast (Ghana). The records of the Consulate General at Monrovia were maintained separately from those of the Legation and were transferred directly to the National Archives in 1950.

DESPATCHES TO THE STATE DEPARTMENT. 1856–1878, 1903–1912. 3 vols. 7 in.   *13*

Included are communications, memoranda, copies of minutes and resolutions of the Liberian House of Representatives, annual commerce and industries reports and papers relating to the estates of deceased American citizens and passports. Also included are documents pertaining to the Liberian boundary disputes with Britain and France, the American Special Commission to investigate the political condition of Liberia (1909), opinions of eminent Liberians on the Commission, American Negro immigration into Liberia, and material for a monograph on Liberia collected by Ernest Lyon, Minister Resident and Consul General. The first volume contains a few letters of the American Agent for Liberated Africans. The last two volumes are indexed alphabetically by subject. Arranged chronologically.

DESPATCHES FROM THE STATE DEPARTMENT. 1903–1910. 1 vol. 2 in.   *14*

Contains acknowledgments of reports, statements of accounts, inquiries, and instructions received by Dr. Ernest Lyon, Minister Resident and Consul General. Included are copies of bonds of appointment for a vice-consul. Indexed alphabetically by subject. Arranged chronologically.

MISCELLANEOUS LETTERS SENT. 1906–1912. 2 vols. 3 in.   *15*

Included are annual reports on commerce and industry, statements of contingent and salary accounts, copies of vouchers, lists of importers and trading firms as possible dealers in American goods and agents for American manufacturing firms, and health reports on American citizens in West Africa. Correspondents include the State Department and American firms and individuals. Indexed alphabetically by subject. Arranged chronologically.

MISCELLANEOUS LETTERS RECEIVED. 1856–1864, 1903–1910. 2 vols. 4 in.   *16*

Included are instructions, notifications, and acknowledgments from the State Department; communications and requests from the Liberian Government, including a request for naval aid against tribesmen; inquiries from American firms and consuls; letters of the American Agent for Liberated Africans; copies of inward cargo manifests; lists of African slaves recaptured from slavers and a contract of the American Colonization Society for their care; and a series of replies to an inquiry concerning economic opportunities open to American Negroes in various American consular districts. Indexed alphabetically by subject. Arranged chronologically.

BUSINESS LETTERS RECEIVED. 1903–1910. 2 vols. 3 in.   17

Letters received from American businessmen and agencies making inquiries about commercial possibilities or advertising goods. Included is a proclamation of the consul general, dated February 11, 1909, enjoining American citizens to neutrality in a threatened local riot between the Liberian Frontier Police Force and Army. Included too is a copy of a pamphlet on 'Patriotism,' the text of a lecture delivered by Dr. Ernest Lyon, Minister Resident and Consul General, at the West African University in Monrovia. Indexed alphabetically by subject. Arranged alphabetically by name of correspondent.

GENERAL CORRESPONDENCE. 1910–1935. 60 vols. 14 ft.   18

Correspondence with the State Department, the Liberian Government, American firms, American and foreign consuls, and individuals. These papers relate to the administration of the consulate, destitute seamen, the estates of deceased Americans, and the supplying of commercial information to businessmen and general intelligence on Liberia to the State Department. Also included are annual commercial and industrial reports and statistics of shipping, customs revenue, imports and exports. There are also letters from stamp collectors. Organized and arranged according to the classification scheme summarized in appendix B below. Some of the earlier volumes have alphabetical subject indexes.

'MISCELLANEOUS RECORD BOOK.' 1856–1863. 1 vol. 2 in.   19

Record of miscellaneous information not entered in other consular books. Included are copies of lists of Treasury fees received and of arrivals and departures of American vessels; letters to persons and to governments and United States agents on the West African coast; answers to State Department questionnaires on commerce and local products. Arranged chronologically.

CERTIFICATES OF REGISTRATION OF AMERICAN CITIZENS. 1907–1916. 1 vol. 2 in.   20

Certificates issued by the consul general declaring that a person has been registered as an American citizen. Information given includes date and place of birth, date of arrival and purpose of stay in Liberia, and names of children. Arranged chronologically.

Records of the United States Consular Agency at Grand Bassa, Liberia

The first United States commercial agent was appointed to Grand Bassa on February 28, 1868. The records of the post are incomplete, and few materials relating to it are to be found among the records of the Legation and Consulate General at Monrovia. Apparently Monrovia served only to transmit communications between Grand Bassa and the State Department.

DESPATCHES TO THE STATE DEPARTMENT. 1870–1884. 1 vol. 2 in.   21

Contain narrative and statistical reports on commerce, industry, and navigation in the consular district. Arranged chronologically.

MISCELLANEOUS LETTERS SENT. 1872–1884. 1 vol. 2 in.   22

To the Minister Resident and Consul General at Monrovia, American firms, and

private persons, relating mainly to visiting American vessels and citizens, inventory-
ing of archives, and other routine consular business. Arranged chronologically.

Records of the United States Consular Agency at Elmina, Gold Coast

The United States Consular Agency at Elmina (Cape Coast Castle) came
into existence when a native of the country, Mr. G. E. Eminsang, was appointed
consular agent on September 15, 1883. Before that date Messrs. P. S. Hamel,
confirmed on January 2, 1879, and Arthur Brunn, confirmed on April 28, 1883, had
served part time. Both men also served as consular representatives of France and
the Netherlands while serving as American representative. The single letter book
described below covers mainly the administration of Mr. Eminsang. The Elmina
post was subordinate to the Consulate General at Monrovia. Most of the agency's
reports, returns, and correspondence are scattered among the diplomatic records
of the Monrovia Legation, although a few are among the records of the consulate
general there. The Elmina office was ordered closed on June 26, 1900, and its
archives were removed to Monrovia.

LETTERS SENT. 1883–1896. 1 vol. 2 in. 23

Mainly to the United States Minister Resident and Consul General at Monrovia, Liberia, but also to British officials in the Gold Coast. Relate to the appointment
of G. E. Eminsang as consular agent, the welfare of American citizens and sailors,
and the transmittal of returns and other consular records to Monrovia. Included
are reports on minor changes in the local government of Elmina and shipping
facilities between Britain and the Gold Coast. Arranged chronologically.

Records of the United States Consulate at Freetown, Sierra Leone, and Dakar, Senegal

The State Department recognized the existence of American interests in
Sierra Leone by appointing John E. Taylor commercial agent at Freetown on
October 15, 1858. He had already been informally appointed acting consul as early
as 1853 by Commodore Mayo of the ship 'Constitution.' Record Group 59, General
Records of the Department of State, has documents for the period 1853–1858.
In 1915 the consul at Sierra Leone was instructed to remove himself together with
the furniture and the archives of his office to Dakar, headquarters of the Government General of French West Africa. The transfer was completed by March 31,
1915. The Dakar consulate was closed on September 3, 1931.

DESPATCHES TO THE STATE DEPARTMENT. 1869–1912. 5 vols. 10 in. 24

Included are copies of and letters transmitting statements of consular accounts
and business; reports of local events and conditions that might affect American
trade; and papers relating to American shipping, seamen, and citizens resident in
West Africa. After 1879 there are annual commercial reports containing statistics
of American shipping, imports, and exports and information on the social and
political condition of the consular district; reports of rainfall and health; reports
on various military expeditions against interior tribes in the Sierra Leone; and
accounts of the activities of an Islamic movement in the Sudan. The earlier reports
deal solely with Sierra Leone affairs, but the later reports touch on Nigeria and

other parts of West Africa. Three volumes are indexed alphabetically by subject. Arranged chronologically.

DESPATCHES FROM THE STATE DEPARTMENT. 1879–1888, 1906–1911. 2 vols. 2 in.   25

Contains acknowledgments, authorizations, and notifications, relating to the administration of the consulate and reports on produce and local conditions. Included is correspondence relating to an alleged British refusal to allow American ships into the Malacong area, agricultural shows in Nigeria, and the production of palm oil and kernel. One volume is indexed alphabetically by subject. Arranged chronologically.

CIRCULARS FROM THE STATE DEPARTMENT. 1875–1891. 2 vols. 4 in.   26

Contains printed or processed copies of circulars, American legislation relating to consular administration or foreign trade, executive orders, Presidential proclamations, and announcements. Included are instructions on procedures for the collection of data on sanitation and the issuing of passports; questionnaires pertaining to raisins, oranges, lemons, olives, and figs; and announcements of departmental appointments. Unarranged.

ACCOUNTS AND RETURNS SENT. 1894–1905. 1 vol. 2 in.   27

Copies of statements of accounts and returns sent to the State Department. Included are accounts for contingent expenses and salaries and fees; and returns of trade between Sierra Leone and the United States and business done at the consulate. Arranged chronologically.

ACCOUNTS LETTERS RECEIVED. 1880–1888. 1 vol. 1 in.   28

Letters from the Treasury Department and the Bureau of Accounts of the State Department relating to statements of consular accounts. Arranged chronologically.

MISCELLANEOUS LETTERS SENT. 1869–1892, 1897–1898. 2 vols. 4 in.   29

Correspondence with West African officials and American customs, consular, and Treasury Department officials, relating to the welfare of American citizens and seamen, the U.S. Eclipse Expedition to the Congo (1889), and consular administrative matters. Arranged chronologically.

MISCELLANEOUS LETTERS RECEIVED. 1879–1909. 8 vols. 1 ft.   30

Correspondents include the State and Treasury Departments, United States consulates in Great Britain and West Africa, American business firms and missionaries, the Sierra Leone Government, and the Compagnie du Sénégal et de la Côte Occidental d'Afrique. Subjects treated include consular accounts and business; the transportation of destitute American seamen; the losses of American citizens in the 1898 native rising in Sierra Leone; the value of imports and exports; tariff charges; harbor dues; pilotage and other local trade regulations; and names of local importers. There are also consular reports on particular American trade goods, such as tobacco, sewing machines, and household tools, and on climate and health. A few volumes are indexed alphabetically by subject. Arranged chronologically.

GENERAL CORRESPONDENCE. 1909–31. 85 vols. 15 ft.   31

Incoming and outgoing correspondence with the State and Treasury Departments, West African governments and officials, United States Foreign Service posts in Great Britain and on the West Coast of Africa, and American firms and citizens in West Africa. These papers relate to consular appointments, supplies, and duties towards American citizens, vessels, and seamen and to businessmen's inquiries concerning trade commodities, opportunities, and contracts. Also included are copies of periodic and special commercial and industrial reports and papers relating to the collection of data for the compilation of reports. Reports and information given in answers to inquiries and circulars cover all the British and French colonies; they deal with mineral resources, agricultural products, population, commercial legislation, political changes in the territories (e.g., the 1914 amalgamation of the Nigerias), and the effect of the World War on West African trade. Volumes prior to 1924 have alphabetical subject indexes. The records prior to August 1, 1912, are arranged chronologically; from that date they are arranged according to the classification scheme summarized in appendix B below.

'REGISTER OF LETTERS SENT.' 1869–1894, 1898–1913. 2 vols. 2 in.   *32*

Entries for each letter include date, to whom and to what place sent, subject, number of enclosures, amount of postage paid, and remarks. Arranged chronologically.

'REGISTER OF LETTERS RECEIVED.' 1869–1894, 1898–1913. 2 vols. 2 in.   *33*

Entries for each letter include name of writer, place and date, date received, subject, number of enclosures, amount of postage paid, and remarks. Arranged chronologically.

'REGISTER OF CORRESPONDENCE RECEIVED AND SENT.' 1912–1929. 4 vols. 4 in.   *34*

Entries for each letter include file number, name of person to whom sent or from whom received, subject, and remarks. Refers to correspondence described in entry 31. Arranged chronologically.

'REGISTER OF PASSPORTS.' 1890–1930. 1 vol. 1 in.   *35*

Included are tabular summaries and lists giving each passport holder's name, state or country, age, and physical description. Arranged chronologically.

'REGISTRATION FILE (AMERICAN CITIZENS).' 1917–1927. 1 vol. 1 in.   *36*

Contains forms completed by persons who wished to register as American citizens. Each form is accompanied by two to three passport-sized photographs of the applicant. Included are naturalization forms and declarations of American citizens explaining the reasons for their long residence outside the United States. Arranged chronologically.

REGISTER OF AMERICAN SEAMEN SHIPPED, DISCHARGED, OR DECEASED ('SEAMEN'S REGISTER'). 1871–1928. 2 vols. 4 in.   *37*

Entries for each seaman or mariner include his name, date shipped, discharged, or deceased and payments made on his account. Arranged chronologically.

REGISTER OF AMERICAN SEAMEN RELIEVED. 1870–1929. 4 vols. 3 in.   *38*

Entries for each seaman include his name, the name of his vessel, its master and owner, and the nature of the relief afforded. Arranged chronologically.

'RECORD OF ARRIVAL AND DEPARTURE OF AMERICAN VESSELS.' 1869–1928. 2 vols. 4 in.   *39*

Entries for each vessel include dates of arrival and departure, tonnage, place built, place sailed from, place bound, and quantity, value, and place of production or manufacture of cargo. Arranged chronologically.

DAILY REGISTER OF AMERICAN VESSELS ('SHIP'S DAILY JOURNAL').
    1870–1931. 4 vols. 6 in.   40
    Entries for each ship include its name, tonnage, when and where built, names
of owners, master, mate, and second mate, values of inward and outward cargoes,
and dates of arrival and clearance. Arranged by date of arrival.

'RECORD OF QUARTERLY STATEMENT OF FEES.' 1873–1891. 1 vol. 3 in.   41
    Summaries of fees received for services to American vessels. Arranged chrono-
logically.

FEES RECEIVED FOR SERVICES TO AMERICAN VESSELS ('FEE BOOKS').
    1879–1924. 3 vols. 5 in.   42
    Entries on each vessel include its name, party paying fee, amount of fee, date,
nature of service rendered, and destination of vessel. Arranged chronologically.

'ACCOUNTS WITH AMERICAN VESSELS.' 1882–1891. 1 vol. 1 in.   43
    Register of accounts relating to shore services performed in the interest of
American vessels. Entries for each vessel include its name, names of its captain
and owner, place sailed from, place built, and number of American and of foreign
seamen employed. Arranged chronologically.

CERTIFICATION OF INVOICES OF GOODS TO THE UNITED STATES ('INVOICE BOOK').
    1870–1920. 1 vol. 1 in.   44
    Quarterly statements of invoices certified for goods purchased or manufac-
tured within the consular district for export to the United States. The information
in each certification includes the name of the vessel or party receiving the service,
the character of the goods, the place of its production or manufacture, and its
value. Arranged chronologically.

'REGISTER OF LANDING CERTIFICATES.' 1912–1928. 1 vol. 1 in.   45
    Certifications of the arrival and unloading of goods listed on bills of lading.
Information given for each cargo includes date of unloading, names of vessel and
master, loading port, identifying marks on goods, numbers and contents of packages,
date on bill of lading, names of shipper and consignee, and date of certificate.
Arranged chronologically.

SHIPMASTERS' DECLARATIONS OF DAMAGE AND LOSS ('MARINE NOTE OF PROTEST').
    1869–1930. 2 vols. 3 in.   46
    Sworn declarations before the consul as to the possible effect of rough weather
on the vessel and its cargo. Arranged chronologically.

SHIPMASTERS' EXTENDED DECLARATIONS OF DAMAGE AND LOSS ('MARINE EXTENDED
    PROTEST'). 1869–1930. 2 vols. 3 in.   47
    Similar to those described in entry 46 but containing detailed information as
to actual rough weather encountered and resultant damage or loss to the cargo or
vessels and delay in arrival. Arranged chronologically.

'FEES AND SALARY ACCOUNT BOOK.' 1898–1908. 1 vol. 1 in.   48
    Statements of accounts for salaries and allowances for individual consuls and
vice consuls. Arranged chronologically.

'MISCELLANEOUS RECORD BOOKS.' 1898–1931. 5 vols. 6 in.   49
    Contains records that could not be conveniently entered in other consular
volumes. Included are copies of local correspondence, notarial and contingent

expense accounts, vouchers, inventories of furniture and of the archives of the Freetown-Dakar, Gorée, Bathurst, and Saint-Louis posts, papers relating to deceased Americans and destitute seamen, and copies of annual commercial, industrial, and agricultural reports covering territories in West Africa. Also included are letters of American missionaries and traders giving estimates of the causes and effects of and American losses in the 1898 uprising in Sierra Leone. Most of the volumes are indexed, alphabetically by subject. Arranged chronologically.

Records of the United States Consulate at Gorée-Dakar, Senegal

Gorée, the first United States consular post in French West Africa, was opened with the appointment of Peter Strickland as consul on September 27, 1883. The office was closed and its archives taken to the United States consulate at Freetown, Sierra Leone, on June 25, 1905. The records inventoried below cover this period of Mr. Strickland's work at Gorée, but Record Group 59, General Records of the Department of State, contains a little correspondence dated in 1906 between Mr. Strickland and the State Department relating to an unsuccessful attempt to re-establish the consulate. Nevertheless, the list of consular representatives in that record group . . . includes a James W. Johnson, who, apparently, served at Gorée-Dakar from March 30, 1907. (During the period 1883–1905, Gorée, the original town in its area, declined in relative importance and tended to be overshadowed by the immediately adjacent and growing Dakar.)

DESPATCHES TO THE STATE DEPARTMENT. 1883–1905. 2 vols. 4 in.   50

Requests for and acknowledgments of instructions and reports on labor, wages, the cost of living, communist tendencies, commercial facilities and possibilities, the yellow fever epidemic, and the consular status of Gorée-Dakar. Arranged chronologically.

DESPATCHES FROM THE STATE DEPARTMENT. 1887–1905. 1 vol. 2 in.   51

Instructions, acknowledgments, and notifications. Included are instructions relating to the organization of the subordinate consular posts at Bathurst, Gambia, and Saint-Louis, Senegal, consular duties generally, the preparation of reports, and the rendering of accounts. Indexed alphabetically by subject. Arranged chronologically.

'REGISTER OF OFFICIAL LETTERS SENT.' 1883–1896. 1 vol. 2 in.   52

See entry 32.

'REGISTER OF OFFICIAL LETTERS RECEIVED.' 1883–1891. 1 vol. 2 in.   53

Subtitled 'Register of Despatches from Washington.' See entry 33.

'RECORD OF AMERICAN SEAMEN RELIEVED.' 1893–1904. 1 vol. 2 in.   54

Entries for each seaman include date on which relief was given, nature of his relief, and an account of the circumstances leading to his need for relief. Arranged chronologically.

ARRIVAL AND DEPARTURE OF AMERICAN VESSELS. 1884–1905. 2 vols. 2 in.   55

See entry 39.

DAILY REGISTER OF AMERICAN VESSELS ('SHIP'S DAILY JOURNAL').

1884–1905. 2 vols. 3 in.   56

See entry 40.

FEES RECEIVED FOR SERVICES TO AMERICAN VESSELS ('U.S. TREASURY FEES').
    1884–1905. 1 vol. 1 in.   57
    See entry 42.
CERTIFICATION OF INVOICES OF GOODS TO THE UNITED STATES ('INVOICE BOOK').
    1884–1892. 1 vol. 1 in.   58
    See entry 44.
'REGISTER OF LANDING CERTIFICATES.' 1883–1894. 1 vol. 1 in.   59
    See entry 45.
SHIPMASTERS' DECLARATIONS OF DAMAGE AND LOSS ('MARINE NOTE OF PROTEST').
    1884–1904. 1 vol. 1 in.   60
    See entry 46.
SHIPMASTERS' EXTENDED DECLARATIONS OF DAMAGE AND LOSS ('MARINE EXTENDED
    PROTEST'). 1885–1904. 1 vol. 1 in.   61
    See entry 47.
'MISCELLANEOUS RECORD BOOK.' 1885–1904. 1 vol. 2 in.   62
    Contains records of transactions and activities at the consulate that could not
be entered in other books. Included are copies of incoming and outgoing correspondence with local officials and persons, ships' insurance papers, records of the
passage of American vessels and cargo, marine protests, and documents relating
to the care of American seamen. Arranged chronologically.

Records of the United States Consulate at Bathurst, Gambia

    The list of United States consular officers in Record Group 59, General
Records of the Department of State, gives Mr. W. M. Haxton as the first consul
for Bathurst, appointed as early as October 17, 1833, but it further remarks that
no records were filed by him. The extant records of the Bathurst consulate start
with the appointment of Daniel R. B. Upton as commercial agent on May 8, 1858,
although a few despatches for 1857 are filed in Record Group 59, General Records
of the Department of State. The consulate was ordered closed on April 14, 1900,
but business actually ceased on June 30, 1900. The archives were transferred to
the United States consulate at Gorée-Dakar, Senegal.
DESPATCHES TO THE STATE DEPARTMENT. 1858–1889. 1 vol. 2 in.   63
    These relate to suggestions for the shipment of supplies to and the status of
the consular post, the increase of American trade on the Gambia River, summaries
of fees collected from American vessels, and consular accounts. Included are a
copy of a decree promulgating the convention between France and England relative
to Portendic and Albreda (1857), copies of narrative and statistical reports on the
population, government, and trade of Gambia, and copies of invoices. Arranged
chronologically.
REGISTER OF AMERICAN SEAMEN SHIPPED, DISCHARGED, OR DECEASED.
    1858–1874. 1 vol. 2 in.   64
    See entry 37.
REGISTER OF RELIEF AFFORDED DESTITUTE AMERICAN SEAMEN. 1859–1885. 1 vol. 1 in. 65
    See entry 38.

'ARRIVAL AND DEPARTURE OF AMERICAN VESSELS.' 1858–1893. 1 vol. 1 in.   66
   See entry 39.
DAILY REGISTER OF AMERICAN VESSELS ('SHIP'S DAILY JOURNAL').
   1858–1890. 1 vol. 1 in.   67
   See entry 40.
FEES RECEIVED FOR SERVICES TO AMERICAN VESSELS. 1858–1888. 1 vol. 1 in.   68
   See entry 42.
CERTIFICATION OF INVOICES OF GOODS TO THE UNITED STATES ('INVOICE BOOK').
   1859–1867. 1 vol. 1 in.   69
   See entry 44.
SHIPMASTERS' DECLARATIONS OF DAMAGE AND LOSS ('MARINE NOTE OF PROTEST').
   1859–1886. 1 vol. 2 in.   70
   See entry 46.
SHIPMASTERS' EXTENDED DECLARATIONS OF DAMAGE AND LOSS ('MARINE EXTENDED
   PROTEST'). 1859–1885. 1 vol. 2 in.   71
   See entry 47.
'MISCELLANEOUS RECORD BOOKS.' 1859–1900. 2 vols. 3 in.   72
   Contains copies of outgoing letters (mainly to Bathurst addresses), sworn statements of seamen as to their American citizenship and the causes of their misfortunes, proceedings of criminal trials involving American citizens, and certificates of ownership and registration of American vessels. Arranged chronologically.

Records of the United States Consular Agency at Saint-Louis, Senegal

At the request of the consul at Gorée, Francis Lawton was appointed consular agent at Saint-Louis on January 16, 1890. Only the few records described below exist, and there are only scattered documents relating to Saint-Louis among the records of the United States consulate at Gorée-Dakar.

ARRIVAL AND DEPARTURE OF AMERICAN VESSELS. 1890–1891. 1 vol. 1 in.   73
   See entry 39. The volume contains only five entries.
DAILY REGISTER OF AMERICAN VESSELS. ('SHIP'S DAILY JOURNAL').
   1890–1891. 1 vol. 2 in.   74
   See entry 40. The volume contains data for only three vessels.
FEES RECEIVED FOR SERVICES TO AMERICAN VESSELS ('U.S. TREASURY FEES').
   July 10, 1890. 1 vol. 1 in.   75
   See entry 42. The volume contains only two entries for one day.
SHIPMASTERS' DECLARATIONS OF DAMAGE AND LOSS ('MARINE NOTE OF PROTEST').
   1890–1891. 1 vol. 1 in.   76
   See entry 46. The volume contains only three protests.
SHIPMASTERS' EXTENDED DECLARATION OF DAMAGE AND LOSS ('MARINE EXTENDED
   PROTEST'). 1890–1892. 1 vol. 1 in.   77
   See entry 47. The volume contains only four protests.

Records of the United States Consulate at Lagos, Nigeria

The consul at Dakar obtained much-needed relief when the consular office at Lagos was opened on March 29, 1928. The two consuls decided on a delimitation of territorial responsibility. The Lagos consulate was to have jurisdiction over Gambia, Sierra Leone, the Gold Coast, Nigeria, the British mandates in Togoland and Cameroon, the French mandates in Togoland and Cameroon, Fernando Po, and Río Muni. The Dakar consulate was to have jurisdiction over Mauritania, Senegal, French Guinea, the Ivory Coast, Dahomey, Upper Volta, the French Sudan, Niger, and Portuguese Guinea.

Records of the Lagos post were transferred to the National Archives in 1951.

GENERAL CORRESPONDENCE. 1928–1935. 61 vols. 14 ft.   78

Incoming and outgoing correspondence with the State Department, West African governments, the United States consul at Dakar, and American business firms, relating to the establishment and administration of the consulate and requests for information. Included are reports on health, agriculture, commerce, and industry and on the economic and commercial potentialities of Nigeria. Arranged by year and thereunder by the classification scheme summarized in appendix B below.

APPENDIX A

SELECT LIST OF SIGNIFICANT DOCUMENTS AMONG WEST AFRICAN POST RECORDS[1]

Bathurst, Gambia

Imperial Decree for Promulgating the Convention Relative to Portendic and Albreda Concluded between France and England. Issued by the French Second Empire. March 7, 1857. 11 pp. Handwritten. (entry 63)

> Enclosure in letter from Daniel R. B. Upton to Lewis Cass, Secretary of State, August 11, 1859.

Report on River Trade on the Gambia. Despatch No. 11. From Daniel R. B Upton to Lewis Cass, Secretary of State. August 11, 1859. 3 pp. Handwritten. (entry 63)

> Analyzes the effect of the Portendic and Albreda convention on American Trade on the River Gambia.

Report on the Colony of the Gambia. Daniel R. B. Upton. [1859.] 6 pp. Handwritten. (entry 63)

> Gives 1851 census figures and statistics of imports and exports by countries.

[Annual Report on the Gambia.] Letter from Daniel R. B. Upton to Lewis Cass, Secretary of State. December 15, 1860. 10 pp. Handwritten. (entry 63)

> Includes import and export statistics for 1858 and 1859.

Freetown, Sierra Leone—Dakar, Senegal

[Commercial Reports on Sierra Leone.] [By various authors to the State Department.] [1880–1884, 1886–1890, 1895, 1898, 1900.] [159 pp.] Handwritten. (entry 24)

---

[1] The documents are listed alphabetically by post and thereunder chronologically. Following each listing is the inventory entry number for the series in which the document occurs.

Contain mainly annual narrative and statistical information on commerce, agriculture, and foreign trade, but also some other economic data and data on population, education, and rainfall.

Account of a Meeting between the Sierra Leone Government and the Rulers of the Timneh Country to Sign a Peace Treaty. Despatch No. 31. From J. A. Lewis to John Hay. September 30, 1880. 8 pp. Handwritten. (entry 24)

Report Regarding Samudu (Samory) and His Army. Despatch No. 188. From J. A. Lewis to James D. Porter. July 14, 1885. 8 pp. Handwritten. (entry 24)
Contains extracts of Sierra Leone newspaper accounts of the Islamic movement in the Sudan.

Settlement of Liberia–Sierra Leone Boundary Dispute. Despatch No. 202. From J. A. Lewis to James D. Porter. November 23, 1885. 4 pp. Handwritten. (entry 24)

Recommending Cornelius May, a Sierra Leonean, for the Vice-Consulship. Despatch No. 291. From J. A. Lewis to George L. Rives. December 17, 1888. 2 pp. Handwritten. (entry 24)

General Narrative Report on Sierra Leone. Despatch No. 13. From R. P. Pooley to Edwin I. Uhl. June 30, 1894. 13 pp. Handwritten. (entry 24)

Report on the Opening of the Sierra Leone Government Railway and on Trade of French Guinea. From R. P. Pooley to W. W. Rockhill. April 10, 1897. 5 pp. Handwritten. (entry 24)

Confusion of American Citizens by Sierra Leone Rising and Spanish-American War. Despatch No. 14. From John T. Williams to T. H. Griddler. October 28, 1898. 2 pp. Handwritten. (entry 24)

Trade in French West Africa during 1911. By W. J. Yerby. August 5, 1912. 4 pp. Typed. (entry 31)
Narrative and statistical.

Review of Trade in French Guinea, West Africa, 1912. By W. J. Yerby. August 19, 1913. 6 pp. Typed. (entry 31)
Narrative and statistical.

Trade in Northern Nigeria, West Africa, 1912. By W. J. Yerby. September 16, 1913. 2 pp. Typed. (entry 31)

Trade of Gambia, British West Africa, 1912. By W. J. Yerby. September 22, 1913. 5 pp. Typed. (entry 31)
Narrative and statistical.

Amalgamation of the Nigerias, British West Africa. By W. J. Yerby. February 11, 1914. 4 pp. Typed. (entry 31)
Report of the union of Southern and Northern Nigeria, January 1, 1914, with an assessment of the administrative changes involved and the effect on the economic potential and trade of the territories.

Trade Report, Gold Coast Colony, West Africa, 1913. By W. J. Yerby. September 1, 1914. 10 pp. Typed. (entry 31)
Narrative and statistical.

West African Market for American Products. By W. J. Yerby. September 14, 1914. 4 pp. Typed. (entry 31)

Narrative report on the effect of the war on West African trade, credits, transportation, exchange, and banking.

Trade Report on Cameroons and Togoland, German West Africa. By W. J. Yerby. October 28, 1914. 2 pp. Typed. (entry 31)

Abeokuta Treaty, Nigeria, British West Africa. By W. J. Yerby. November 30, 1914. 3 pp. Typed. (entry 31)

An extract from 'The African World,' November 14, 1914: report of Sir Frederick Lugard's treaty with the Egba United Government claiming jurisdiction over Egbaland.

Apparent Balance of Trade between British West Africa and U.S.A., 1912 and 1913. By W. J. Yerby. December 3, 1914. 10 pp. Typed. (entry 31)

Contains statistics of American goods imported into Nigeria, the Gold Coast (Ghana), Sierra Leone, and Gambia.

Gorée-Dakar, Senegal

Report on Labor Conditions in the Senegal. Despatch No. 13. From Peter Strickland to John Davis. July 19, 1884. 8 pp. Handwritten. (entry 50)

Contains sections on the distribution of labor, wages, the cost of living, communism, and intemperance.

French Senegal, Its Commercial Facilities and Possibilities. Despatch No. 16. From Peter Strickland to John Davis. October 22, 1884. 5 pp. Handwritten. (entry 50)

Effect of French Tariff on American Trade in Senegal. Despatch No. 195. From Peter Strickland to W. W. Rockhill. August 31, 1896. 7 pp. Handwritten. (entry 50)

Monrovia, Liberia (Legation)

Natural Capacities, Present Condition, and Future Prospects of the Republic of Liberia. Despatch No. 45. From J. Milton Turner to Hamilton Fish, Secretary of State. May 25, 1872. 17 pp. Handwritten. (entry 1)

Narrative report on the political situation.

Grebo Outbreak at Cape Palmas. Despatch No. 178. From J. Milton Turner to Hamilton Fish, Secretary of State. September 7, 1875. 5 pp. Handwritten. (entry 1)

Report on a war between the Liberian Government and a tribe.

Report on American Shipping and Trade in the Gold Coast. From P. S. Hamel to John H. Smyth. October 10, 1878. 2 pp. Handwritten. (entry 5)

Contains a few statistics for 1875–1877.

Threat of War between the British and Ashanti. From Joseph Upton to J. H. Smyth. March 11, 1881. 2 pp. Handwritten. (entry 5)

The Needs of the Consular Service on the West African Coast. Despatch No. 33. From John H. Smyth to John Davis. June 14, 1883. 13 pp. Handwritten. (entry 1)

Narrative commercial report and assessment of West Africa.

Annual Report for Liberian Fiscal Year Ended September 30, 1884. Despatch No. 96. From J. H. Smyth to James D. Porter, Assistant Secretary of State. May 11, 1885. 10 pp. Handwritten. (entry 1)
> Narrative report on trade, navigation, and agriculture.

Petition against Proposed Franco-Liberian Treaty Ceding Territory. From American Colonization Society to Walter Gresham, Secretary of State. June 26, 1893. 13 pp. Typed. (entry 2)
> Gives history of Liberia and of the Society together with extracts of agreements entered into between American and Maryland State Colonization Societies and the Liberian Government.

Report of the Commission of the U.S.A. to the Republic of Liberia. [From the Commissioners to the Secretary of State.] October 6, 1909. 45 pp. Typed. (entry 5)
> An account of Liberia's financial, political, and frontier problems and related recommendations. The commissioners were Roland P. Falkner, George Sale, and Emmett J. Scott.

Settlement of the War of 1875-76 between the Liberian Government and the Grebo United Kingdom. Captain A. A. Semmes, United States Navy. n.d. 12 pp. (entry 5)
> Contains report of proceedings of Captain Semmes' arbitration meetings with representatives of both parties.

APPENDIX B

FOREIGN SERVICE OF THE UNITED STATES OF AMERICA
CLASSIFICATION OF CORRESPONDENCE

Summary [1]

CLASS	0	Miscellaneous.
	000	General.
	010	Letters of Introduction.
	020	Publications.
	030	Visits. Expeditions, Tours.
	050	Pouch Service.
	090	Testimonials.
CLASS	1	Administration, United States Government.
	100	General.
	110	Department of State.
	120	Foreign Service of the United States.
	130	Citizenship.
CLASS	2	Extradition.
CLASS	3	Protection of interests.
	300	General.

[1] From a manual issued by the Bureau of Indexes and Archives, Department of State, 1924.

310   Personal interests. (Ill-treatment at the hands of unofficial persons.)
320   Personal rights. (Ill-treatment at the hands of officials.)
330   Deaths. Estates.
340   Litigation (or controversy) between persons or concerns.
350   Property rights (as against the Government).
360   Philanthropic institutions maintained in one country by national interests of another.
370   Relief from military service or taxation.
380   Fraudulent enterprises.
CLASS   4   Claims.
CLASS   5   International Congresses and Conferences. International Treaties.
CLASS   6   Commerce. Commercial relations.
600   Statistics of trade.
610   Trade extension.
620   Customs laws and regulations. Customs administration.
630   Import tariff.
640   Food and drugs regulations.
650   Meat and live animals regulations.
660   Exclusion of goods.
670   Export tariff.
680   Export bounty.
690   Other administrative measures affecting export trade. Embargo.
CLASS   7   Relations of States.
700   General.
710   Political relation. Treaties.
720   Commerce and navigation.
730   Extra territoriality.
740   Naturalization.
750   Immigration.
770   Fur seals.
780   Fisheries.
790   Slave trade. Liquor traffic. Opium traffic and other habit-forming drugs.
CLASS   8   Internal Affairs of State.
800   Political affairs.
810   Public order. Safety. Health. Works. Charities.
820   Military affairs.
830   Naval affairs.
840   Social matters.
850   Economic matters.
860   Industrial matters.
870   Communication and transportation.
880   Navigation.
890   Other internal affairs.

SUPPLEMENT II

GUIDES TO GERMAN RECORDS MICROFILMED AT ALEXANDRIA, VA.

Guides to Records of Reich Ministries and Offices

Records of the Reich Ministry of Economics (Reichswirtschaftsministerium). 1958. 75 pp. (Guide No. 1)

Records of the Office of the Reich Commissioner for the Strengthening of Germandom (Reichskommissar für die Festigung deutschen Volkstums). 1958. 15 pp. (Guide No. 2)

Records of the Reich Ministry for Armaments and War Production (Reichsministerium für Rüstung und Kriegsproduktion). 1959. 109 pp. (Guide No. 10)

Fragmentary Records of Miscellaneous Reich Ministries and Offices. 1959. 19 pp. (Guide No. 11)

Records of the Reich Air Ministry (Reichsluftfahrtministerium). 1959. 34 pp. (Guide No. 13)

Records of the Reich Ministry for Public Enlightenment and Propaganda. 1961. 41 pp. (Guide No. 22)

Records of Reich Office for Soil Exploration (Reichsamt für Bodenforschung). 1961. 11 pp. (Guide No. 26)

Records of the Reich Leader of the SS and Chief of the German Police (Reichsführer SS und Chef der Deutschen Polizei):

    Part I. 1961. 165 pp. (Guide No. 32)

    Part II. 1961. 89 pp. (Guide No. 33)

    Part III. 1963. 198 pp. (Guide No. 39)

Miscellaneous SS Records: Einwandererzentralstelle, Waffen-SS, and SS-Oberabschnitte. 1961. 34 pp. (Guide No. 27)

Miscellaneous German Records Collection:

    Part I. 1958. 15 pp. (Guide No. 5)

    Part II. 1959. 203 pp. (Guide No. 8)

    Part III. 1962. 61 pp. (Guide No. 36)

Guides to Records of German Military Organizations

Records of Headquarters, German Armed Forces High Command (Oberkommando der Wehrmacht/OKW):

    Part I. 1959. 222 pp. (Guide No. 7)

    Part II. 1960. 213 pp. (Guide No. 17)

    Part III. 1960. 118 pp. (Guide No. 18)

    Part IV. 1960. 76 pp. (Guide No. 19)

Records of Headquarters, German Army High Command (Oberkommando des Heeres/OKH):

    Part I. 1959. 19 pp. (Guide No. 12)

    Part II. 1961. 154 pp. (Guide No. 29)

    Part III. 1961. 212 pp. (Guide No. 30)

Records of Headquarters, German Air Force High Command (Oberkommando der Luftwaffe/OKL). 1961. 59 pp. (Guide No. 24)

German Air Force Records: Luftgaukommandos, Flak, Deutsche Luftwaffen-
mission in Rumänien. 1961. 41 pp. (Guide No. 25)
Records of Headquarters, German Navy High Command (OKM). 1962. 5 pp.
(Guide No. 37)
Records of German Army Areas (Wehrkreise). 1962. 234 pp. (Guide No. 34)
Records of German Field Commands: Army Groups. Part I. 1963. 126 pp.
(Guide No. 40)
Records of German Field Commands: Armies:
      Part I. 1959. 61 pp. (Guide No. 14)
      Part II. 1964. 110 pp. (Guide No. 42)
Records of German Field Commands: Divisions. Part I. 1963. 160 pp. (Guide
No. 41)
Records of German Field Commands: Rear Areas, Occupied Territories, and
Others. 1963. 200 pp. (Guide No. 38)
Miscellaneous SS Records: Einwandererzentralstelle, Waffen-SS, and SS-Oberab-
schnitte. 1961. 34 pp. (Guide No. 27)
Miscellaneous German Records Collection:
      Part I. 1958. 15 pp. (Guide No. 5)
      Part II. 1959. 203 pp. (Guide No. 8)
      Part III. 1962. 61 pp. (Guide No. 36)

Other Guides

Records of the National Socialist German Labor Party (Nationalsozialistische
Deutsche Arbeiterpartei):
      Part I. 1958. 141 pp. (Guide No. 3)
      Part II. 1960. 45 pp. (Guide No. 20)
      Part III. 1962. 29 pp. (Guide No. 35)
Records of Nazi Cultural and Research Institutions and Records Pertaining to
Axis Relations and Interests in the Far East. 1958. 161 pp. (Guide No. 6)
Records of Former German and Japanese Embassies and Consulates, 1890–1945.
1960. 63 pp. (Guide No. 15)
Records of the Deutsches Ausland-Institut, Stuttgart:
      Part I: Records on Resettlement. 1960. 105 pp. (Guide No. 16)
      Part II: The General Records. 1961. 180 pp. (Guide No. 21)
Records of Private Austrian, Dutch, and German Enterprises, 1917–1946. 1961.
119 pp. (Guide No. 23)
Records of Private German Individuals. 1959. 23 pp. (Guide No. 9)

NEW HAMPSHIRE HISTORICAL SOCIETY

The New Hampshire Historical Society, Concord, New Hampshire, has papers of
Edmund Roberts, New England merchant and later diplomatic agent to Zanzibar,
1815–1836, 1 box. The Society also has papers of Levi Woodbury (1789–1851),
New Hampshire Senator and Secretary of the Navy, who was one of the prime
movers in the establishment of official relations between the United States and
Zanzibar in the 1830's, 1 box.

NEW YORK HISTORICAL SOCIETY

The manuscript collection of the New York Historical Society, 170 Central Park West, New York, New York 10024, includes materials dealing with the African slave trade during the eighteenth and nineteenth centuries, among them trade and account books of slave ships. Of particular interest are the letters from Jacobus Van Cortlandt and Philip Livingston and Sons on the slave trade in the first half of the eighteenth century. There are also about 100 volumes of papers of Gerard G. Beekman (1719–1797) and his descendants; he was a New York merchant involved in the slave trade. Similarly involved were Dutilh and Wachsmuth, eighteenth- and early-nineteenth-century Philadelphia shipping merchants, 1 volume, 1 folder. The Society also holds the journals, 1791–1792, of John Clarkson (1764–1828), British naval officer and Governor of Sierra Leone. These journals are concerned with his missions to America and Africa relating to the slave trade.

In the Society's rather extensive material that relates to Africa there is also a letter of September 10, 1788, from John Ledyard to Thomas Jefferson. Ledyard, a Connecticut Yankee, was the first man sent by the British African Association to explore the Niger River. Other scattered letters on Africa include one pertaining to Liberia by E. J. Roye in 1850.

NEW YORK PUBLIC LIBRARY

It is the policy of the New York Public Library, Fifth Avenue and 42d Street, New York, New York 10018, to acquire for the Reference Department one copy of every book which is thought to have permanent reference value in all subject areas except law, religion, theology, education, medicine, and biological sciences. This broad policy applies to Africa as well as other major areas of the world. The Reference Department has extensive holdings in African materials, and all of its divisions collect in this area. The material is dispersed, however, throughout the subject divisions of the Library; there is no separate collection of African material.*

Under the Farmington Plan, the New York Public Library is responsible for publications issued in Algeria, Eritrea, Ethiopia, Morocco, Somalia, Somaliland, Spanish Sahara, Sudan, and Tunisia; the history of the foregoing countries plus Egypt and Carthage; general history of African civilization and culture; and African aboriginal languages.

Under Public Law 480, the New York Public Library receives current publications from Egypt and has extensive collections in modern Arabic.

HOLDINGS OF VARIOUS DIVISIONS IN AFRICAN MATERIALS

Oriental Division collects North African material in Arabic and other non-European languages (material in English and European languages about North Africa goes into the appropriate subject division). This division has strong collec-

---

* About 50 percent of the Schomburg Collection of Negro Literature and History of the New York Public Library, which is described below, is comprised of African materials. This is a special collection of the Circulation Department of the Library and is geared to the needs of the general reader as well as the researcher.

tions in Arabic and the languages of Ethiopia, as well as material in or about more than 360 indigenous African languages.

Economics Division has an excellent collection of government documents from British and other colonial powers, including annual reports of various departments, blue books, gazettes, and codes of laws. It now attempts to collect the government documents of the independent nations of Africa. It is also a depository for all United Nations documents. Economics Division acquires all suitable material in its area—finance, business, commerce, transportation, etc.—as well as material in related sociological fields, e.g., politics, demography, slavery, colonization, associations, criminology, race relations, women, and education.

Periodicals Division collects intensively in this field and has almost 300 periodicals from or about Africa. Included are many valuable scholarly journals from all parts of Africa, mostly in foreign languages, and many highly specialized ones in the fields of economics and technology. Much valuable African material in older scholarly journals from England and Europe dating from the late nineteenth century has been indexed and is made available through the card catalogue.

Information Division has extensive African holdings in the areas for which it is responsible: anthropology and ethnology (there is material on over 430 African tribes), history, geography, travel, religion, biography, literature, fiction, poetry, essays, and philosophy.

Rare Books Division has a fine collection of Ethiopian material: religious writings, dictionaries and grammars of its languages by the early Portuguese explorers and missionaries, and works on travel and exploration. Here can be found books by the Arab scholars and travelers of the Middle Ages, as well as the later works by European explorers and colonists.

Map Division has an outstanding collection of maps of Africa or parts of Africa, both historical rarities and current maps.

Other divisions—*Art, Music, Science and Technology*—have important holdings in African material which, however, in sheer volume, do not constitute significant proportions of their total collections.

In general, strong points of the Reference Department's holdings in Africana are Ethiopia, medieval through modern, with much 'rare book' material; modern Arabic material, from Egypt primarily; government documents from British and other colonial powers and extensive material on the former Belgian Congo and the Republic of South Africa; maps; and African languages.

Manuscript Division of the New York Public Library contains materials dealing with the Boer War and the Ethiopian War of 1935, several nineteenth-century journals of Americans touring in Egypt, and several diaries kept by travelers to other parts of Africa. Also important are the B. Griswold Miscellaneous Papers, which include a description of the early years of Liberian colonization; the 1826–1830 account books of Jeremiah Evarts, secretary of the American Board of Commissioners for Foreign Missions; and the 1904–1911 papers of Emil Gribeschock, which include correspondence and a typewritten manuscript about 'The First American Trading Mission to Ethiopia.' A few items relating to American interests in Africa, particularly the Congo, can be found in the papers of the long-time president of the American Geographical Society, Charles P. Daly.

The papers of Miss Alice Donlevy (received in 1917) contain 3 boxes of material on the Boer War, including items of Miss Donlevy and of Jessie Fara, her associate in the Women's South African League and the Woman's Auxiliary League of New York, Boer Relief Fund.

The Library also has a microfilm negative copy of John Scott's (1844–1922) 'Notes from My Notebook' (an account of the 9th Kaffir War, Zulu War, and Cape Town Highlanders).

Documents which relate to the Island of Bourbon (now Ile de la Réunion) are those on the administration of Sieur Jean Baptiste de Villers (Governor, 1701–1710), 410 pp., 2 volumes of census returns, the *mémoires* of Chevalier de Recous, 1681, and Antoine Boucher's journal, 1702–1705. Also held are papers (about 75 items) of Aaron Ward Weaver (1832–1919), who served with the African Squadron, 1857–1859.

The Library's collection of original manuscripts and typescripts by modern authors includes materials by Stuart Cloete and Robert Ruark.

THE SCHOMBURG COLLECTION

The Schomburg Collection of Negro Literature and History is kept at a branch of the New York Public Library on 135th Street near Lenox Avenue in New York City.*

THE LIBRARY

The Schomburg Collection, a library and archive of materials devoted to Negro life and history, is considered one of the most important centers in the world for the study of the Negro. The Collection includes books by authors of African descent, regardless of subject matter or language. This is the first principle of selection. The second is that the Schomburg Collection should contain all *significant* materials *about* peoples of African descent.

The basis of the present collection was the private library of Arthur A. Schomburg (1874–1938), a Puerto Rican of African descent, who through years of patient devotion amassed one of the largest and most important libraries devoted to the Negro. In 1891 he came to the United States. For a number of years he was clerk in the Bankers Trust Company. However, the motivating force in his life seems to have been the goal of collecting all evidence he could find that the 'Negro had a long and honorable past.' He became a scholar and expert in this field.

At present this record of the experience of peoples of African descent throughout the world is not limited to books but includes art objects, musical recordings, sheet music, manuscripts, newspaper files (many microfilmed for permanent preservation), and periodicals. The selection of art objects was influenced by Alain

* For the catalogue of the Collection see *Schomburg Collection* (9 vols., Boston, G. K. Hall and Co., 1962). The survey of the library holdings is adapted from the Preface to the 'Catalogue of the Schomburg Collection' by Jean Blackwell Hutson, Curator, Schomburg Collection; the survey of the manuscript collections is drawn from the *Historical Records Survey: Calendar of the Manuscripts in the Schomburg Collection of Negro Literature* (New York, Work Projects Administration, 1942).

Locke, who was the prime mover in having about half the Blondeau-Theatre Arts Collection deposited here. The Eric de Kolbe Collection of African arms consists of about 250 weapons, mainly from south of the Sahara.

The Schomburg Collection also has roots in the community of Harlem. When the 135th Street Branch Library was established in 1905, the neighborhood which it expected to serve was a quiet, well-to-do American-Jewish section. By 1920 it had become half-Negro. Miss Ernestine Rose, a librarian with vision and persever-ance, was appointed to adapt this library to the needs of the growing community of Negroes. By 1924 Harlem had become the acknowledged capital of Black America. Its population, thanks to the migrations of the preceding decade, had reached approximately 150,000. At the same time it had drawn Negro talent and leadership from all parts of the United States and the Caribbean.

By then books on the Negro were in such demand that they could not be kept on the library shelves, and they were read so avidly that they were soon worn to shreds.

The following year, Schomburg's library was purchased by the Carnegie Corporation for the New York Public Library. Another gift from the Carnegie Corporation in 1932 enabled the New York Public Library to retain Mr. Schomburg as curator, a position he held until his death in 1938.

Among the items in Schomburg's collection when it came to the Library were the following:

A copy of Juan Latino's Latin verse (Granada, Spain, 1573). Remembered as incumbent of the chair of poetry at the University of Granada during the reign of Philip V and spoken of as the 'best' Latinist of Spain in his day, Latino had not been thought of as a Negro for generations. Schomburg reminded scholars that Juan Latino was a full-blooded African Negro.

The work of America's first Negro poet—Jupiter Harmon's *Address to the Negroes in the State of New York* (1787).

Manuscript poems and early editions of the works of Phillis Wheatley, slave girl.

The autobiography of Gustavus Vassa, which led to Granville Sharp's attack on slavery in the British colonies.

Copies of the *Almanacs* (1792 and 1793) compiled by Benjamin Banneker, the Negro whose unusual abilities were employed by Thomas Jefferson and others.

The sermons of Lemuel Haynes, the Negro who served as pastor of a white church in Rutland, Vermont, for thirty years following the Revolutionary War.

The scrapbook of Ira Aldridge, Negro actor who won fame in Europe as a Shakespearean actor during the nineteenth century.

Clotel, or the President's Daughter: A Narrative of Slave Life in the United States, the first novel by an American Negro.

Schomburg had found Latin and Dutch treatises such as those by Capitein (1717–1747), an African educated in Holland whose writings are still admired by students of the African in Europe. The first edition (1600) of Leo Africanus and many of the subsequent editions were present, as was Ludolf's *History of Ethiopia* (1681–1693) in Latin, English, and French. Many works which are better appreciated now than formerly, such as Rattray's works on the Ashanti and the Gold Coast, were in the original Schomburg Collection. Ibn Batuta's *Travels in Asia and Africa, 1325–1354* furnished an eyewitness account of medieval West African kingdoms at the height of their splendor. *Tarikh el-Fettach* and *Tarikh es-Soudan* were books by indigenous African writers which not only give firsthand accounts but also are histories of the royal houses and dynasties which ruled the western Sudan. The manuscripts of Alexander Crummell and the writings of Edward Blyden, American Negroes who influenced the development of Liberia, were also acquired.

As of 1962, the Schomburg Collection had more than 36,000 bound volumes, of which about half concern people on the African continent. The largest number are in English, the next largest in French, German, and Spanish. Eighty drawers of vertical file materials, such as clippings, articles taken from magazines, programs, broadsides, etc., supplement the book and periodical collection. The vertical file material is valuable because it is classified in detail, mainly on biographical but also on geographical and other lines. Files have been amassed on African personalities such as Tom Mboya, Sékou Touré, Félix Houphouet-Boigny, and Gamal Abdel Nasser and on new countries such as Ghana, Nigeria, Togoland, the French Community, and the Mali Federation.

Men such as Nkrumah and Azikiwe have been represented in the files for at least twenty years; in fact, both these men used the Schomburg Collection during their years in America. In the past it has probably been true that African students learned more about their homelands here than they could at home, because of the lack of local facilities.

The Collection continues to serve in making information in this field available to the general public. Students, magazine writers, and research assistants read side by side with housewives, nationalists, and senior citizens. A great deal of information is given by telephone and correspondence extending all over the world.

As the emergence of new nations in Africa goes on, this collection has become increasingly valuable in helping Americans understand the many aspects of Africa which made this emergence a reality. With growing awareness of the American Negro's stature, the Collection presents source material on his contributions, his roots, his struggles and victories.

MANUSCRIPT COLLECTIONS

The major topics of interest to Africanists include the slave trade, the abolition movement, African congresses, Negro missionaries, the Black Star Line, Liberia, Sierra Leone, and Nigeria.

I. The Slavery and Abolition Collections, 1700–1876

The activities of the abolition movement in the United States and England are covered by letters from William Lloyd Garrison, Theodore Weld, Frederick

Douglass, William Wilberforce, and Thomas Clarkson. Slave sales, passes, wills, speeches, and letters dealing with slavery are included. Especially important are letters relating to the Amistad mutiny (1839) and other slave cases which got into court.

II. The Crummell Collection, 1837–1898

Alexander Crummell (1819–1898), A.B., D.D., LL.D., was born in New York City. His father was reputedly the son of a West African chief. Crummell became an Episcopal minister in 1842. In 1847 he went to England and was awarded a degree from Queens' College, Cambridge University, in 1853. His health caused him to move to Liberia in 1853 and he remained for twenty years as a missionary and teacher. He taught at Liberia College and visited Sierra Leone. In 1873 he returned to the United States.

The Crummell letters and sermons (more than 500 items) are valuable for religious and educational affairs and for local news about Liberia and its connections with the United States.

III. The Bruce Collection, 1872–1924

John Edward Bruce (1856–1924) was born a slave in Piscataway, Maryland, and grew up in Washington, D.C. A self-taught journalist and editor, he wrote for many periodicals, among them the *West African Record, South African Spectator*, and *African Times and Orient Review*. He was a colorful, dynamic, and controversial Negro writer and leader.

Bruce was at first hostile to Marcus Garvey and his 'Back to Africa' movement but later became a staunch defender and trusted friend of Garvey. He was also active in the African Society (in London), the African Methodist Episcopal Zion Church (in the United States), the Order of African Redemption (in Liberia), and the American Negro Society for Historical Research. The letters he received and wrote cover three continents and deal with political, social, and economic reform.

Letters, editorials, newspaper articles, and addresses in the collection number more than 400. Some refer to persons and events in Africa, Liberia, Sierra Leone, and Nigeria and to the Garvey movement.

IV. Miscellaneous Letters and Papers, 1757–1918

This holding, consisting of 105 items in 1942 when the *Calendar* was prepared for publication, has been growing in recent years. Some of the items deal with West Africa, but the larger number pertain to distinguished persons of African descent (such as Ira Aldridge and Victor Sejour) and their activities on the European continent.

NEW YORK ZOOLOGICAL SOCIETY

The New York Zoological Society, Bronx, New York, has an unpublished autobiography of William Temple Hornaday (1854–1937), leading zoologist and zoo director. His book *Free Rum on the Congo* (1887) and articles initiated a widespread movement in the United States and Britain against the liquor traffic in tropical Africa.

NEWBERRY LIBRARY

The general collection of the Newberry Library, Chicago, Illinois, holds about 2,500 volumes on Africa and is strong in nineteenth-century material and in the North African area. About 1,100 of these volumes are not listed in the Library of Congress printed catalogue. The William B. Greenlee Collection on Portugal is excellent in diplomatic and colonial affairs; the bibliographical section is especially complete. The Greenlee Collection is noteworthy in the literature of the Portuguese expansion overseas—in Africa, the Far East, and Brazil.

Although the general collection of Newberry sometimes makes interlibrary loans, the scholar should be warned that the terms of the Greenlee bequest forbid interlibrary loans of materials in the Greenlee Collection. The catalogue of this collection was published in 1953, but present-day holdings are considerably greater than represented therein. The Greenlee Collection (as it was in 1950) was described in a still useful article by C. R. Boxer in the *Newberry Library Bulletin*, 2d ser., No. 6 (May 1951), pp. 167–178.

NEWPORT HISTORICAL SOCIETY

The Newport Historical Society, Newport, Rhode Island, has in its files 112 pieces on Aaron Lopez (1731–1782), a merchant and slave trader of Newport.

UNIVERSITY OF NORTH CAROLINA

The Southern Historical Collection of the University of North Carolina Library, Chapel Hill, North Carolina, has the papers of Raleigh E. Colston, a brigadier general in the Confederate States Army and explorer for the government of Egypt. There are 10 volumes and 743 pieces in the collection. Colston arrived in Egypt in 1873. He led various expeditions to explore and survey roads and ports between the Nile and the Red Sea.

Other papers dealing with Africa include:

Edwin Alexander Anderson, letters from Liberia, the Congo, and Egypt, 1886–1887.

Charles Iverson Graves, reminiscences, letters, and papers—letters from Graves to his wife while he was serving as lieutenant colonel in the Egyptian army, 1873–1877, letters to him from other Americans in Egypt, and miscellaneous papers relating to his Egyptian service.

Samuel Henry Lockett, papers dealing with his service in Egypt, 1874–1876, as colonel of engineers and his later activities in Egypt.

Silas McBee, papers, including extensive correspondence of the editor of the *Churchman*, some of which deals with South Africa and the Boer War.

James Morris Morgan (1845–1928), papers, 16 folders, with various items relating to Morgan's Egyptian service, 1870–1871.

James Graham Ramsay, papers and books, 1885–1889. Included are letters from William G. Ramsay to his family in North Carolina; Ramsay went out to work for the mines in Axim, Gold Coast (Ghana).

Service family, papers, 1803–1892, 400 items. Martha Williford (daughter of
Mrs. Martha Service by a previous marriage) was a missionary in Africa
under the Episcopal missionary bishop John Payne (1815–1874), Cape Palmas,
Liberia, whom she later married. Besides her letters, there are letters from
Payne.

NORTH CAROLINA STATE DEPARTMENT OF ARCHIVES

The holdings of the North Carolina State Department of Archives (formerly the
North Carolina Historical Commission), at Raleigh, North Carolina, include the
papers of David L. Swain, some of which are concerned with the African slave
trade. Letters relating to slaves who were freed and sent to Liberia by the American
Colonization Society are contained in the C. B. Heller Collection.

NORTHWESTERN UNIVERSITY

The African collection at Northwestern University, Evanston, Illinois, has grown
most rapidly during the last two decades, although the University Library has
had books on Africa from its very beginning.

A special impetus for collecting material on Africa was given in 1927 when
Melville J. Herskovits, who had just completed a thesis on the cattle complex of
East Africa, joined Northwestern's faculty. Dr. Herskovits retained an unflagging
interest in the University Library in general, and its African collection in particular,
until his death in 1963.

In 1948 the need for greater knowledge of Africa and its inhabitants had
become so apparent that the Anthropology Department announced the establishment of an African research program, to be guided by an interdisciplinary committee. Coincident with this, the University Library acquired a large collection of
African newspapers, periodicals, pamphlets, and monographs, as a gift from the
Museum of the University of Pennsylvania. The report in the *Northwestern Library
News* of December 17, 1948, describing the gift, concluded with these words:

> Not the least significant aspect of this acquisition is the demonstration of inter-
> university cooperation and division of labor it gives. The University of Penn-
> sylvania is now placing emphasis on studies of North Africa, while North-
> western will specialize on Negro Africa. Between the two, American resources
> in training and research in the field of African Studies will, for the first time,
> afford coverage of the entire continent.

Successive grants from the Carnegie Corporation enabled the Program of
African Studies to expand considerably, and an annual sum was allocated for
library acquisitions. In 1954 and in 1960, the Program received grants from the
Ford Foundation, part of which were specifically budgeted for library development.
However, the bulk of the cost of the Program and the Library's activities in the
African field is increasingly borne by the University. The appointment in 1964 of
Dr. Gwendolen M. Carter as the director of the Program ensures the continued
growth of the collection.

The collection now consists of about 30,000 volumes, including files of 300 periodicals and 30 newspapers, archival material, manuscripts, maps, phonograph records, photographs, and language tapes. The focus is the human aspect of Africa; the aim is to meet the demands of the entire academic community. An attempt is made to acquire as much as possible of what is published in Africa and about Africa.

The general resources of Northwestern University Library offer a great deal of relevant material. The Library has large foreign serial holdings, including British government documents, and is a depository for official United States and United Nations documents including those of the Economic Commission for Africa. Nearly complete holdings are available for League of Nations publications, those of the specialized agencies of the United Nations, and those of intergovernmental agencies such as the Organization for Economic Cooperation and Development and of the International Bank for Reconstruction and Development. The Library also receives the Foreign Broadcast Information Service's *Daily Reports of Foreign Radio Broadcasts* and the Joint Publications Research Service's *Translations on Africa*. The Library is a charter member of the Center for Research Libraries (originally the Midwest Inter-Library Center) and cooperates in the various activities of the Association of Research Libraries, such as the Farmington Plan, the Foreign Newspaper Microfilm Project, and the Official Gazette Project. It is also a member of the Cooperative African Microfilm Project (CAMP), which provides access to bulky or rare research materials, such as the records in Britain on the Belgian Congo, microfilmed for the Fonds National de la Recherche Scientifique in Brussels.

However, the Library's resources of Africana and the contingent services have been organized as a separate department of Deering Library. Although initially the acquisitions policy emphasized anthropology and travel, largely confined to tropical Africa, it now encompasses all of Africa and surrounding islands and embraces all subjects irrespective of language. Of particular strength are anthropology, art, economics (including trade, commerce, and labor), geography, health and hygiene, history, law, political science, psychology, sociology, and language and linguistics. Some 800 grammars, dictionaries, and other language instruction materials are available. Many books and pamphlets are available in African languages. An attempt is being made to identify and collect works, in both African and European languages, written by contemporary African writers. The extensive literature on travel and exploration includes early editions of Dapper, Ogilby, Bruce, Tuckey, Serpa Pinto, and Sparrman.

Efforts are made to collect bibliographic material both old and new. Publications and index cards are currently received from the International Centre of African Social and Economic Documentation (CIDESA) in Brussels. Close contact is maintained with the Centre d'Analyse Documentaire pour l'Afrique Noire (CADAN) in Paris as well as with libraries and special collections all over the world.

Geographically, modern Algeria is well represented, unlike the rest of Northern Africa. West Africa is a major area of strength, with regard to both official documents of former British West Africa and contemporary material from Ghana, Nigeria, Gambia, and Sierra Leone. The Library has an almost complete set of the publications of the Institut Français d'Afrique Noire, of regional agencies, and of the succeeding national organizations. Somewhat unusual are publications from Niger, including some of the writings of Boubou Hama in mimeographed form. The collection's outstanding area of strength is the Congo. In 1950 Northwestern University Library acquired more than 1,300 volumes (including the official gazette of the Congo Free State) pertaining to the Congo, originally the personal library of Félix-Alexandre Fuchs, a former governor. East Africa is well represented, in particular with current material. Southern Africa material is being acquired at an increasing rate. It includes a complete set of the publications of the Van Riebeeck Society; the Basutoland National Council *Proceedings*, in English and Sesuto, from 1910 on; and a copy of the transcript of the South African Treason Trial. The Library has been greatly strengthened by the recent addition of official documents of South Africa, on the High Commission Territories and on South-West Africa, and the records of African and Indian nationalist groups.

Archival resources include the 57 file drawers of the late Melville J. Herskovits, which, until 1988, may be used only with special permission; 10 drawers of material relating to the Northwestern University *Economic Survey of Liberia*, 1962; and a box of the correspondence of Lavinia Scott, a missionary in South Africa for the period 1932–1959. The archives also contain a microfilm copy of the Church Missionary Society Archives pertaining to Africa and dating from the foundation of the Society in 1799 to about 1910. Among these documents are the minutes of the central committee in London, correspondence with missionaries, and their reports and journals. Of much smaller scope are the records of the Presbyterian Historical Society in Philadelphia about West Africa. The collection possesses the microfilmed section of the United States National Archives that have a bearing on Africa, such as the consular reports and the letter books, 1843–1845, of Commodore Matthew Perry, first commander of the African Squadron sent to help suppress the slave trade. Numerous doctoral dissertations and master's theses submitted to British universities between 1950 and 1960 are also available on microfilm.

A large collection of maps—over 2,000 sheets—has been assembled and catalogued. It includes historical and decorative maps of the seventeenth and eighteenth centuries.

Commercial releases of phonograph records of African music have been purchased for the last fifteen years. The collection also has a complete set of the International Library of African Music records.

In 1962 an author and title *Catalog of the African Collection, Northwestern University Library* was issued by G. K. Hall and Company in Boston. More recent material is recorded in the *Joint Acquisitions List of Africana* which since 1962 has listed, bimonthly, the material published within the last five years and received by at least one of the United States libraries most actively interested in Africana.

The bulk of the collection is housed in Room 102, Deering Library, where it may be consulted between 8:30 A.M. and 5:00 P.M. Monday through Friday. Most of the monographic material is also available on interlibrary loan. In the library complex soon to be erected, the African collection will have more space.

Almost all members of the library staff are to some degree concerned with Africana, but the operation of the Department of Africana is the exclusive duty of a curator, a bibliographer, and an assistant.

HANS E. PANOFSKY

OLD DARTMOUTH HISTORICAL SOCIETY

The Old Dartmouth Historical Society and Whaling Museum, New Bedford, Massachusetts, has preserved business papers relating to whaling, seafaring, and merchant trade out of New Bedford, including those of various New Bedford merchants and firms, 1796–1923, and logbooks, chiefly of whaling vessels, 1745–1923, more than 700 volumes. There are also papers of William Rotch (1734–1828), major Nantucket and New Bedford whaling merchant, and of Jonathan Bourne (1811–1889), prominent New Bedford whaling shipowner (3 linear feet). (There may be more documentation on Bourne among the papers—totaling 46 linear feet—of his son, Senator Jonathan Bourne of Oregon, in the University of Oregon Library, Eugene, Oregon.)

The Society contains the following missionary archives:

Extracts from a journal of the Reverend D. Baldwin on board the ship *New England* in 1830–1831, 8 pp., typed.
Journal of Mrs. Andrew D. Colcord on board the missionaries' brig *Morning Star* in 1875, 42 pp., typed.
A rare pamphlet, *The Story of the Morning Star*, published by the American Board of Commissioners for Foreign Missions, 1866, 71 pp.

UNIVERSITY OF OREGON

The University of Oregon Library, Eugene, Oregon, contains letters and documents (1 ft.) of the International Association of the Congo, 1881–1883, collected by Lt. Lieven Van de Velde. Included are letters and correspondence of Henry Morton Stanley, whom Van de Velde accompanied to the Congo.

The Van de Velde Collection* consists of one bound volume and a portfolio of loose papers. The bound volume, with 468 letters and documents, including two treaties and 31 Henry M. Stanley letters, has a binder's title 'Documents de l'expedition au Congo de L. Van de Velde, 1881–1882–1883.' The portfolio holds a few loose letters, family and military documents, pamphlets, official papers, photographs, and 11 water colors by Lieven Van de Velde. Most of the water colors relate to the Congo region. The correspondence in this collection is official, either originals or official copies. The letters of Stanley and of J. Grant Elliott, together with duplicates of those addressed to Stanley, are in English. Others are in French, German, Portuguese, and Dutch. The collection was obtained from Paul Van de Velde of Salem, Oregon, in 1950.

---

* For a description of the collection see the *Call Number*, Vol. XXII, No. 2 (Spring 1961), published by the Library of the University of Oregon.

PACIFIC SCHOOL OF RELIGION

The Pacific School of Religion Library, 1798 Scenic Avenue, Berkeley, California, holds the diary of William Taylor, Methodist evangelist, missionary, and missionary bishop to Liberia, Angola, and the Congo in the late nineteenth century.

PEABODY MUSEUM AND ESSEX INSTITUTE

Many of the papers relating to American commercial contact with Africa have been preserved by the Peabody Museum and Essex Institute in Salem, Massachusetts. Logbooks, merchants' account books, and letters from agents and captains provide a rich historical record of Americans in Africa and of events in Africa in the eighteenth and nineteenth centuries. Entries for each institution are arranged chronologically.

The *Essex Register* (1800–1893) and the *Salem Gazette* (1768–1892), held by the Essex Institute, give valuable information on the activities of merchants in Africa. Articles based on the materials held by the Museum and the Institute are published in the *Historical Collections* and *Bulletin of the Essex Institute*.

(See also the Peabody Museum entry under Art and Ethnographic Collections below.)

PEABODY MUSEUM

James D. Philips Papers, containing extremely useful research tools—ship arrivals and departures from Salem, news of business transactions (all from the Salem press)—for the eighteenth and early nineteenth centuries.

Logbook, *Henry* (1788–1791), account of a voyage to India, with stops at Cape Town and Mauritius.

Logbook, *Richard and Edward* (1789), has good information on market conditions in Mauritius and Cape Town.

Logbook, *Lighthorse* (1791–1792), including transactions at Cape Town, with a harbor journal by Benjamin Crowninshield.

Jacob Crowninshield, letter book (1791–1797); commercial affairs.

Logbook, *Fanny* (1792–1793), record of a voyage to Cape Town.

Nathaniel Silsbee, account book (1792–1795), including material on the Cape Verde Islands, Mauritius, and South Africa.

Logbook, *Britannide* (1792–1796), with description of Cape Town harbor defenses.

Logbooks, *America* (1796–1806). A 1796–1797 voyage includes information of dealings by the ship's captain with the revolutionary government established in Mauritius as a result of the French Revolution. A few matters of commercial interest are also included. A 1801–1802 voyage describes a stop at Mauritius and the difficulties experienced by Americans there due to measures resulting from the Napoleonic Wars. Another logbook, for 1804–1805, gives information about Réunion.

Logbooks, *William & Henry* (1797–1798, 1798–1800); many transactions at Cape Town.

Logbook, *Belisarius* (1799). The log contains a good description of Tenerife.

Dudley L. Pickman, journal (1799–1804). The author visited Mauritius and Réunion and gives a brief history of these islands, as well as a description of contemporary conditions.

Logbook, *Herald* (1801–1809). An informative account, by Capt. Moses H. White, is given of Cape Town and Mauritius. The unsettled commercial situation, owing to the Napoleonic Wars, and the condition of the slave population are of particular interest.

Crowninshield family papers (1804–1864), miscellaneous papers dealing with trade, including an account of the visit of the Confederate vessel *Alabama* to Cape Town in 1864.

John Bryant, letter book (1806–1807), describes conditions of trade in Cape Town and Mauritius.

Logbook, *Recovery* (1806–1807), lists American vessels at Cape Town.

Samuel Swan, letter book (1806–1809) and journal (1815–1818), including a valuable account of trading conditions along the West African coast. A series of letters to an unnamed friend contains an extensive description of Senegal and Sierra Leone.

Logbook, *Columbia* (1811–1812), record of an unsuccessful voyage to the Cape Verde Islands.

Logbook, *Packet* (1816–1817). Trade conditions and the effects of a great fire at Port Louis, Mauritius, are detailed.

Samuel Hodges, Jr., papers (1818–1827). Hodges was American consul in the Cape Verde Islands. His collection includes commercial papers, consular dispatches, and letters relating to West Africa.

Logbook, *Potomac* (1825–1826). A rough colored illustration of Table Mountain, Cape Town, is included.

Logbook, *Spy* (1826–1827), one of the earliest accounts of an American voyage to eastern Africa. The vessel visited the Portuguese possessions, Madagascar, the Comoro Islands, and Zanzibar.

Logbook, *Susan* (1828–1829), an account of visits to Portuguese ports, the Comoro Islands, Zanzibar, Lamu, and Majunga.

Logbook, *Virginia* (1828–1829), includes a report of a visit to Majunga, Madagascar, and of the unsettled conditions owing to a campaign by the Hova ruler, Radama. The most important section of the logbook relates to Mombasa, where Said ibn-Sultan, ruler of Zanzibar and Muscat, was attacking the city. The *Virginia* also visited Zanzibar and the Portuguese possessions.

Michael Shepard, papers (1836–1853). Shepard's letter collection contains information on commercial affairs for the entire East African area. They are of particular importance for Zanzibar since they give details of American maneuvering to secure the major portion of the trade of that port. Accounts of the freeing of slaves in the French possessions are also included.

Richard P. Waters, papers (1836–1847). Waters was the first American consul at Zanzibar. His papers, including some duplicates of official documents, are of primary importance for the history of Zanzibar. They deal with political affairs, with the American effort to secure a monopoly of trade, and with the conditions which caused this effort to fail. Three letters from J. L. Krapf (German missionary-explorer), recounting his arrival at Mombasa, and some of his early letters are included. Accounts of visits to Majunga and Mozambique are also of interest.

Benjamin Shreve (?), accounts (1837–1838). Though listed under Shreve's name, this daily account book recording trade at an Ambriz factory may have belonged to another person, possibly Alfred H. Beckett. The pages contain several water colors of local sights.

J. A. West, George West, and Benjamin A. West, papers (1837–1853, 1849–1861). These papers are very important for the penetration of Americans into East Africa. Though not so valuable as the Waters collection, they include information on commercial rivalry between British and Americans and on American trade with Madagascar. Letters from several American consuls are included. The second collection of West papers has material relating to West African trade—particularly at the Cape Verde Islands and the Gambia River from 1849 to 1861.

Sandwith Drinker, typed extract from his 'A Private Journal of Events and Scenes, 1838–1841.' Drinker sailed the Zanzibar vessel *Sultani* from New York to Zanzibar. Included is good information on various Zanzibari personalities.

Logbook, *Neptune* (1841), including a colorful description of trade along the West African coast. A visit with Governor Russwurm of Cape Palmas is recorded.

Logbook, *Cherokee* (1841–1842), contains a description of market conditions at Majunga.

Logbook, *Herald* (1843–1847). This vessel traded a variety of goods with the settlement of Monrovia, Liberia.

B. Frank Fabens, papers (1843–1857). Fabens was a prominent commercial agent in Zanzibar; his papers are especially valuable for information on the American effort to meet the increasing competition for the Zanzibar trade. They are of value also for the Madagascar trade, American-Zanzibar diplomatic relations, and the role of the Indian Customs Master in Zanzibar commercial life.

Michael W. Shepard, letter (1844). This valuable letter from Shepard, inserted in the logbook of the *Star*, gives a very full account of affairs in Zanzibar.

Logbook, *Ann Parry* (1845–1848). The *Parry* was a Portsmouth whaler which visited widely in East African waters. Information is given on shore visits for Zanzibar and Madagascar.

Henry L. Williams, papers (1846). Included are a few particulars on commercial matters at Zanzibar.

Logbook, *Albatross* (1847–1848), with a description of a Malabar christening on Mauritius.

Thomas P. Pingree, David Pingree, and Charles Pingree, papers (1849–1877). The collection is almost entirely concerned with commercial matters in East Africa, Sierra Leone, and the Gold Coast.

Logbook, *Vintage* (1850–1851), record of a trading voyage to Angola.

Logbooks, *Arthur Pickering* (1850–1860), covering several voyages to East African waters. Some commercial information is included.

Logbook, *Catherine* (1853–1855), account of visits to several Angolan ports.

Joseph Winn, Jr., papers. Included are an interesting sketch of Zanzibar in 1855 and photographs of some of the inhabitants of the island.

Logbook, *Sea Mew* (1856). The *Sea Mew* visited several ports in Angola. The entries deal mainly with cargo loading and other vessels encountered.

Logbook, *Arabia* (1857–1858). Commercial information on a visit to Zanzibar is given.

Horace B. Putnam, papers (1858). One valuable letter is on trading conditions in the western Indian Ocean.

N. B. Mansfield, papers (1860–1885), including a collection of 111 boxes of cargo manifests, owners' instructions, letters from agents, and other material relating to West African trade; also a large collection of daybooks, account books, and books of letters relating to this same trade. Mansfield and his associates were among the principal merchants trading to West Africa.

Aaron W. Berry, papers (1863–1864); information on commerce and general conditions in the Gold Coast.

John Cole, papers (1864). A note on social life among the Europeans in Mauritius is included.

Logbook, *Glide* (1865); commercial information on Majunga and Zanzibar.

Edward Bertram Trumbull, 'Twenty-two Years on Deep Blue Water' (a typescript). The author, a master of Salem vessels trading to eastern Africa, gives a general account of his life at sea and in port in the latter third of the nineteenth century.

Logbook, *A. Houghton* (1866–1867), account of visit to Ambrizette and South Coast.

Logbook, *Hellespont* (1866–1867), visits to Zanzibar and Muskat.

Logbook, *Para* (1867–1871), a whaling voyage with stops at many East African ports.

Edward D. Ropes, Sr., and Edward D. Ropes, Jr., papers (1867–1888). The collection, made up mostly of letters from the younger Ropes, is of great value. Among the matters dealt with are the personal life in Zanzibar of an American agent, the strong position held by the British representatives Churchill and Kirk, the competition of the various resident firms, the entry of Germany into East Africa, and the personal and business life of the noted Indian merchant, Taria Topan.

William H. Hathorne, papers (1877–1880). Hathorne was both a commercial agent and a U.S. consul at Zanzibar. His papers are similar to those of Ropes in import. Of special interest are his letters to H. M. Stanley while the latter was beginning his venture on the Congo River for Leopold of Belgium.

Logbook, *Benefactor* (1881–1884), account of two voyages to the Gold Coast.

Impost Books, Port of Salem. These contain entries for every ship entering the port from 1790 to 1853. In some instances, return cargoes are detailed.

Essex Institute

Aaron Lopez (1731–1782), papers, 1 envelope. Lopez was a merchant and slave trader of Newport, Rhode Island.

Derby family papers (1785–1797). Elias H. Derby was the pioneer of American trade to St. Helena, South Africa, and the Mascarenes from the mid-1780's into the early 1800's. This voluminous collection contains several very full letters on the trading conditions of the various ports visited.

Logbook, *Fanny* (1788), a brief voyage to the Cape Verde Islands for salt. A number of other American vessels were there at the time.

Nathaniel Silsbee Papers. Much valuable information is given on trade at Cape Town in the 1790's.

Brookhouse family papers (1791–1861). There are letters to Brookhouse's agent A. B. Gorea from 1855 to 1861 concerning trade to Angola and also Gorea's correspondence (in Portuguese) with various of his factors.

Logbook, *Augusta* (1803–1804); good description of the Cape Verde Islands.

Logbook, *Aeolus* (1805), with an interesting account of riding out one of Table Bay's famous gales.

Logbook, *Louisa* (1806), including information on a stay at Cape Town.

Logbook, *Gentoo* (1816); colorful account of efforts to trade and to repair the vessel at Cape Town and Simons Town.

Logbook, *General Lincoln* (1816–1817); records of a ship seized off Sierra Leone.

Logbook, *Seaman* (1822–1825). This vessel was one of the earlier ones to trade with Majunga, in Madagascar. A few commercial details are given.

Logbook, *Monroe* (1825). The *Monroe* traded along the windward and leeward coasts. Of special interest is the description of trading in the Gambia, which was closed to American merchants at that time.

Logbooks, *Ann* (1826–1827, 1827–1829); one of the earliest recorded visits to Zanzibar and the ports of Lindi, Berbera, Anjouan, and Mombasa. The captain especially notes the efforts of the French to secure slaves for Réunion.

Logbook, *Osprey* (1830–1831). A note of a meeting with the inhabitants of St. Augustine Bay, Madagascar, is included.

Logbook, *Sciot* (1831). The *Sciot* visited the windward and leeward coasts of West Africa. It mentions smuggling goods off the island of Gorée.

Richard P. Waters, shipping records (1832–1844), additional information from the first American consul to Zanzibar. (See Waters entry, 1836–1847, in Peabody Museum listing.)

Logbook, *Quill* (1833–1834), with an interesting note on the blockade of Mombasa by Said ibn-Sultan.

The Dunlap Papers (1835). Volume 15 contains an interesting circular printed by the U.S. consul at Cape Town, Isaac Chase, soliciting American business.

Logbook, *Gleaner* (1835–1836); excellent log by A. H. Beckett, merchant in the West Africa trade.

Logbook, *Gleaner* (1836–1838). The American goods shipped and the purchases made at a factory at Ambriz are recorded, as well as some of the names of individual Africans traded with.

Logbook, *Reaper* (1837–1838). This whaler visited the ports of Madagascar.

Logbooks, *Richmond* (1837–1839, 1842–1843, 1843–1844, 1845), with details on Portuguese ports in Mozambique.

Logbook, *Rolla* (1838); information on trade at Zanzibar.

Account book, *Elizabeth* (1839). The book contains several sets of owners' instructions relating to the groundnut trade in Gambia. There are also cargo manifests, port charges, expenses, and an account of the return cargoes.

Logbook, *Palestine* (1839–1842). There is a brief account of the people of the Comoro Islands and of their relations with American whalers. A notice on Majunga is also included.

Logbook, *Oregon* (1840). This journal by the captain, Edward Harrington, is of notable value for its description of the American settlement at Cape Palmas and the English fort at Dix Cove.

Logbook, *Star* (1842), covers a visit to Zanzibar and has information on a shore visit by the crew.

Logbooks, *Ann Parry* and *Izette* (1842–1845). Both vessels were whalers in the waters off Madagascar, and the logbooks give details of visits to the island.

Logbook, *Vintage* (1843–1844); trade with Angola-Congo ports.

John Felt Osgood, sketches and diary (1843–1867). Most of Osgood's material has appeared in the work *Notes or Recollections of Majunga, Zanzibar, Muscat, Aden, Mocha, and Other Eastern Ports* (Salem, 1854). The notes seem to have been worked over by Joseph B. F. Osgood, who has, until now, been regarded as the author of the account.

William B. Bates, journal (1845). The captain of the *Richmond* gives a full account of trading conditions in the ports of Mozambique and of the effects of British measures against the slave trade from this area. There are a few notes of a stop at Zanzibar.

Logbook, *Ceylon* (1845–1846), record of a trading voyage to Gambia, Portuguese Guinea, and Sierra Leone.

Logbook, *Herald* (1846–1847); trade with São Tomé and Angola.

Horace B. Putnam, 'Notes of a Cruise to the Indies' (1847), journals (1847–1848, 1850–1851), 'A Cruise to the Indies and a Life on Shore' (1848–1849). Valuable manuscript accounts of the ports of Majunga, Mayotte, Nosy-Bé, Zanzibar, and Brava, including many details of the social life and political organization in each area. An especially valuable report concerns the attack of the Sakalavas on Nosy-Bé.

E. A. Emmerton, journal (1848–1849), 'Sketch of His Life,' has valuable information on Zanzibar and the Mozambique ports.

Logbooks, *Lewis* and *Potomac* (1848–1849). Both give examples of the restrictions imposed on foreign trade by the Portuguese in Mozambique.

Logbook, *Sophronia* (1848–1849), with a report on certain American vessels being held by the Portuguese for suspicion of participation in the slave trade from the Mozambique coast.

Logbook, *Susan Kelley* (1851). This vessel traded at the Los Islands and in the Rio Pongo and Rio Nunez.

Logbook, *Allen* (1851–1852). The *Allen* traded in the Rio Pongo and the Rio Nunez in company with the *Susan Kelley*. The brief entries are occasionally of value.

Logbook, *Elizabeth Hall* (1851–1852). A note about the U.S.S. *Susquehanna*'s visit to Zanzibar in 1851 is given.

Logbook, *Winnegance* (1851–1852). The vessel stopped at most of the ports on the leeward coast, including Fernando Po, not often visited by American vessels.

John J. Coker, papers (1852–1867), 8 volumes containing letters and invoices on trade to the west coast of Africa, principally Angola. Coker was sometime acting U.S. commercial agent in Loanda.

Logbook, *William H. Shailer* (1853); trade on the Angolan coast.

Logbooks, *Catherine* (1853, 1854–1855, 1855–1856), records of trading voyages to São Tomé and Angola.

Logbook, *Peacock* (1855). There is an account of wreck near Majunga.

Journal, *Goldfinch* (1857–), incomplete journal of a voyage to Angola.

Logbooks, *Ionia* (1859–1860, 1863), give information concerning business arrangements between legitimate traders and slave merchants on the West African coast.

Caleb Cook, journal (1860–1862). Cook was sent to Zanzibar by Louis Agassiz to study the natural history of the island. His journal is not of primary significance, but it does include references to many of the important persons visiting the island.

Pingree family papers (1860–1879). Thomas P. Pingree and his associates traded extensively with West Africa, principally Sierra Leone and the Gold Coast. The papers include letters from Pingree's agents, his business associates in Sierra Leone and the United States, and vessel manifests and accounts of sales of African cargoes.

Logbook, *Tremont* (1863). The vessel made a direct voyage to Sierra Leone, loaded with ginger and hides, and returned to Boston in a remarkably short voyage of four months' duration.

Logbook, *Glide* (1867–1868), of interest for a visit to Tamatave, Madagascar.

Logbook, *Gertrude Howes* (1867–1869). The vessel spent nearly two years in whaling, shark fishing, and coastal trading on the southwest African coast. The log contains an account of a fight with Africans at Walvis Bay.

Logbook, *W. H. Thorndike* (1876–1877), a visit to Zanzibar.

William H. Trumbull, diary (1876–1881). Trumbull served a Salem firm in Zanzibar. The diary records the daily events of his life.

Miscellaneous shipping and commercial records (1805–1849, 1850–1870). The collection contains diverse materials relating to trade with West, East, and South Africa. It includes letters from Americans in East Africa and cargo manifests for West Africa.

Salem Custom House records. The records consist of bales of customs papers separated by the year of a vessel's return. Included are occasional bills of sale for African ports visited.

NORMAN R. BENNETT and SUSAN J. HERLIN, Boston University
George E. BROOKS, Indiana University
Alan R. BOOTH, Ohio University

THE HISTORICAL SOCIETY OF PENNSYLVANIA

The Historical Society of Pennsylvania, 1300 Locust Street, Philadelphia, Pennsylvania, holds 'Slave Trade on the Western Coast of Africa,' 1822, 1 volume. This volume is a copy of a report by Commodore Sir Robert Mends of H.M.S. *Iphigenia*, at Sierra Leone, to the British Admiralty; it also contains a genealogical list of the Mends family.

Manuscripts relating to American activities in Africa include papers of William Rotch (1734–1828), major Nantucket and New Bedford whaling merchant; a brief narrative of the adventures and experiences of John Menzies as a sailor and traveler to Portugal, Africa, and China, 1793–1794; material on Stephen Decatur, U.S. naval officer, 1801–1805, 1-volume letter book; papers of George C. Read (1787–1862), commander of the African Squadron, 1846–1847, 7 volumes; the papers of the Pennsylvania Society for Promoting the Abolition of Slavery, 1748–1916 (containing the minutes of the Committee on African Slave Trade, 1805–1807); 1 volume of biographical sketches of the African Colonization Society, 1832–1872; and papers of John Cox and family, including correspondence, documents, reports, religious and literary manuscripts, papers on slavery and the abolition movement, and trade with Africa and elsewhere.

The Society also has papers, 1626–1834, of the Dutch West India Company, which had trade with West and South Africa, about 500 items. There are also papers of Dutilh and Wachsmuth, eighteenth- and early-nineteenth-century Philadelphia shipping merchants involved in the slave trade, about 1,000 items which constitute the company's own records plus the large segment of the approximately 10,000-item Charles W. Unger collection pertaining to the company.

UNIVERSITY OF PENNSYLVANIA

The Van Pelt Library of the University of Pennsylvania, Philadelphia, Pennsylvania, holds about 3,000 volumes and over 250 serials on Africa. The University Museum and Museum Library contain strong collections of African ethnology and archaeology.

PRINCETON UNIVERSITY

The Library of Princeton University, Princeton, New Jersey, holds the papers of Robert Field Stockton (1795–1866), naval officer, the agent of the American Colonization Society who negotiated for the Society's first foothold on the Liberian coast in 1821, 12 boxes. It also has the papers of Herbert Gibbons (1880–1934), foreign correspondent and traveler in Africa, author of *The New Map of Africa* (1916), about 15 boxes. (See also Princeton University entries under Art and Ethnographic Collections below.)

PROVIDENCE PUBLIC LIBRARY

The Providence Public Library, 150 Empire Street, Providence, Rhode Island, has a special Nicholson Whaling Collection in which are found the following:

Logbook, *Octavia* of New Bedford (1838), visits to Madagascar, the Comoro Islands, and Mauritius.

Logbook, *Bogota* of New Bedford (1843), visits to the east coast of Africa and the Comoro Islands.

Logbook, *Roscoe* of New Bedford (1847–1848), visits to Madagascar, Réunion, the Comoro Islands, Mozambique, and Mauritius.

Logbook, *A. Hicks* of Westport (1877–1878), visits to the Comoro Islands and the Seychelles.

RHODE ISLAND HISTORICAL SOCIETY

The Rhode Island Historical Society, 52 Power Street, Providence 6, Rhode Island, has four items relating to Africa:

Logbook, *Providence* (1795–1797), a visit to Réunion.

Logbook, *Benjamin Rush* (1832), a visit to the Comoro Islands.

Logbooks, *Maryland* (1854–1860), visits to East African ports.

Import Books, Providence Custom House, information on nineteenth-century voyages to Africa.

UNIVERSITY OF ROCHESTER

The University of Rochester Library, Rochester, New York 14627, contains 8 boxes of materials of Carl Ethan Akeley, naturalist and explorer, for the period 1895–1926. Akeley and both his first and his second wife have written extensively about their trips to Africa. The collection includes material relating to the African Hall in the American Museum of Natural History. Also held by the Library are papers (18 linear feet) of Henry Augustus Ward (1834–1906), eminent naturalist of the University of Rochester who visited West Africa in 1859–1860 and made two journeys hundreds of miles into the interior.

ROOSEVELT UNIVERSITY

The Roosevelt University Library, 430 South Michigan Avenue, Chicago, Illinois 60605, has a collection of between 1,200 and 1,500 volumes on Africa, with greatest strength in history and politics, geography, and anthropology.

RUTGERS UNIVERSITY

The Library of Rutgers University, New Brunswick, New Jersey, holds 1 volume of papers of William Wilberforce (1759–1833), M.P. and long-time leader of the British abolitionist movement.

SANFORD MEMORIAL LIBRARY

Papers of Henry Shelton Sanford (1823-1891) are kept at the Sanford Memorial Library, Sanford, Florida.* He served as minister to Belgium, 1861–1869, as

---

* See *Register: Henry Shelton Sanford Papers Processed by Manuscript Section, Archives Division, Tennessee State Library and Archives* (Nashville, Tenn., 1960, 73 pp.).

representative of the American Geographical Society at the African International Conference, 1876, and as representative of the United States at the Berlin Conference, 1884. He was also the representative of the United States at the Anti-Slavery Conference in Brussels, 1890.

Sanford served on the executive committee of the International Association which sent Henry Morton Stanley to the Congo to set up stations manned by Europeans and Americans. He helped the International Association of the Congo (later known as Congo Free State) secure diplomatic recognition from the United States and European powers. The Sanford Exploring Expedition, which he organized, went to the Congo in 1886 to open the interior of Africa.

The Sanford papers dealing with Africa are in 12 boxes and span the years 1870–1891. The material is separated into accounts, correspondence, legal documents, and memorandums and is arranged chronologically.

The most significant correspondents for the African part of the papers are H. P. Bailey, Chatrobe Bateman, James G. Blaine, F. F. Carter, F. Dewinton, Frederick T. Frelinghuysen, Baron Greindl, George Grenfell, E. J. Glave, Cam Janssen, John A. Kasson, J. B. Latrobe, Amos A. Lawrence, Leopold II, Henry Morton Stanley, Col. M. Strauch, A. B. Swinburne, E. H. Taunt, Edwin Terrell, Capt. Albert Thys, W. P. Tisdel, A. J. Wauters, and T. Wauters.

SCHENECTADY COUNTY HISTORICAL SOCIETY

The Schenectady County Historical Society, 32 Washington Street, Schenectady 5, New York, has some data on the American Colonization Society concerned with Liberia.

SMITHSONIAN INSTITUTION

The Division of Ethnology's Accession Papers, dating from 1880, have been retained by the Smithsonian Institution in Washington, D.C., and contain data on the populations, cultures, and environment of various African areas. (See also Smithsonian Institution entry under Art and Ethnographic Collections below.)

STANFORD UNIVERSITY

The Africa collections at Stanford University, Stanford, California, are housed largely in the University Library, the Library of the Food Research Institute, and the Hoover Institution on War, Revolution, and Peace. Although the major portion of the material is found in the Hoover Institution, the other two libraries constitute important resources. Special collections are found in the Branner Library (Geology), the Cubberley Library (Education), the Lane Medical Library, and the Law Library.

The *University Library* buys widely in the African field but accepts primary responsibility for all African material before 1870 and in the areas of art, ethnography, geography, linguistics, literature, religion, sociology, statistics, and technical documents. The Government Documents Division receives general statistical annuals and bulletins from all African countries and statistical reports of foreign trade from most countries. An effort is made to acquire all census and development-planning material. Most departmental reports are also received. The Documents Division had long been an official depository for British government documents and thus contains an outstanding collection of parliamentary debates, blue books, command papers, Foreign Office papers, and annual reports of the Colonial Office from the early nineteenth century. For France the debates of the Assemblée Nationale are held from 1871 and the *Journal Officiel* from 1914; for Germany the Reichstag debates are complete from 1867. These together with the depository publications of the United Nations make a substantial collection of material relevant to Africa.

Books and monographs number over 10,000 volumes, primarily in the field of early travels, history, economics, politics, and ethnography. The University Library also subscribes to approximately 100 serials on Africa, among them the Académie Malgache, *Bulletin* (1902–); *African Studies* (formerly *Bantu Studies;* 1921–); and Société des Africanistes, *Journal* (1931–).

The *Branner Library* (Geology) contains an excellent collection of older geological surveys of various African countries and subscribes to most of the current African geological journals. An effort is made to acquire the important geological monographs on Africa.

The *Cubberley Library* (Education) is collecting documentary and secondary material on education in Africa. The main categories of material to be found in the Library are government (Ministry of Education) reports from various African countries, including statistics, development plans, etc.; catalogues of African universities and colleges; various journals on, or containing articles on, education in Africa; and secondary material on education in Africa, especially comparative studies, including material prepared by the U.S. Office of Education.

The *Lane Medical Library* has important holdings on the literature dealing with African medicine and subscribes to nearly all the current African medical journals.

The *Law Library* secures the basic legal material, e.g., the legislative enactments and the decisions of the higher courts from many African countries as well as supporting material (constitutions, monographs, all journals) on African law. Several hundred volumes of older statutory laws are also held.

FOOD RESEARCH INSTITUTE

The Library of the Food Research Institute is mainly a noncirculating research and reference library. The Food Research Institute was established in 1921 under a grant from the Carnegie Corporation and later received grants from the Ford Foundation for research in the production, distribution, and consumption of food. In addition to books, official and unofficial journals, reprints, and pamphlets, the collection includes many statistical annuals, quarterly and monthly statistical bulletins, and reports of the Department of Agriculture and other government departments concerned with food, agriculture, nutrition, population, and economic development.

The Food Research Institute Library maintains current files of such periodicals as *Agronomie Tropicale, Ghana Farmer, East African Agricultural and Forestry*

Journal, Journal d'Agriculture Tropicale et de Botanique Appliquée, Tropical Abstracts, Marchés Tropicaux du Monde, and *Journal of the West African Science Association.* Some important agricultural journals such as the *Bulletin Agricole du Congo Belge* date back to 1910.

The Institute maintains files of publications of the Food and Agriculture Organization and the Economic Commission for Africa. In addition, an effort is made to procure all the publications of the Conseil Scientifique Africain and the Commission de Coopération Technique en Afrique au Sud du Sahara pertinent to the Institute's research. The Library holds approximately 8,000 African titles. The librarian maintains an organized file of bibliographical cards issued monthly by CIDESA. These cards analyze current books, monographs, government documents, and periodical literature on Africa.

A number of monographs on Africa have been published by the Institute.

HOOVER INSTITUTION

The beginnings of the Africa Collection in the Hoover Institution go back to 1919 when the Belgian government presented Herbert Hoover with a collection of official Belgian documents and reports, including many pertaining to the Belgian Congo and Ruanda-Urundi. In the fall of 1919, an agent of the provisional German government contributed a large number of maps and documents on Africa. After the establishment of the Hoover War Library in 1922, Miss Nina Almond, the first librarian, expanded the collection by securing the reports of the League of Nations Mandates Commission and many official gazettes of colonial powers. The Library now has reports from all the mandates in Africa under the League (and also the United Nations) and files of older official gazettes from the various African countries—Tanganyika (1919–1937, 1957–), South-West Africa (1916–1963), the Gold Coast (1917–1957), Nigeria (1914–1937, 1952–), Gambia (1914–1955), and the Camerouns (1926–), to mention but a few. With the appointment of Mrs. Ruth Perry as half-time curator of the Africa Collection in 1956, a relatively extensive program of acquisitions was undertaken. Mrs. Perry's trips to Africa greatly strengthened the Ghana (former Gold Coast) and Nigeria collections. Since the appointment of Dr. Peter Duignan as full-time curator in 1959 the holdings have been significantly increased.

The Africa Collection is integrated into the general collections and holdings of the Hoover Institution, which uses the Library of Congress classification scheme; approximately 80 percent of the Africa Collection's holdings are catalogued. The remaining 20 percent are listed under the country, society, language, and organizational heading.

The collection concentrates on the period from 1870 to the present in Africa south of the Sahara and on the fields of history, politics, government, and economics. There are no specific limitations on language coverage, but the bulk of the material is in English and French, with important holdings in German, Italian, Portuguese, and Russian. An effort is being made to collect Swahili language material. The Hoover Institution has an outstanding Middle East Collection (over 40,000 volumes) which grows each year through membership in P.L. 480. As a result North Africa is well covered—over 5,000 books and 50 serial titles in Western languages and in Arabic.

The Africa Collection contains approximately 25,000 books, 8,000 government documents, and 3,000 pamphlets. Currently 300 periodicals and 55 newspapers dealing with Africa are received. In addition to subscribing annually to the debates, gazettes, and many departmental reports for all African states, the Hoover Institution has a valuable assortment of older government documents. The Library's holdings in this respect are most extensive for the former Gold Coast and Belgian Congo, South Africa, the Rhodesias, and Senegal. They include Legislative Council debates from the Gold Coast (1928–1951) and Legislative Council and Legislative Assembly debates (1914–) as well as Native Affairs Department reports (1904–) from Southern Rhodesia. Besides the official journal for French Equatorial Africa (1939–1949) and French West Africa (1905–1959), the Africa Collection has some debates from several assemblies—Chad (1952–1958), Senegal (1879–), and Ubangi-Shari (1947–1956).

Among the important francophone African materials on microfilm are 15 reels of items selected from the proceedings of the Grand Conseil de l'Afrique Occidentale Française (1947–1954). The Grand Conseil film has holdings for Senegal, Guinea, Ivory Coast, Niger, Haute-Volta, Middle Congo, and Ubangi-Shari. The largest runs are the *Procès Verbaux* (1949–1950, 1952–1954) of the Conseil Général of Dahomey and the debates (1947–1953) and budget sessions (1949–1954) of French Equatorial Africa. (An inventory of this material has been prepared.)

Recent important acquisitions of government documents from former French West Africa include the *Bulletin Administratif du Sénégal* (1819–1908) and the *Journal Officiel* of Dahomey (1918–1959), Guinea (1901–1957), Soudan and Mali (1906–), Ivory Coast (1904–), and Senegal (1914–1961).

The Africa Collection is further strengthened by the documentation of the countries of Western Europe relating to their overseas territories—those of England, France, Germany, Portugal, Belgium, and Italy. The Western Europe Collection and the British Collection contain over 100,000 books, pamphlets, and government documents, 11,000 recorded periodical titles, and 800 newspaper titles. For up-to-date documentation on this area, over 300 current periodicals and 46 newspapers are available.

For Italian Africa, the Library has the *Rivista Coloniale* (1906–1927), *Rivista delle Colonie Italiane* (1927–1943), and *Annuario delle Colonie Italiane* (1926–1939). For French Africa it has the *Bulletin Officiel* prepared by the Ministère des Colonies from 1914 to 1945, when it was replaced by the Ministère de la France d'Outre-Mer. For the Belgian colonies the Library has the *Bulletin Officiel* (1885–1896, 1910–1959), *Bulletin de l'Office Colonial* (1910–1940), and *Bulletin de Colonisation Comparée* (1908–1914). For Ruanda-Urundi the Institution holds the *Bulletin Officiel* (1924–1937) and *Rapport sur l'Administration Belge du Ruanda-Urundi* (1921–1960). Also held are the *Annuaire Statistique de la Belgique et du Congo Belge* (1870–). Pamphlets and serials published in Western Europe and dealing with colonial Africa are also numerous.

Among the many French and Belgian serials in the collection are *Afrique Française* (1900–) and *Revue Française d'Histoire d'Outre-Mer* (1913–). The Africa Collection has fairly complete holdings of the various series of the Institut Français d'Afrique Noire and of the Institut's branches, e.g., *Etudes Camerounaises, Etudes Dahoméennes*, etc. Also held are *Congo Illustré* (1891–1895), *Congo: Revue Générale de la Colonie Belge* (1920–1940), and *Notre Colonie* (1919–1929). The collection has in addition a complete file of the publications of the Académie Royale des Sciences Coloniales in Brussels; other serials include *Voix du Congolais* (1945–1959), *Essor du Congo* (1934–1960), and *Moniteur Katangais* (1960–1963).

The Hoover Institution has approximately 1,000 volumes dealing with the history and administration of the German colonies and the German attitude toward the colonial question. Every aspect of German colonization is widely covered in the publications of the Kolonialamt, which the Institution has. These include source books and interpretations of laws touching such subjects as commerce and banking, agriculture, education, labor, insurance, taxes, income and inheritance, military and maritime law, constitutional law, electoral law, prices, and wartime economy affecting the supply and distribution of food. Important official publications include the *Deutsches Kolonialblatt* (1890–1921) and the *Verhandlungen des Reichstags: Stenographische Berichte* (1871–1938) of the Reichstag—these and the accompanying Anlagebände and the Beilage to the *Deutsches Kolonialblatt* contain not only all the debates on colonial questions but also numerous documents, committee reports, correspondence, and the official reports on the colonies given by the Colonial Office. There are also reports of colonial societies like the Deutsche Kolonialgesellschaft, whose official organ, the *Deutsche Kolonialzeitung*, is available for the years 1884–1922. Other important titles for German colonial affairs in the early part of the twentieth century are the *Zeitschrift für Kolonialpolitik, Kolonialrecht und Kolonialwirtschaft* (1899–1911) and *Koloniale Rundschau* (1909–1927). Since special attention was given to collecting colonial publications for the war years, the Library has holdings of the *Mitteilungen des Kolonial-Instituts* in Hamburg for the period 1914–1917 and the *Abhandlungen* (1910–1921). National Socialist publications treating the history of the German colonies are also numerous. The valuable archival material held on German Africa is listed below under 'Manuscript and Archival Collections.'

Coverage of Portuguese Africa is being strengthened. The most valuable items include the *Boletim Geral do Ultramar* (1925–1963), *Colecção Oficial de Legislação Portuguesa* (1922–1958), *Anuário do Império Colonial Português* (1935–1946), and *Revista Portugueza Colonial e Maritima* (Nos. 1–156, 1897–1910). (Professor Richard Hammond has acquired an extensive collection of books and pamphlets on nineteenth- and twentieth-century Portuguese Africa for a research project of the Food Research Institute, and this material will be available to scholars.)

The Hoover Institution also has an outstanding collection of Soviet and international Communist material relating to Africa. No numerical estimation has been made, but most items referred to in Rudolf Loewenthal's *Russian Materials on Africa: A Selective Bibliography* (1958)—and others as well—are to be found here. An increased effort is being made to document the interest in Africa of the Soviet

Union and its allies. It is estimated that about 90 percent of the material published in Russia since 1960 on Africa is available at the Hoover Institution.

The serial holdings of Stanford University and the Hoover Institution were partially revealed in the publication *A Checklist of Serials for African Studies, Based on the Libraries of the Hoover Institution and Stanford University* in 1963. This list showed 1,221 serial items (exclusive of most government department annual reports) and 196 newspapers. Since that time over 150 serial titles and 25 newspapers have been added and many gaps in the holdings filled. The Institution now has the complete run of such rare journals as the *Zambesi Mission Record* (Vols. I–IX, 1898–1934), which is, in effect, a history of the Catholic Church in Rhodesia from 1870 to 1934, and the *Nouvelles de Zambèze* (1898–1934).

POLITICAL EPHEMERA

Political ephemera, i.e., rare government documents, party pamphlets, rare newspapers, constitutions, reports of congresses, and trade-union literature, constitute an important element in the Africa Collection. The Institution has sizable collections on Nigeria, Ghana, Portuguese Africa, the Rhodesias, and South Africa.

The Rhodesian holdings can be classified under three main categories: conference records; original documents that pertain to African political, trade-union, and separatist church movements; and miscellaneous government reports from 1894 to 1953. The unprinted government records from 1890 to 1930 deal with various African associations and separatist churches which developed in Southern Rhodesia, such as the Bantu Voter's Association (founded in 1905) and the Southern Rhodesia Native Association (started in 1919). The Library also has on microfilm the various papers put out by modern political and trade-union groups, such as *Chapupu, Freedom,* and *Voice of the Unions.* Very useful too are the reports of committees on native affairs—'Report of the Native Labour Enquiry Committee,' 1906; 'Report of the Commission on the Strike among African Employees of the Rhodesia Railways, 1945'; and 'Report on African Local Government for Southern Rhodesia,' 1954.

On South Africa the collection of documents deals primarily with nationalist and radical political movements over the past sixty years. Several thousand items are held, such as copies of the *A.P.O.,* a newspaper published by the African People's Organization between 1909 and 1923; notices and minutes of meetings, constitutions, and presidential addresses; materials published by the African National Bond, African National Congress, and South African Congress of Democrats; and pamphlets and conference proceedings of the Communist Party of South Africa. The collection also includes rare South African newspapers: *The International* (1915–1924), *Umsebenzi: South African Worker* (1926–1938), *The Spark* (scattered issues, 1935–1938), *Guardian* (1937–1952), *Inkundla ya Bantu* (1944–1950), *Challenge* (1951–1953), *Advance* (scattered issues, 1952–1954), *New Age* (1952–), *African Bulletin* (1954–1957), *African Communist* (1961–), *Counterattack* (1961–), and *Fighting Talk* (1961–).

The Hoover Institution purchased a copy of the 'Treason Trial Record in South Africa, 1956–1961' and has prepared a guide for that part of the trial that has been microfilmed (August 1959–October 1960). Microfilms are being made of all subsequent trials of African nationalists and radicals. These will be deposited in the Center for Research Libraries, Chicago, for use by CAMP members.

CENTER FOR RESEARCH LIBRARIES

Stanford University is a member of the Association of Research Libraries which maintains the Center for Research Libraries (formerly the Midwest Inter-Library Center) at Chicago. A wide range of important materials may be borrowed on interlibrary loan from the Center, e.g., foreign gazettes, foreign newspapers, and foreign theses. (See Center for Research Libraries entry for detailed description.)

CAMP

As a member of the Cooperative African Microfilm Project (CAMP) of the Center for Research Libraries, the Hoover Institution has available the expanding resources of this African collection. Included are the Herbert J. Weiss Collection on the Belgian Congo, the collection of British material on the same area, Cameroun and Northern Rhodesia political ephemera, and the South African treason trial documents introduced in evidence. (See Center for Research Libraries entry for full description.)

MANUSCRIPT AND ARCHIVAL COLLECTIONS

Among these valuable collections are the following:

Sir Joseph Banks (1743–1820), president of the Royal Philosophical Society and one of the founders of the Association for Promoting the Discovery of the Interior Parts of Africa (founded in 1788), approximately 500 items (all microfilmed) concerned with Africa for the period from 1788 to 1817. The originals are at the Sutro Library, San Francisco, California. (See California State Library entry for fuller description.)

Germany, important archival material on German Africa, including Deutsches Zentralarchiv, Potsdam, minutes and correspondence of the Board of Directors of the Deutsche-Ostafrikanische Gesellschaft, 1885–1898; official documents of the German protectorate Deutsch-Südwestafrika for 1914–1915; selected files of the Reichskolonialamt, 1907–1919; and minutes, protocols, and reports of the Committee of the Deutsche Kolonialrat, 1890–1906—all on microfilm.

Great Britain, confidential prints relating to Africa, 1870–1914, microfilm copies. Since the mid-nineteenth century it has been the practice of both the Foreign Office and the Colonial Office to print, for internal circulation, all important letters, dispatches, memoranda, and minutes. The format was identical with the published blue books on foreign and colonial affairs, which were often based on these confidential prints. Memoranda were customarily printed separately and given a separate series; correspondence and minutes were collected under the subject-matter headings in chronological order of receipt. All collections are furnished with a contents table. The volumes vary greatly in length but may run to as many as 400 pages, or 1,000 documents. The contents are virtually unedited. They are available for study and microfilming within the time limits laid down by the 'fifty-year rule,' i.e., as far as the end of 1914. The uniformity of format and the use of print make them exceptionally suitable for microfilm, and they are, of course, far more convenient than the originals for research and reference. For a time the Colonial Office destroyed the original documents after printing, so that the prints sometimes constitute the only source material.

Dr. A. B. Xuma, president of the African National Congress in the 1940's, 10 microfilm reels of papers, an important source for political material on South Africa. These papers contain not only his private correspondence but also political pamphlets and party policy statements.

Because of its research on United States involvement in Africa the Hoover Institution has begun to collect, on microfilm, copies of valuable papers dealing with American activity in Africa:

African Squadron, 1843–1861, letters received by the Secretary of the Navy from commanding officers of squadrons. The originals are in the National Archives.

Thomas Jefferson Bowen (1814–1875), papers, the original manuscripts held by the Southern Baptist Convention Historical Commission, Nashville, Tennessee. The Reverend Thomas Jefferson Bowen served in Nigeria from 1849 to 1856 and played an important role as missionary, explorer, and linguist. (See Historical Commission of the Southern Baptist Convention entry for fuller description.)

R. Dorsey Mohun, microfilm of papers covering the period 1892–1913, the originals of which are in the National Archives. Mohun's papers deal with his activities as U.S. commercial agent, Boma, Congo Free State, 1892–1895; U.S. consul, Zanzibar, 1895–1897; chief, Congo Free State Telegraphic Expedition, 1898–1901; chef de Mission de Recherches Minières for Forminière in the Congo, 1907–1909; and agent of the Rubber Exploration Co. of New York in South Africa, Mozambique, and Madagascar, 1910–1911. (See National Archives entry for fuller description.)

Commodore Matthew C. Perry, letter book, March 10, 1843—February 20, 1945, 1 roll. The original is in the National Archives.

Henry Shelton Sanford, 12 boxes of microfilmed material, separated into accounts, correspondence, legal documents, and memoranda, arranged chronologically. Sanford served as minister to Belgium, 1861–1869, as representative of the American Geographical Society at the African International Conference, 1876, and as representative of the United States at the Berlin Conference, 1884, and at the Anti-Slavery Conference in Brussels, 1890. He served on the executive committee of the International Association which sent Henry Morton Stanley to the Congo, and he helped the International Association of the Congo (later known as the Congo Free State) secure diplomatic recognition from the United States and European powers. The original material is at the Sanford Memorial Library, Sanford, Florida. (See that entry for a fuller description of the material.)

Robert W. Shufeldt, 22 boxes of material on microfilm, the originals in the Naval Historical Foundation Collection on deposit in the Library of Congress. Shufeldt, U.S. naval officer, 1864–1884, sailed to Africa and Asia in 1878 under instructions to extend American influence along the coasts of these continents and among the islands of the Indian Ocean, to investigate changes in Zanzibar and their effect on the United States, and to determine if improvements could be made in the 1867 treaty with Madagascar.

Lt. Lieven Van de Velde, who accompanied Stanley to the Congo, microfilm copy of his papers. These contain records of the International Association of the Congo, 1881–1883, and letters and correspondence of Henry Morton Stanley. The originals are held at the University of Oregon Library, Eugene, Oregon. (See University of Oregon entry for fuller description.)

PUBLICATIONS

In addition to various monographs on Africa, a number of bibliographical studies have been prepared by the African section:

Africa South of the Sahara: A Select and Annotated Bibliography, 1958–1963, by Kenneth M. Glazier. 1964. 65 pp. $1.50.

Americans in Africa: A Preliminary Guide to American Missionary Archives and Library Manuscript Collections on Africa, by Robert Collins and Peter Duignan. 1963. 96 pp. $2.00.

A Checklist of Serials for African Studies, Based on the Libraries of the Hoover Institution and Stanford University, by Peter Duignan and Kenneth M. Glazier. 1963. 104 pp. $3.00.

German Africa: A Select Annotated Bibliography, by Jon Bridgman and David E. Clarke. 1965. 120 pp. $3.00.

The Treason Trial in South Africa: A Guide to the Microfilm Record of the Trial, by Thomas Karis. 1965. 124 pp. $3.00.

United States and Canadian Publications on Africa in 1961. 1963. 114 pp. $3.00.

United States and Canadian Publications on Africa in 1962. 1964. 104 pp. $3.00.

United States and Canadian Publications on Africa in 1963. 1965. 136 pp. $3.00.

United States and Canadian Publications on Africa in 1964. 1966. 180 pp. $5.00.

The *Africana Newsletter* from 1962 to 1964 published information on current research projects and library, bibliographical, and archival matters dealing with Africa south of the Sahara. In January 1965 the *Newsletter* merged with the *African Studies Bulletin* of the African Studies Association of the United States. The new journal combines the features of the *Bulletin* and the *Newsletter*.

PETER DUIGNAN

SWARTHMORE COLLEGE

The Friends Historical Library of Swarthmore College, Swarthmore, Pennsylvania, contains the papers (2 feet) of Moses Sheppard, Quaker humanitarian and businessman of Baltimore, who was active in the antislavery movement, the American Colonization Society, and colonization in Liberia. The papers cover the period 1794–1927. Also held are papers of William Rotch (1734–1828), major Nantucket and New Bedford whaling merchant.

SYRACUSE UNIVERSITY

Syracuse University, Syracuse, New York, has its collection of books, articles, periodicals, and government documents in functionally located branch libraries on campus. At the center of the Program of Eastern African Studies a selection of periodicals, books, and government documents dealing with contemporary Eastern Africa is available, and circulation procedures are being developed which will enable recent research and source materials to be circulated among program staff and graduate students as soon as possible.

Under the direction of Mr. Edward E. Brown, the Syracuse University Library is developing a bibliographic file of Eastern Africa which already includes over 40,000 titles. This file will soon be 'computerized,' and, with the cooperation of several other universities, it will be possible to produce complete annotated bibliographies on any subject in Eastern Africa at read-out speed.

The first complete bibliography of books and articles on Malawi (*A Bibliography of Malawi*, compiled by Edward E. Brown, Carol A. Fisher, and John B. Webster, 161 pp.; Syracuse University, Eastern Africa Bibliographical Series, No. 1) was compiled under the direction of Mr. Brown and was released by the Syracuse University Press in 1965. No references to government publications are included since this material forms the subject matter of a bibliography to be published by the Library of Congress.

Negotiations are under way to microfilm the government archives of the countries of Eastern Africa. Once the microfilming has been completed, these materials will be deposited at the Syracuse University Library. Arrangements have also been made with various government agencies to receive declassified documents pertaining to Eastern Africa.

The library and bibliographic resources of Syracuse University's Program of Eastern African Studies are being developed through a cooperative effort on the part of the library staff and the staff of the Eastern African Studies program. Mr. Brown is acting as the coordinator of these efforts, and considerable growth in resources is expected in the immediate future.

Two recent acquisitions in the Africana collection include the letters of Lieutenant Hall dealing with colonial administration from 1894 to 1900. The Syracuse University Library also has the correspondence of Gerrit Smith, Peter Smith, and Gerrit Smith Miller, 1780–1890, 52,000 pieces. The collection is comprised mostly of letters to Gerrit Smith, 'moral reformer' of central New York, from prominent persons; there is some material on abolition, antislavery, and Negro colonization movements, the American Colonization Society, Liberia, missionary efforts in Africa, and proposals for an African company to trade in African lands and products. (See *Calendar of the Gerrit Smith Papers in the Syracuse*

University Library [2 vols., Albany, N.Y., Works Projects Administration, Historical Records Survey, 1941–1942].)

TELFAIR ACADEMY OF ARTS AND SCIENCES, SAVANNAH

The Telfair Academy of Arts and Sciences, Savannah, Georgia, has the papers of William B. Hodgson (1801–1871), Orientalist and consular official at Algiers, Tunis, and Egypt, 1826–1842, who published a pioneer study of the Berber language and other linguistic and ethnographic materials pertaining to the Maghreb, the Sahara, and the Sudan.

UNITED NATIONS LIBRARY

The United Nations Library, New York, New York, has substantial holdings of current government documents and newspapers from African countries. These materials are retained for varying periods of time as a working collection rather than as a research library for use by scholars. Materials are discarded when judged no longer useful. Permission must be obtained to use the African documents and newspapers.

UNIVERSITY OF VIRGINIA

The Library of the University of Virginia, Charlottesville, Virginia, holds the papers of John Hartwell Cocke (1780–1866), planter, publicist, reformer, and army officer, for the period 1825–1831, 53 feet. Included are letters of freedmen from Monrovia, Liberia. There are papers of Bushrod Washington (1762–1829), first president, 1817–1829, of the American Colonization Society, about 50 pieces.

The Library also holds the papers of Samuel L. Clemens, among them a diary, 1895–1896, and family letters and notes from a tour to Australia, India, and South Africa.

VIRGINIA HISTORICAL SOCIETY

The Virginia Historical Society, Boulevard and Kensington Avenue, Richmond 21, Virginia, contains 2 volumes of records of the Colonization Society of Virginia from 1823 to 1859, when it was an auxiliary of the American Colonization Society. An additional holding concerning the American Colonization Society includes the diary of William Proby Young, 1860, as a doctor on board the *Castilian;* ports of call were New York, Key West, Cape Mount, Robertsport, Monrovia, Grand Bassa, and New Orleans. Held also are papers of Matthew Fontaine Maury (1806–1873), noted oceanographer and astronomer who conducted oceanographic studies of the Indian Ocean and the South Atlantic, 130 items.

WEST VIRGINIA UNIVERSITY

The West Virginia University Library, Morgantown, West Virginia, has an extensive collection—approximately 10,000 volumes—on East Africa. An effort is made to obtain all current material on this area, including government publications. Materials held include:

American Colonization Society. Liberia.

> John Moore McCalla, Jr., edited typescript copy of the journal Dr. McCalla kept on a voyage, June–December 1860, as special agent for the U.S. government and physician appointed by the American Colonization Society, on board the *Star of the Union*, a ship chartered by the Society for the transportation of 'recaptured Africans' to Liberia, 87 pp. (Original journal held by Duke University.)

> Peter G. Van Winkle Papers, 17 pp.; speech on the American Colonization Society.

Southern Rhodesia.

> Edward C. Tabler, typed manuscript and page proofs of Tabler's *The Far Interior: Chronicles of Pioneering in the Matabele and Mashonga Countries, 1847–1879* (Cape Town, 1955), 1 box.

WILBERFORCE UNIVERSITY

The Wilberforce University Library, Wilberforce, Ohio, contains the papers of Benjamin William Arnett (1838–1906) from 1860 to 1900 (about 1,000 items), Levi Jenkins Coppin (1848–1923) from 1888 to 1920 (about 350 items), and Reverdy Cassius Ransom (1861–1959) from 1893 to 1951 (about 1,000 items), all of whom were bishops of the African Methodist Episcopal Church and active in its mission work in Africa. The papers include letters, clippings, records, reports, and addresses relating to the Negro, both African and American, and records and minutes of the African Methodist Episcopal Church conferences and reports.

' COLLEGE OF WILLIAM AND MARY

The Library of the College of William and Mary, Williamsburg, Virginia, holds papers of Samuel Barron (1809–1888), commander of the U.S.S. *John Adams* in the African Squadron, 1849–1853, about 1,750 items.

STATE HISTORICAL SOCIETY OF WISCONSIN

Manuscript collections of the State Historical Society of Wisconsin, 816 State Street, Madison, Wisconsin 53706, include the following:

Walter B. Cockerill, papers, 1911–1915, 1950–1958, 1 box; largely composed of correspondence of Mr. Cockerill, a missionary to Nyasaland in 1914–1915. The early group of letters relates to conditions in Nyasaland and to Chilembwe's uprising, a native revolt. Letters, 1950–1958, include many from George Shepperson, Scottish historian of the uprising.

Dutilh and Wachsmuth, eighteenth- and early-nineteenth-century Philadelphia shipping merchants involved in the slave trade, papers, 1 box.

Richard W. Guenther (1845–1913), papers, 1878–1910, 56 items. The collection includes correspondence and memorabilia of a Wisconsin political figure who served as consul to Cape Town.

William Walker (1808–1896), papers, 1801, 1837–1896, 3 boxes including 31 volumes. Walker, a Wisconsin Congregational minister, was a missionary in West Africa from 1842 to 1883. Letters, diaries, and other papers describe his missionary activities. The collection includes some material on the history of French Equatorial Africa and some papers in the Mpongwe language.

THE UNIVERSITY OF WISCONSIN

The strong African interest of the University of Wisconsin, Madison, Wisconsin, is of relatively recent date. A systematic program in African studies was begun only in 1959, and it was not until mid-1961 that a bibliographer for African materials was added to the library staff.

Geographically, the collecting policy of the Library concerning Africa embraces the entire continent and its offshore islands, with the greatest emphasis on the area between the Sahara and the northern borders of the Republic of South Africa. With regard to discipline, the collecting policy focuses on the social sciences and African languages and literatures.

The book collection, which has doubled in the last two and a half years, now stands at 11,268 bibliographic volumes. This number includes 495 serial titles. In terms of physical volumes, the Library's holdings relating to Africa number approximately 15,000. For the most part, these are shelved throughout the main library stack. There are additional groupings of books outside the main library building in the Law Library and the Geography Library.

At present the book collection's major strengths are in the literature of exploration and travel, history, and ethnography. Although the University has only lately begun to concentrate on African studies, it has long had an interest in the British Empire, and the Library's resources for the study of this subject are noteworthy, particularly in the area of government publications. For this reason it is in those parts of Africa which were formerly British possessions that the Library's holdings are strongest.

The Library's resources with respect to newspapers consist of 16 titles on microfilm which are available on loan from the Center for Research Libraries (formerly the Midwest Inter-Library Center).

In addition to books, serials, and newspapers, there are also a collection of approximately 600 maps of Africa and a collection of 200 LP phonographic recordings of African music.

In order to build up rapidly a holding of pamphlet material, the Library has recently had filmed the British Colonial Office Library's pamphlet collection on Africa. This consists of 74 volumes containing more than 2,000 pamphlets. The areas dealt with are Central, West, and East Africa. The dates of the pamphlets range from the early 1850's to the late 1940's. The subject matter has to do chiefly with administration, economics, linguistics, and ethnography.

The single great manuscript resource which the Library possesses is its microfilm of those parts of the archives of the Church Missionary Society that deal with Africa. These documents are available from the foundation of the Society in 1799 to a date fifty years earlier than the present time and cover the Society's missionary activities in Sierra Leone, Nigeria, South Africa, Abyssinia, Madagascar, Kenya, Uganda, Tanganyika, the Sudan, and Egypt. The archive contains the minutes of the central committee in London, correspondence with missionaries in the field, and reports and journals of missionaries. In addition to a vast amount of material of interest for missionary history, there is much concerning the social and economic history of Africa. Also interesting are papers (140 items) of Sir Joseph Banks (1743–1820), eminent scientific administrator and prime mover in the British African Association's effort to locate the sources of the Niger River.

Located on campus but in the custody of the Department of Art History is a collection of 14 pieces of African art. These are of West African provenience and are chiefly masks and sculpture.

RICHARD BERNARD

XAVIER UNIVERSITY

The Xavier University Library, 3912 Pine Street, New Orleans, Louisana, has approximately 5,500 pieces dealing with the manifests for slave ships arriving, generally, in the ports of Louisiana, Texas, and Mississippi, 1832–1857.

YALE UNIVERSITY*

Area studies at Yale University, New Haven, Connecticut, embrace Africa, East Asia, Southeast Asia, Latin America, Russia, and Eastern Europe. There is also interest in Near Eastern, Indic, and Commonwealth studies. Each area has a curator or adviser to the Library who ensures that all important publications issued in or about his area are secured.

Although the Council on African Studies at Yale goes back only to 1957, interest in Africa extends much further into the past. Individual members of the faculty have pursued Africanist researches from the beginnings of such studies. African history and the African collections in the Yale Library owe much to Professor Harry Rudin. Professor G. P. Murdock and associates founded the Cross Cultural Survey at Yale, and out of it grew the Human Relations Area Files. (The complete files of both are housed in the Sterling Memorial Library.)

Current Africa-orientated teaching and research include most of the social sciences, some linguistics, Egyptology and the history of North Africa in classical times, missiology, law, and tropical forestry and medicine. Languages taught at the moment are Swahili, Ethiopic, Coptic, Egyptian, and Arabic, with Hausa possibly to come.

The diversity of area and academic discipline means that the various campus libraries are called upon to provide a very wide range of supporting literature, though the depth of coverage varies a great deal according to present and likely future demands.

---

* This survey of Yale's Africana collections was prepared by J. M. D. Crossey. Peter Duignan contributed the section on manuscripts.

The collections of relevant materials on the campus are considerable. The exact number of volumes is difficult to ascertain accurately owing to the scattering of the material through so many libraries and the use of several different classifications. A rough estimate, however, would put total holdings at about 16,000 volumes, the bulk of which are in the Sterling Memorial Library, the main library on campus.

Sterling Memorial Library houses books on all subjects not the particular province of one of the major school or departmental libraries. So far as Africana are concerned, Sterling has most standard publications in the social sciences, languages and literature, and geography and travel. There are also significant amounts of material in the biological sciences and technology. Particularly strong are the collections of bibliographies, anthropology, and early travels; indeed, few books published prior to 1900 are lacking.

Sets of most of the standard Africanist periodicals and serials are held. Somewhat unusual items are the *Bulletin Officiel* (1908–1942) and *Bulletin Administratif* (1925–1951) of the former Belgian Congo; *Boletim Geral do Ultramar* (incomplete); *Rivista Coloniale, Organo dell'Instituto Coloniale Italiano* (1906–1927); and *Rivista delle Colonie: Rassegna dei Possedimenti Italiani e Stranieri d'Oltremare* (1927–1943). A list of Yale's African periodicals was issued in October 1963, but it is rather incomplete as a great many new titles were recently started and more are rapidly being added.

Newspaper holdings are not very strong; only about 15 are being received currently. Another dozen or so are on order but have not yet been received. The Library of Congress titles on microfilm are being subscribed to, and more titles on film will be added as the opportunity arises. The newspaper project of the Center for Research Libraries (formerly the Midwest Inter-Library Center) is also utilized.

Government document holdings vary from one country to another. Best are those for the Rhodesias and the Republic of South Africa, followed by former British East and West Africa. The French-speaking and North African countries are weakest. A recent large purchase will remedy most of the deficiencies in the literature on Portugal's African territories. Partial sets of parliamentary debates were recently received from Nigeria, Kenya, Tanganyika, Northern Rhodesia, Uganda, Cameroun, and the Malagasy Republic. It is hoped that cooperative microfilming will fill in for the earlier years of all or most countries.

The Howell Wright Collection of Rhodesiana and South Africana is particularly noteworthy. (See also the last section, 'Manuscript Collections.') Mr. Wright was acquainted with Cecil Rhodes and bequeathed various momentos and letters besides his own books and manuscripts. A small endowment helps maintain the collection. A recent acquisition was one of the Ladysmith siege newspapers. The Farmington Plan brings in a great many of the more recent historical and other social science publications of and on South Africa.

The Garvan Sports Collection and smaller related collections contain all the classical works on big-game hunting in Africa.

The Map Collection has most of the standard maps and atlases of Africa and includes some rare items. Efforts are being made to complete the collection with all useful maps which may be lacking.

Most French and German dissertations are received on exchange. American and nonprinted foreign dissertations are purchased on microfilm when requested by faculty or students.

The Public Law 480 Project brings in all new Egyptian publications including government documents (Indian and Pakistani publications are also obtained this way, as will be those of Indonesia, Israel, and some others).

New books are being acquired on publication and older out-of-print items sought in the antiquarian market. Reprints, if needed, are procured as they appear. Added strength derives from the Library's being a depository for the publications of the United Nations, the U.S. federal government, and other agencies. A six-page statement on acquisitions policy was issued in October 1963. Facilities for interlibrary loan and photocopying of books, manuscripts, etc., are available on request to the Reference Department.

The *Beinecke Rare Book and Manuscript Library* holds all books, etc., which were formerly in the Rare Book Room in Sterling, together with several other previously separate collections. Besides rare items in the general collection such as early voyages and travels, the G. W. Johnson Collection consists of literary and other works by and about Africans and American Negroes.

The *Divinity Library*'s Africana holdings have been briefly described in the *African Studies Bulletin*, III, No. 2 (May 1960), 6. Professor George Edward Day began to collect books on missions in the 1870's, and he later turned them over to Yale. The numerical count of the holdings does not tell the whole story—much material of high quality has been collected. The collection is primarily Protestant in orientation but has a sizable amount of Catholic material as well. The Day Missions Library and other collections are very complete for monographs on both Catholic and Protestant missions in Africa. There are also significant holdings of missionary periodicals and some manuscripts, especially the archive of the Student Volunteer Movement for Foreign Missions. A certain number of works on travel, ethnology, comparative religion, and history are also held, mostly duplicated in Sterling Memorial. Additions are made regularly of both new and antiquarian works, mainly on missions and church history. On the basis of measurement of catalogue cards, the African holdings number at least 2,300 to 2,500 monographs. To this should be added periodicals (41 titles), which doubtless would add 1,500 to 2,000 volumes, and reports of mission boards and societies, which would be extensive. The American Board of Commissioners for Foreign Missions has worked in Africa for many years, and their reports and many others are held. Thus 5,000 to 5,500 separate bibliographical items would be a conservative estimate. A sizable body of mission material remains to be organized. This will contain material on Africa.

The *Economic Growth Center Library* is devoted to publications on economic development of countries with a population in excess of 2 million. Its African holdings comprise official and nonofficial publications on economic planning, budgets, statistics, and other financial and economic matters. For recent years these publications are nearly complete. A quarterly list of new serials is issued, as well as an occasional list of other accessions.

The *Law Library* has very extensive holdings of current and older legal Africana. Sets of statutes, reports, journals, and treatises for almost every country issuing them are available. New titles are acquired on publication and, owing to faculty interest, constant effort is made to fill any gaps which come to light.

The *Medical Library* has a large amount of medical Africana, mostly on tropical medicine, public health, history of medicine, and medical missions. A number of African medical journals are received. The Streeter Collection of weights and measures includes a few African specimens.

The *Geology Library* contains standard treatises on the geology of African countries, official publications of the various geological surveys and mining departments, geological maps, periodicals, etc.

The *Forestry Library* has reports and other publications of the forestry departments of various African countries and relevant monographs and periodicals. Wildlife and some general agricultural publications are also held, e.g., the *Bulletin Agricole du Congo Belge*.

Some Africana in their appropriate fields are held by the Peabody Museum Library (anthropology and biology mainly), Political Science Research Library, and Ornithology, Botany, Zoology, Geography, Labor Management, and Art Libraries.

The *Art Gallery* has a fine collection of African sculpture on permanent display (see also Yale University entry under Art and Ethnographic Collections). The *Peabody Museum* has a large African anthropological collection which is catalogued and available to researchers.

Manuscript Collections

The Historical Manuscripts Department of the Sterling Memorial Library contains 45 boxes of correspondence and 10 boxes of memorabilia in the Howell Wright Collection, which covers the period 1880–1955. Wright, a writer, was an extensive collector of South Africana and Rhodesiana; hence the collection contains much information concerning the early colonial days of these two former British colonies. Specifically, there are large sections of the collection that deal with the 1890 Pioneer Expedition to Rhodesia, the Jameson Raid, and the Johannesburg Reform Committee, as well as personal reminiscences of Cecil Rhodes, President Kruger, and Lobengula. Approximately 30 boxes of correspondence and papers of John Hays Hammond for the period 1893–1936 are also held. As chief mining consultant to Cecil Rhodes, Hammond played an important role in Transvaal and Southern Rhodesian affairs. He was also involved in the planning of the Jameson Raid and the attempt to unseat President Kruger of the Transvaal.

Other collections are:

Sir Joseph Banks Papers, about 3,500 items. Sir Joseph (1743–1820) was an eminent scientific administrator and prime mover in the British African Association's effort to locate the sources of the Niger River.

Elizabeth Donnan Materials, 2 boxes of manuscript notes (600 items) on the slave trade (ca. 1806–1863) taken from newspapers, ships' logs, and letter books at the Library of Congress. Much of this material was used in her book *Documents Illustrative of the History of the Slave Trade to America* (4 vols., 1930–1935). Elizabeth Donnan, who died in 1955, was professor of economics at Wellesley College.

Edwards Family Papers, 1805–1874, 1,900 items. Included is correspondence of George Champion, a missionary to the Zulus in 1838. Champion was a brother-in-law of Jonathan Edwards (1789–1875), a politician from upper New York State.

Hugh Marshall Hole Papers on South Africa, 1885–1928, 1 reel of microfilm. Hole (1865–1941), an official of the British South Africa Company in Rhodesia, was author of books and articles on Rhodesia.

Charles Templeman Loram Papers. Loram (1879–1940) was a teacher in South Africa, inspector and superintendent of education in native schools there, and later Sterling professor of education, Yale University. His papers consist of 17 boxes of notes and reports, including carbon copies of reports to the Minister of Native Affairs in South Africa.

Richard Thurnwald Papers. Thurnwald (1869–1954) was a noted German ethnologist and sociologist. These papers range over the years 1901–1936 and contain about 2,000 items. Correspondents include the Deutsche Kolonialgesellschaft, *Koloniale Rundschau*, International Institute of African Languages and Culture (London), and Philip E. Mitchell and H. M. T. Kayamba (both in Tanganyika). There are also lecture notes, articles, and reports on his South Seas expedition.

CHURCH AND MISSIONARY LIBRARIES AND ARCHIVES

THE AFRICA COMMITTEE

The Africa Committee, as a department of the Division of Foreign Missions of the National Council of Churches of Christ in the U.S.A., unites some forty foreign mission boards and agencies in the United States and Canada for mutual consultation and joint action in Africa south of the Sahara. Although its current formal structure came into being with the National Council of Churches, the Africa Committee had its beginnings in the 1920's and became a Standing Representative Committee as a part of the Foreign Missions Conference in North America in 1939. The Africa Committee also serves as a center of counsel and information for African students in North America, missionary candidates, and other persons interested in African studies and affairs. Through its staff, contact is maintained with other volunteer organizations having interest in Africa. The Committee maintains current and archival files of its activities and correspondence in its offices at 475 Riverside Drive, New York, New York 10027. It issues an annual report and frequent items of information for members and others who are interested.

AFRICA INLAND MISSION

The Africa Inland Mission, 253 Henry Street, Brooklyn 1, New York, was organized in 1895. That same year its first missionaries, led by Peter Cameron Scott, founder of the mission, went to Kenya. Since then work has been carried on in Tanganyika (1909), Congo (Leopoldville; 1912), the West Nile district of Uganda (1918), Central African Republic (1924), and Sudan (1949). The Africa Inland Mission maintains an extensive collection of records, journals, missionary correspondence, and books by its missionaries at the Brooklyn offices and publishes a bimonthly periodical, *Inland Africa*. Two monthly publications are printed in Kenya: *Doing in Kenya* and *Afrika ya Kesho* (Africa of Tomorrow).

AFRICAN METHODIST EPISCOPAL CHURCH

The Home and Foreign Missionary Department of the Board of Home and Foreign Missions of the African Methodist Episcopal Church, 475 Riverside Drive, New York, New York 10027, was organized in 1900. The first officially sponsored mission work was begun in Sierra Leone in 1886, but AME missionaries worked in Liberia and Sierra Leone as far back as 1821. The work in Liberia was officially resumed in 1891. Mission work was begun in the Republic of South Africa in 1892; Nyasaland and Northern and Southern Rhodesia, 1900; Bechuanaland, 1901; Basutoland, 1903; Swaziland, 1904; Tanganyika, 1920; Ghana, 1935; South-West Africa, 1953; and Nigeria, 1956. Attempts have been made to establish churches in other areas, but only a few references to these efforts survive. Extensive correspondence files dating back to 1900, as well as biographical and photographic material about the missionaries, are available at the New York office. Bound volumes of the annual and quadrennial official reports of the Department as well as the monthly missionary magazine since 1900, *Voice of Missions*, are also kept in New York. Pre-1900 records are held by the *A.M.E. Christian Recorder*, the weekly official organ of the denomination since 1850, at 414 8th Avenue South, Nashville 3, Tennessee. A number of books have been written on the mission work abroad, including *A Century of Missions* by L. L. Berry and *The African Methodist Episcopal Church in Africa* by Artishia Wilkerson Jordan.

AFRICAN METHODIST EPISCOPAL ZION CHURCH

The Board of Foreign Missions of the African Methodist Episcopal Zion Church, Room 1910, 475 Riverside Drive, New York, New York 10027, was organized in 1892. The Board has had mission work in Liberia since 1876, Ghana since 1896, and Nigeria since 1930. It holds extensive correspondence in a dead-letter file. The Board issues official annual and quadrennial reports. A monthly periodical, the *Missionary Seer*, has carried material on the African work since 1880. The office record of this publication goes back only to 1948, but the names of the libraries holding earlier copies are available through the office.

AMERICAN BAPTIST CONVENTION

The American Baptist Foreign Mission Society, 475 Riverside Drive, New York, New York 10027, was organized in 1814 and for more than thirty years, beginning in 1821, was active in Liberia. Since 1884 the Society's major field of missionary work in Africa has been the Congo (Leopoldville); in that year, under the name of the American Baptist Missionary Union, it took over from the English Baptists the six-year-old Livingstone Inland Mission. The archives have recently been moved to Valley Forge, Pennsylvania. They contain biographical files of the missionaries, missionary correspondence relating to both the Congo and Liberia, and other unpublished material, including several doctoral dissertations dealing with the Congo. An official periodical which appeared between 1914 and 1940 under the names *The Handbook, The Guidebook, Overseas,* and *All Kindreds and Tongues* contained much information on the Society's work in Africa to supplement the annual reports. The post-1940 publication, *Overseas Outreach*, is simply the annual report without statistical tables. Other periodicals on file are *Missions* (which began in 1833 as the *Baptist Missionary Magazine*) and the very informative quarterly *Congo Newsletter*, published by the Congo missionaries since 1910. Information about Baptist work in the Congo is also included in the *Congo Mission News*, issued by the Congo Protestant Council since 1924. Many of the Society's files were deposited in the Missionary Research Library before the headquarters of the American Baptists were moved from New York City to Valley Forge.

AMERICAN BIBLE SOCIETY

The American Bible Society, 450 Park Avenue, New York, New York 10022, was organized in 1816 as a publishing and distributing organization; it has no mission stations in Africa, although it maintains many offices there. The Society's nine-teenth-century missionary correspondence, most of which concerns the publication of the Scriptures in various languages, is being microfilmed. An annual report and the *Bible Society Record* (issued 10 times yearly since the 1840's) contain material on Africa.

Translation and distribution work has been carried on over long periods in the following areas: Congo (since 1915), Egypt (1827), Ethiopia (1824), Liberia (1840), Sudan (1920). In 1962, the Society began a project to underwrite Bible translation and distribution in almost all the major areas of Africa.

AMERICAN LEPROSY MISSIONS, INC.

American Leprosy Missions, Inc., 297 Park Avenue South, New York, New York 10010, was organized in 1906 to give aid to the more than thirty Protestant mission boards interested in caring for leprosy patients. It has supported leprosy work established by other boards in Tanganyika (1893), Sudan (1908), Mozambique (1913), Congo (Leopoldville; 1922), Angola (1924), Liberia (1928), Nigeria (1929), Cameroun (1935), and Burundi (1950). It has also supplied medicines to leprosy stations in Egypt, Ethiopia, and Sierra Leone. The national headquarters have six drawers consisting of correspondence and another five drawers of reference and clipping files, as well as a collection of approximately 3,600 photographic negatives of Angola, Burundi, Cameroun, Congo, Liberia, Mozambique, Nigeria, and Tanganyika. Annual data sheets from the mission stations receiving aid and special reports are held. Magazine material dating back to 1906 is available and includes copies of the American section of *Without the Camp*, the *American Leprosy Missions Digest*, and the *Digest*'s successor, *American Leprosy Missions News*. A survey, *Leprosy Work in Africa*, by Dr. O. W. Hasselblad, was published by the headquarters in 1963.

AMERICAN LUTHERAN CHURCH

The Division of World Missions of the American Lutheran Church, 422 South 5th Street, Minneapolis 15, Minnesota, was organized in 1961 as a result of the merger of the American Lutheran Church, the Evangelical Lutheran Church, and the United Evangelical Lutheran Church in 1960. The Evangelical Lutheran Church began mission work in the Malagasy Republic in 1888, Cameroun in 1923, and the Central African Republic in 1930. In 1927 this church assumed control of the mission work which the Norwegian Lutheran Church started in the Republic of South Africa in 1844. The United Evangelical Lutheran Church began mission work in Nigeria in 1913. The old American Lutheran Church initiated its mission work in Ethiopia in 1957. The archives for the former Evangelical Lutheran Church and the former United Evangelical Lutheran Church are in the library of Luther Theological Seminary, 2375 West Como Avenue, St. Paul 8, Minnesota; the archives for the former American Lutheran Church are at Wartburg Seminary, Dubuque, Iowa. Bound copies of missionary magazines and the general records of the former mission societies are kept in the archives.

AUGUSTANA LUTHERAN CHURCH
(Now part of the Lutheran Church in America)

The Board of World Missions of the Augustana Lutheran Church was formed in 1923 as a result of the reorganization of the Central Mission Board, which had been founded in 1866. In 1962 the Augustana mission board merged with the mission boards of the United Lutheran Church in America, the American Evangelical Lutheran Church, and the Suomi Synod (Finnish) to form the Board of World Missions of the Lutheran Church in America with offices at 231 Madison Avenue, New York, New York 10016. The first Augustana missionary in the African field was sent out in 1919 to investigate the West African area. In 1922 he was sent to Tanganyika to administer the mission work of the expelled German Lutherans. In 1926 the Board established its own mission station in Tanganyika. The official archives of the Augustana Lutheran Church are in the Augustana Theological Seminary, Rock Island, Illinois. The only manuscript materials available are the extensive correspondence and papers of Dr. G. A. Brandelle, who was president of the Church during and after the establishment of the Tanganyika mission. The archives have a complete collection of all the official records and periodicals related to the African mission work. These include the minutes of the Tanganyika mission, the annual reports of the Board of World Missions and of the president of the Church, and complete files of the *Augustana Foreign Missionary, Mission Tidings, Lutheran Companion, Augustana,* and *World Missions News-Letter.* The Augustana Book Concern has published three books about the Augustana work in Tanganyika: *Touring Tanganyika* (1950) and *Foundation for Tomorrow* (1960), both by S. H. Swanson, and *Letters from Africa* (1951), by Martin Bystrom.

BAPTIST GENERAL CONFERENCE

The Board of Foreign Missions of the Baptist General Conference, 5750 North Ashland, Chicago 26, Illinois, has supported missionaries in Africa since 1950. The Conference now has mission stations in four areas of Ethiopia. Missionary records, reports, and materials are on file at the Chicago headquarters. Publications of the Conference include an annual and a biweekly magazine, *The Standard.* The Board of Foreign Missions publishes the following: *Daily Prayer Calendar* (annual), *Foreignews* (bimonthly), *News and Needs* (monthly), and missionary prayer letters as received. Photographs and biographical sketches of the missionaries, maps, and a limited selection of field photos can be secured from the Chicago office.

BAPTIST MID-MISSIONS

The Baptist Mid-Missions, 1740 East 12th Street, Cleveland 14, Ohio, was organized in 1920. It has had mission work in Chad and the Central African Republic since 1920; Liberia, 1940; Ghana, 1950; and Congo (Leopoldville), 1953. General hospitals are maintained in Chad and the Central African Republic, a leprosy colony in Liberia. The office files contain a great deal of confidential missionary correspondence. A periodical, *The Harvest,* carried a limited amount of information concerning the African missions.

BEREAN MISSION, INC.

The Berean Mission, Inc., 3536 Russell Boulevard, St. Louis 4, Missouri, was organized in 1934. It has worked in the Congo (Leopoldville) since 1938 and is starting mission activity in Tanganyika. A limited amount of material on the mission work is kept in folders in the office. The official organ, *Missiongrams*, and other occasional publications carry reports on the work done.

BRETHREN IN CHRIST WORLD MISSIONS

The Brethren in Christ World Missions, first known as Foreign Missions and organized under the Brethren in Christ Foreign Mission Board in 1895, has had mission work in Southern Rhodesia since 1898 and in Northern Rhodesia since 1906. The present headquarters are at 48-1/2 South Market Street, Elizabethtown, Pennsylvania. The Board has issued an annual report since 1913, occasional news-letters, and pamphlets. The *Evangelical Visitor*, the denominational biweekly, carries a missionary section in each issue. Most of the published materials are available at the Messiah College Library, which also houses the archives of the church. These include mission correspondence, minutes, diaries, and newsletters. See H. Frances Davidson, *South and South Central Africa: A Record of Fifteen Years' Missionary Labors among Primitive Peoples* (Elgin, Ill., Brethren Publishing House, 1915), and *Sowing and Reaping: The Story of God in Rhodesia, 1898–1948* (Rhodesian Printing and Publishing Co., Ltd., 1959).

BROTHERS OF HOLY CROSS

The Brothers of Holy Cross was founded in France in 1820 and came to the United States in 1837. The Eastern Province of the Brothers of Holy Cross, 24 Ricardo Street, West Haven 16, Connecticut, conducts two schools in Uganda, one opened in 1959, the other in 1961. Archival materials, consisting of some printed reports (governmental as well as a few school publications), a few maps, photographs, and slides are located at the Provincial Offices in West Haven.

CHICAGO THEOLOGICAL SEMINARY

The Chicago Theological Seminary Library, 5757 University Avenue, Chicago, Illinois, has a large body of papers, 1825–1929, relating chiefly to Congregational Church history. Included are 21 letter books of the American Board of Commissioners for Foreign Missions, 1871–1906.

CHRISTIAN AND MISSIONARY ALLIANCE

The Christian and Missionary Alliance, 260 West 44th Street, New York, New York 10036, was first organized as the International Missionary Alliance in 1887 and incorporated as the International Missionary Alliance in 1889. The present name was adopted after the 1897 merger with the Christian Alliance, which had been incorporated in 1890. The first missionaries sent to the Congo (Leopoldville), in 1884, were graduates of the Nyack (New York) Missionary College. Since then mission work has been carried out by the Alliance in the Cabinda enclave, Angola (1907), Guinea (1918), Mali and Upper Volta (1923), Ivory Coast (1930), and Gabon (1934). The Alliance maintains an extensive collection of records, journals, missionary correspondence, etc., in its New York offices for the convenience of its officers. The Alliance issues an annual report; a biweekly, *The Alliance Witness;* and a monthly, *Foreign Field Flashes.* The fields in Africa publish *Congo Tidings, Ivory Coast Today, Mali–Upper Volta Tidings, Panorama* (Guinea), and *Gabon Tribes,* copies of which are available in New York. Three books written by Alliance missionaries concerning missionary work in Africa are *Congo* (Harrisburg, Pa., Christian Publications, Inc., 1937), by Mrs. Alexander Macaw [Grace Anna (Main) McCaw], and *The Niger Vision* (Harrisburg, Pa., Christian Publications, Inc., 1934) and *The Soul of French West Africa,* both by the Reverend R. S. Roseberry.

CHRISTIAN REFORMED CHURCH

The Christian Reformed Board of Foreign Missions, 2850 Kalamazoo Avenue, S.E., Grand Rapids, Michigan 49508, was organized in 1888. The Board began its work in Nigeria in 1940 when it occupied a station established by the Sudan United Mission in the 1900's. Evangelical, educational, and medical work is carried on by approximately 70 missionaries and a great number of Nigerian co-workers. The annual reports of the mission work are published in the *Acts of Synod of the Christian Reformed Church,* and a complete file is available in the Library of Calvin College, Grand Rapids, Michigan. A bimonthly *Newsletter* is distributed, and *The Banner* and *Missionary Monthly* contain reports from the Board's missionaries. Four books, now out of print, have been written about the Board's African mission work.

CHURCH OF GOD

The Missionary Board of the Church of God, 1303 East 5th Street, P.O. Box 2498, Anderson, Indiana, was organized in 1909. The Church of God has been active in mission work in Kenya since 1922, when it took over the work of another group founded in 1905. At present it maintains four mission stations in Kenya, with hospitals, schools, and churches. The Board's files include missionary correspondence, documents, and records. The official publication of the Board is the *Church of God Missions,* a monthly.

THE CHURCH OF JESUS CHRIST OF LATTER-DAY SAINTS

The Office of the Church Historian for The Church of Jesus Christ of Latter-day Saints is located at 47 East South Temple Street, Salt Lake City 11, Utah. The Church first sent a mission to the Republic of South Africa in 1853. Notes from minute books, letters, and quarterly reports have been collected into a manuscript history from 1853 to 1866, for the year 1886, and from 1903 to the present. Minute books from the various branches, districts, and the general mission in South Africa are also held. A record of members and annual genealogical report on the South African mission, from the early years of activity to 1951, is maintained.

CHURCH OF THE BRETHREN

The Church of the Brethren General Brotherhood Board, 1451 Dundee Avenue, Elgin, Illinois, began mission work in Nigeria in 1922. Records and reports of the activities of the Church of the Brethren mission are filed with the Foreign Mission Commission in Elgin. Printed materials such as annual reports and copies of publications which carry educational materials are also housed with this commission in Elgin. Publications include the *Gospel Messenger* and the *Church of the Brethren Leader;* and bibliography and mission study order forms are produced and distributed annually.

CHURCH OF THE NAZARENE

The Department of Foreign Missions, General Board, Church of the Nazarene, 6401 The Paseo, Kansas City 10, Missouri, was organized in 1907. Missionary activity began in the Cape Verde Islands in 1907; Swaziland, 1910; Republic of South Africa, 1919; Mozambique, 1922; Nyasaland, 1957; Northern Rhodesia, 1958; and Southern Rhodesia, 1963. The archival material in Kansas City includes missionary correspondence, records of mission stations, journals, official reports, and other publications. A monthly journal, *The Other Sheep*, carries news of missionary activities.

In May 1963, church activities in Africa were broadened with the opening of the Nazarene Publishing House, Johannesburg, South Africa. A general history of Nazarene missionary work, *Fifty Years of Nazarene Missions*, Vol. II, is available from the Nazarene Publishing House, P.O. Box 527, Kansas City, Missouri.

COLLEGE OF THE BIBLE

The College of the Bible Library, Lexington, Kentucky, contains the papers of Andrew F. Hensey from 1905 to 1940, 6 bound volumes. Dr. Hensey was concerned with the missions in the Congo of the Disciples of Christ. His papers and correspondence deal generally with mission problems. Of special interest are the accounts of Bantu folklore and languages.

Extensive files of correspondence up to the present day from missionaries in the Congo are also held.

A complete file of a denominational missionary magazine, *World Call* (1919–), the *Rheinische Missionsgesellschaft* (1834–1939), and similar publications are available. These contain frequent articles on missionary work in the Congo, Southern Rhodesia, and South Africa. Additional holdings include unpublished theses and privately printed studies of missionary activities in the Congo.

COLLEGE OF THE HOLY CROSS

College of the Holy Cross, Worcester, Massachusetts, possesses about 800 unpublished papers of Joseph John Williams and letters to him concerned with his book *Hebrewisms in West Africa* (1930) and his proposed study 'Religion and the Primitive in Africa.' Father Williams collected documentary evidence from the most experienced missionaries in Africa.

CONCORDIA HISTORICAL INSTITUTE

The Concordia Historical Institute, St. Louis, Missouri, has about 450 items of material on Elmer Christian Zimmerman (1896–), post-World War I Lutheran missionary in Nigeria. Its collections also include records, 1906–1953, about 15,000 items, of the Missionary Board of the Evangelical Lutheran Synodical Conference of North America. These records have material on the missionary work among Ibesikpo tribes in Nigeria, and there are reports on negotiations with the Qua Iboe Mission, on the work of Henry Nau, on the establishment of a central hospital, and on the Nigerian Lutheran Seminary.

CONGO INLAND MISSION, INC.

The Congo Inland Mission, Inc., 251 West Hively Avenue, Elkhart, Indiana, was organized in 1911 as the United Mennonite Board of Missions to coordinate the Congo (Leopoldville) mission work of the Central Conference of Mennonites and the Defenseless Conference of Mennonites. In 1912 the present name was adopted. The present mission board consists of representatives from the successors to the original founders: the Evangelical Mennonite Church, the Evangelical Mennonite Brethren Conference, and the General Conference Mennonite Church. The work in the Congo (Leopoldville) has been carried on since 1912. The holdings in the mission office include missionary correspondence, records of mission stations, journals, and bound volumes of the official organ, *Congo Missionary Messenger*, in which are published the annual reports of the Congo work.

CONGREGATIONAL CHRISTIAN CHURCHES OF THE UNITED STATES
(Now part of the United Church of Christ)

The American Board of Commissioners for Foreign Missions was organized in 1810. In 1961 it became the United Church Board for World Ministries in a merger that included the Evangelical and Reformed Commission on World Service and the Congregational Christian Service Committee. African areas and periods of work are Angola, since 1880; Gabon, 1842–1870; Ghana, since 1947; Liberia, 1834–1842; South Africa, since 1835; Southern Rhodesia (and, for part of the time, Mozambique), since 1893; and Togo, since 1947. The archives of the Board contain over 500,000 pieces, from 1810 to date, including missionary correspondence, diaries, reports, and other papers. Among these are 2,600 volumes of missionary correspondence, mission reports, and minutes. A large amount of this material is deposited in Houghton Library, Harvard University. Contemporary correspondence is retained in the Board offices for ten years, after which it is prepared for transfer to Harvard.

The other major repository for the American Board archives is the United Church Board for World Ministries, 14 Beacon Street, Boston, Massachusetts. This collection is strong in biographies of the individual missionaries, especially the Vinton Books, which are handwritten compilations of brief biographies of missionaries of the American Board from 1810 to 1910. They were begun by the Reverend John A. Vinton in 1869 and continued after his death in 1877 by Dr. Alfred O. Treat and Miss A. M. Chapin. They are arranged by country or area and then by mission. Official annual reports dating from 1811 and various missionary periodicals from 1803 are also held. Complete files of the annual reports and the official periodicals of the separate Women's Mission Board, which merged with the American Board in 1926, are available. In addition, the United Church Library has numerous pamphlets about African missions, miscellaneous unpublished manuscripts by missionaries, and several as yet unsorted boxes of scrapbooks, letters, minutes, diaries, and other manuscript materials. There is also a sizable collection of photographs of missionaries, mission stations, institutions, etc. Many of these have been copied for the Johannesburg Public Library. Complete files of the printed annual reports and the magazine *Missionary Herald* are held both in the Boston office and at Harvard. Special application must be made to gain access to the indexed records of the Prudential Committee, the board of directors of the American Board, which made major policy decisions on the society's missionary work in Africa. Permission to use the manuscripts must be obtained from the librarian of the Board.

For further information on these records, see Mary Alden Walker, 'The Archives of the American Board for Foreign Missions,' *Harvard Library Bulletin*, IV (Winter 1952), 52–68, and Dorothy Oxman Kelly, 'The American Board for Foreign Missions in South Africa,' *Quarterly Bulletin of the South African Library*, XI (June 1957), 129–143.

(The libraries of the Chicago Theological Seminary and Princeton Theological Seminary also hold material on the American Board of Commissioners for Foreign Missions.)

CONSERVATIVE BAPTIST ASSOCIATION OF AMERICA

The Conservative Baptist Foreign Mission Society, P.O. Box 5, Wheaton, Illinois, was organized in 1943. The Society has had mission work in the Congo (Leopoldville) since 1945; Ivory Coast, 1947; Uganda, 1961; and Senegal, 1962. The Society's office files contain correspondence, manuscripts, memoranda, and letters on their work in all these African countries. An annual report and a monthly paper, the *Conservative Baptist*, also contain information on the Society's missionary activity.

DISCIPLES OF CHRIST HISTORICAL SOCIETY

The Disciples of Christ Historical Society, 1101 Nineteenth Avenue, South, Nashville, Tennessee 37212, holds material (18 boxes) dealing mostly with the former Belgian Congo although there is some material from South Africa. The contents include correspondence, reports, and station records, from the late 1920's until 1958. The general correspondence of the Foreign Christian Missionary Society also has many letters concerning Africa before 1920.

EASTERN MENNONITE BOARD OF MISSIONS
AND CHARITIES

The Eastern Mennonite Board of Missions and Charities, Salunga, Pennsylvania, was organized in 1914. It has had its own mission work in Tanganyika since 1934, Ethiopia since 1948, and Somalia since 1953. The headquarters office keeps files of correspondence on the various fields. The annual report is included in the *Missions Yearbook*. A mimeographed bimonthly called the *African Circle Letter* carried missionary correspondence and articles from 1934 through February 1952. This publication was then incorporated into the *Missionary Messenger*, the monthly official organ, bound copies of which are kept in the Salunga offices. The Board has published three mission study booklets and a small booklet commemorating 25 years of mission activity in Tanganyika.

ELIM MISSIONARY ASSEMBLIES

Elim Missionary Assemblies, Lima, New York, was first operative in Africa in 1940 under the name Elim Missionary Home, Inc., a faith fellowship and Bible training center. The present name and church body (1944) grew out of a need for a missionary sending agency and church fellowship for the graduates of the Elim Bible Institute, then at Hornell, New York. Mission work in Africa began in 1940 in Kenya and later developed in Tanganyika (1955), Ethiopia (1955), Ghana (1959), and Uganda (1961). All the records of the agency are retained at its Lima headquarters and include reports and manuscripts with maps and photographs. The bimonthly publication, *Elim Herald*, is the official organ of the association.

THE EVANGELICAL ALLIANCE MISSION

The Evangelical Alliance Mission, 2845 West McLean Avenue, Chicago, Illinois 60647, was founded in 1890 as the Scandinavian Alliance Mission of North America. It has had mission work in the Republic of South Africa since 1892 and in Southern Rhodesia since 1942. Missionary correspondence files are maintained. Bound copies of the bimonthly publication, the *Missionary Broadcaster*, are kept in the office.

EVANGELICAL BAPTIST MISSIONS

Evangelical Baptist Missions (formerly Africa Christian Missions, then Christian Missions, Inc.) maintains headquarters at 146 North Seventh Street, Paterson 2,

New Jersey. Work has been carried on in West Africa since 1928 and at present is actively pursued in Niger and Mali. Archives are held at the home office in Paterson. Publications include the *Evangelical Baptist*, as well as descriptive brochures. Works in the French and Djerma languages are printed for distribution in Africa. Works in French are printed in Martinique for distribution there and in Arabic for use in the Middle East and for Arabic-speaking peoples in the United States.

EVANGELICAL COVENANT CHURCH OF AMERICA

The Department of World Missions, Evangelical Covenant Church of America, 5101 North Francisco Avenue, Chicago 25, Illinois, was organized in 1885. It has had a mission field in the Congo (Leopoldville) since 1937. The Department's files include correspondence, articles, and manuscripts. Official reports on the work in the Congo appear in the *Covenant Yearbook*. The official weekly, the *Covenant Companion*, and a quarterly, the *Covenant Missionary Newsletter*, carry articles on the Congo mission.

EVANGELICAL FREE CHURCH OF AMERICA

The Department of Overseas Missions of the Evangelical Free Church of America, 1515 East 66th Street, Box 6399, Minneapolis 23, Minnesota, began mission work in the Congo (Leopoldville) in 1922, concentrating in the Ubangi section. Cooperative work has been carried on since 1937 with the Evangelical Covenant Church of America, which was invited to share the territory under the Free Church's charter. Correspondence and official mail are held at the Minneapolis office. Information appears in the *Evangelical Beacon*, the official organ of the Evangelical Free Church of America, and in *Missions on the March*, a quarterly insert on missions.

EVANGELICAL MENNONITE BRETHREN CONFERENCE

The Evangelical Mennonite Brethren Conference, 839 Pine Street, Omaha 8, Nebraska, was organized in 1914 under the name Defenseless Mennonite Brethren of North America. It does not operate its own mission stations but has more than 100 missionaries serving under various mission boards including the Gospel Missionary Union, Congo Inland Mission, and Sudan Interior Mission. The field and administrative reports of the sending agencies as well as correspondence from the individual missionaries come to the Omaha office.

EVANGELICAL MENNONITE CHURCH

The Evangelical Mennonite Church, 3100 West Addison Avenue, Fort Wayne, Indiana, formerly called the Conference of Defenseless Mennonite Church of North America, began in 1866. The first missionary supported was sent to West Africa in 1866 under The Christian and Missionary Alliance. In 1906 a mission station was opened in British East Africa under the African Inland Mission, which was sold to them in 1910. A corporation was formed with the Central Conference of Mennonites in 1912, namely, The Congo Inland Mission. During the past 50 years eight stations have been built and over 100 missionaries supported by four branches of Mennonites. They have carried on educational, medical, agricultural, and evangelism work. All records, financial reports, and missionary correspondence are kept at the Congo Inland Mission headquarters at 251 West Hively Avenue, Elkhart, Indiana. The Evangelical Mennonite Church publishes a monthly magazine, the *Evangelical Mennonite*, and an annual report.

EVANGELICAL UNITED BRETHREN CHURCH

The Board of Missions, Division of World Missions, of the Evangelical United Brethren Church was organized in 1946 with the merger of the Evangelical Church and the Church of the United Brethren in Christ. (Predecessor mission boards were organized in 1839 and 1841, respectively.) Mission stations have been maintained in Sierra Leone since 1855 and Nigeria since 1922. The archives are located in the Historical Society of the Evangelical United Brethren Church, 1810 Harvard Boulevard, Dayton 6, Ohio, and the Board of Missions, 601 West Riverview Avenue, Dayton 6, Ohio. These archives contain manuscripts, journals, proceedings, diaries, and correspondence. Available periodicals which contain material about missionary work are *Evangelischer Missionsbote*, *Evangelical Missionary World*, *Searchlight*, *Missionary Advance*, *Missionary Gem*, *World Evangel*, *Sierra Leone Outlook*, and *Missionary Yearbook*, which are the missionary publications, and the official denominational periodicals of the merged church and its predecessor communions.

FIVE YEARS MEETING OF FRIENDS

The American Friends Board of Missions, 101 Quaker Hill Drive, Richmond, Indiana 47374, was organized in 1894. It has had work in Kenya since 1902. The archival material, consisting of two file drawers of records, letters, articles, leaflets, and a few old photos, is kept in a vault at the Richmond office. A complete file of the annual *Report of the Board of Missions* is also available. Two monthly magazines, *Quaker Life* (the successor to the *American Friend*) and *Friends Missionary Advocate*, contain information about the Kenya mission. Two publications bearing on the Board's Africa mission work are *Among Friends in Kenya, Africa*, published by the Board, and *Emory J. Rees, Language Pioneer* (Gowanda, N.Y., Niagara Frontier Publishing Co., 1958).

FRANCISCAN FATHERS

The Franciscan Fathers opened their mission in Northern Rhodesia in 1931 from the Rome headquarters, and the Province of Our Lady of Consolation, Mount Saint Francis, Indiana, sent its first missionaries in 1947. Maps, letters, etc., are kept in the archives both in Indiana and in Rome. The magazine *Friars Fields*, published in Union City, New Jersey, carries most of the activity of the missions in Northern Rhodesia under the care of the Franciscan Conventual Fathers and Brothers. Annual reports on the 'Status Animarum' can be obtained from the superior in charge of the mission.

FREE METHODIST CHURCH OF NORTH AMERICA

The General Missionary Board of the Free Methodist Church of North America, Winona Lake, Indiana, was organized in 1885. It has had mission work in Mozambique since 1885; Republic of South Africa, 1891; Egypt, 1899; Ruanda-Urundi, 1935; Southern Rhodesia, 1938; and Congo (Leopoldville), 1963. The Board has holdings of approximately 100 box files and 50 file drawers of missionary correspondence, plus a few reports in a fireproof vault at the headquarters building. The general missionary secretary issues quadrennial reports. The *Free Methodist*, the denominational weekly, carries a column of news of the African missions. Bound volumes of *Missionary Tidings*, the monthly missionary publication, are available from its origin in the late 1800's. Works published by the Board on its work in Africa include *Lights in the World* (1951) and *Venture* (1960), both by Byron S. Lamson.

FREE WILL BAPTIST BOARD OF FOREIGN MISSIONS

The Board of Foreign Missions, 3801 Richland Avenue, Nashville 5, Tennessee, was organized in 1935 as the foreign missionary agency of the National Association of Free Will Baptists in the United States. The first missionaries were sent to the Ivory Coast in 1956. The Board maintains an extensive collection of records, journals, missionary correspondence, etc., in its Nashville office for the convenience of board members and staff. A monthly magazine, *Heartbeat*, is published. An annual report of Free Will Baptist foreign missionary activity appears each July in *Digest of Reports of the National Association of Free Will Baptists*. The April issue of *Contact*, official publication of the National Association of Free Will Baptists, each year is given to a survey of foreign missionary activity. The Board maintains a photographic file in its Nashville office. A pamphlet series, *Ivory Coast*, was begun with the 1963 edition. Copies of this and *Heartbeat* are available without charge from the Nashville office.

FULL GOSPEL CHURCH OF GOD

The Full Gospel Church of God, with headquarters at Cleveland, Tennessee, was formed in 1951 by a merger of the Church of God and the Full Gospel Church. The latter had grown up among the whites in South Africa as a result of missionary work begun between 1908 and 1910. The Mission Department of the Church maintains congregations among the several racial groups in Natal, Mozambique, South-West Africa, Angola, the Rhodesias, and Nyasaland and in other parts of South Africa.

GARRETT THEOLOGICAL SEMINARY

The Garrett Theological Seminary Library, 2121 Sheridan Road, Evanston, Illinois, contains the papers of Ezekiel Cooper, who was concerned with mission work in Sierra Leone at the beginning of the nineteenth century. A *Calendar of the Ezekiel Cooper Collection of Early American Methodist Manuscripts, 1785–1839* was prepared by the Illinois Historical Records Survey Project, Division of Professional and Service Projects, Work Projects Administration, Chicago, Illinois, in 1941.

GENERAL CONFERENCE OF SEVENTH-DAY ADVENTISTS

The General Conference of Seventh-day Adventists, 6840 Eastern Avenue, N.W., Takoma Park, Washington 12, D.C., was organized in 1863. The Seventh-day Adventists began their mission work in Africa in the Republic of South Africa and are now active in almost every nation of the continent. The 55 African mission stations are administered through four divisional offices located in Europe, Africa, and the Levant. The Trans-Africa Division, P.O.H.G. 100, Highlands, Salisbury, Southern Rhodesia, is responsible for work in the Republic of South Africa (since 1887), Southern Rhodesia (1894), Nyasaland (1902), Tanganyika (1903), Northern Rhodesia (1905), Kenya (1906), Congo (Leopoldville; 1921), Ruanda-Urundi (1921), and Uganda (1927). The Northern European Division, 41 Hazel Gardens, Edgware, Middlesex, England, administers the work in Ghana (since 1894), Sierra Leone (1905), Ethiopia and Eritrea (1907), Nigeria (1913), Liberia 1927), and Ivory Coast (1946). The Southern European Division, Hoheweg 17, Berne, Switzerland, administers the work in Algeria and Tunisia (since 1905), Mauritius (1914), Angola (1925), Cameroun (1928), Morocco (1928), Mozambique (1933), Cape Verde Islands (1935), Réunion (1936), Seychelles (1936), Malagasy Republic (1949), Senegal (1952), and Central African Republic (1960). The Middle East Division, Box 2020, Beirut, Lebanon, administers the work in Egypt (since 1899) and the Sudan (1953). The General Conference files in Washington, D.C., include correspondence from American Adventist missionaries in Africa and biographical records of all overseas workers. The *Annual Yearbook* and a weekly, the *Review and Herald*, contain reports from Africa.

GENERAL COUNCIL OF THE ASSEMBLIES OF GOD

The General Council of the Assemblies of God, 1445 Boonville Avenue, Springfield, Missouri, which, with several other full gospel groups comprises the Pentecostal movement, was founded in 1914. The first missionaries went to Sierra Leone in 1905 before the Assemblies of God was officially organized. They were appointed for a second term of service by the newly formed Assemblies of God Foreign Missions Board. Since then the Assemblies of God have established works in the following countries: Liberia (1908), South Africa (1910), Congo (1918), Upper Volta (1921), Nyasaland (1930), Ghana (1931), Tanganyika (1938; reorganized 1953), Nigeria (1939), Togo (1940), Dahomey (1945), Basutoland (1950), and Senegal (1956).

The Assemblies of God Foreign Missions Department in Springfield has missionary correspondence, a collection of records, photographs, microfilms, and pamphlets giving a résumé of the work in various fields. The Foreign Missions Department issues a quarterly report and an annual report of the *Key* and has a section each week in the *Pentecostal Evangel; Global Conquest* and the *Missionary Forum* are published quarterly. The *Nigerian Evangel*, the *Ghana Evangel*, and the *Pentecostal Evangel* in the Swahili language are published in Africa; copies are available in the Springfield office.

GETTYSBURG SEMINARY

The Gettysburg Seminary Library, Gettysburg, Pennsylvania, contains the diary of the Reverend Morris Officer, A.M. (1823–1874), a Lutheran missionary to Liberia. The diary covers the period from October 1852 to May 1864. The library also has his biography by the Reverend A. J. Imhoff, *The Life of Rev. Morris Officer* (Dayton, Ohio, United Brethren Publishing House, 1876).

GOSPEL FURTHERING FELLOWSHIP

The Gospel Furthering Fellowship, 537 West Springfield Road, Springfield, Pennsylvania, was organized in 1935. Mission work has been carried out in Kenya and Tanganyika since 1936. The Fellowship has several file drawers of missionary correspondence and issues an occasional newsletter. One of the Fellowship's retired missionaries, the Reverend Frederick E. Holland, has recently written a book, *Kulikuwa Hatari* (New York, Exposition Press, 1963), a story of his life and experiences as senior missionary at the Babati, Tanganyika, center.

GOSPEL MISSIONARY UNION

The Gospel Missionary Union, Smithville, Missouri, was organized in 1892. It has worked in Morocco since 1894 and in Mali since 1919. A small number of manuscripts are available. Bound volumes of the official monthly magazine, the *Gospel Message*, which has carried letters and articles on the work in Africa since its inception, are available at the office. *Memories of Morocco, 1897–1914*, by George C. Reed, recounts some of the mission work in Africa.

HARTFORD SEMINARY FOUNDATION

The Case Memorial Library of the Hartford Seminary Foundation contains a large collection of mission reports and mimeographed and manuscript letters from missionaries in the African field. There are also about fifty unpublished theses and a large collection of anthropological studies on various tribes. Detailed information about the collection may be obtained by writing to the archivist of the Case Memorial Library, 55 Elizabeth Street, Hartford 5, Connecticut.

HISTORICAL COMMISSION OF THE SOUTHERN BAPTIST CONVENTION

The Historical Commission of the Southern Baptist Convention is located at 127 Ninth Avenue, North, Nashville 3, Tennessee. The Commission was first organized as the Southern Baptist Historical Society and in 1951 was incorporated as the Historical Commission of the Southern Baptist Convention. This organization is the official archive of the Southern Baptist Convention and maintains a library jointly with the Baptist Sunday School Board, Nashville, Tennessee. The Historical Commission gathers Baptist materials from all over the world, either in the original form or in micro form. The Commission has prepared a catalogue of its archival material.

Among the holdings concerned with Baptist missionary work in Africa are the Bowen Papers (1 reel). The Reverend Thomas Jefferson Bowen (1814–1875) and his wife were missionaries to the Egba of Nigeria. The Reverend Mr. Bowen visited Liberia and the Gold Coast and served at Abeokuta in Nigeria from 1849 to 1856. Bowen used his military skill to defend the Egba against a Dahomean invasion in the Battle of Aro in 1851. He published two books about his mission experiences in Africa, compiled a dictionary and grammar of the Yoruba language,* and drew up maps of Yorubaland for the British government.

The Bowen Papers were compiled, copied, and arranged by the Reverend and Mrs. Cecil Roberson. The material is separated into letters, journals, diaries, notebooks, newspaper articles, and speeches and deals with personal affairs, mission work, African customs, languages, and beliefs, politics and economics of West Africa, and history and geography of Yorubaland. Parts of Mrs. T. J. Bowen's diary and her letters from Africa are also held.

Other materials held on microfilm are as follows: 'History and Journal of Kabba Baptist Mission of Nigeria, 1900–1957,' copied by C. J. Roberson; Dr. George Green, 'Travels and Works as a Medical Missionary to Nigeria, 1907–1942' (typescript of Journal); *Missions Magazine*, 1803–1953 (title varies); *Nigerian Baptist*, 1923–1961; *Royal Service* (women's missions magazine), 1906–1961; various periodicals of the Southern Baptist Foreign Mission Board, 1846–1953. There is also a selection of British Baptist materials, including reports of the Baptist Missionary Society of London, 1792–1957. Microfilmed dissertations include several dealing with Africa, e.g., Svende A. Hogspron, *A History of the Danish Baptist Mission in Ruande Urundi, 1928–1957* (Zurich, Switzerland, Baptist Theological Seminary, 1958).

The Foreign Mission Board of the Southern Baptist Convention, located in Richmond, Virginia, maintains original files of correspondence from missionaries, along with their annual reports of mission.

---

* Thomas Jefferson Bowen, *Central Africa: Adventures and Missionary Labors in Several Countries in the Interior of Africa from 1849 to 1856* (Charleston, Southern Baptist Publication Society, 1857), *Merokee; or, Missionary Life in Africa* (Philadelphia, 1858), and *Grammar and Dictionary of the Yoruba Language, with an Introductory Description of the Country and People of Yoruba* (Washington, D.C., Smithsonian Institution, 1858).

THE HOLY CROSS FOREIGN MISSION SOCIETY, INC.

The Holy Cross Foreign Mission Society, Inc., 4301 Harewood Road, N.E., Washington 17, D.C., was organized in 1924 as a support and sending operation for the overseas work of the Congregation of Holy Cross in the United States. Long identified with work in India and Pakistan, it has been connected with activities of the Congregation in West and East Africa since 1957, particularly the countries of Ghana, Liberia, and Uganda. The Society maintains the reports of and correspondence with these overseas operations, as well as a library of photographs and color slides. A former publication, the *Bengalese*, later called *Holy Cross Missions*, was supplanted in 1959 by various newsletters, including the *Uganda Drum*, distributed from Washington, D.C.

HOLY GHOST FATHERS

(Congregation of the Holy Ghost)

The Congregation of the Holy Ghost was founded in Paris, May 27, 1703. It has been in the United States since 1795. Its headquarters are in Pittsburgh, Pennsylvania (915 Dorseyville Road), for the Eastern Province and in Glenwood Springs, Colorado, for the Western Province. The Public Information Office is at 1615 Manchester Lane, N.W., Washington, D.C. Its first missionaries to Africa went to Senegal in 1779, but its major efforts in Africa date from the middle of the nineteenth century when the Congregation of the Holy Heart of Mary merged with that of the Holy Ghost. Since then it has carried on missionary work in Mauritania, Senegal, Guinea, Cameroun, Gabon, Congo-Brazzaville, Central African Republic, Gambia, Sierra Leone, Nigeria, Angola, Portuguese Congo, Congo-Leopoldville, South Africa, Tanganyika, Kenya, Zanzibar, and most of the adjacent islands, including Madagascar. The central archives of the Congregation, located in Paris (30, rue Lhomond), are open for scholarly research with certain restrictions. They contain many hundreds of dossiers, diaries, and written and printed reports. About fifty volumes of printed records *(Bulletin General)*, a number of microfilms, and files of periodicals are preserved in the archives of Duquesne University Library (limited access). The Congregation publishes numerous missionary periodicals, some of which are available through the African Library of Duquesne University.

THE INDEPENDENT BOARD FOR PRESBYTERIAN FOREIGN MISSIONS

The Independent Board for Presbyterian Foreign Missions, 246 West Walnut Lane, Philadelphia 44, Pennsylvania, was organized in June 1933 and sent its first missionaries to Kenya in 1946. The archives are in its Walnut Lane headquarters offices and are kept for the official use of the Board. This board publishes a monthly magazine, *Biblical Missions*, which carries news and information concerning its activities all over the world.

INTERNATIONAL CONVENTION OF CHRISTIAN CHURCHES (DISCIPLES OF CHRIST)

The United Christian Missionary Society was organized in 1919 as the successor to the Foreign Christian Missionary Society, founded in 1875. Three societies went into the making of UCMS: American Christian Missionary Society (1849), Christian Woman's Board of Missions (1874), and Foreign Christian Missionary Society (1875). Most of the archival material is held by the Disciples of Christ Historical Society, 1101 Nineteenth Avenue, South, Nashville, Tennessee 37212. Some correspondence is also kept in the Society's library in its headquarters at 222 South Downey Avenue, Indianapolis, Indiana 46207. Mission work has been carried out in the Congo (Leopoldville) since 1898 and the Republic of South Africa since 1932. The Historical Society's archives contain unprocessed letters, reports, and manuscripts and the minutes of the mission meetings. The Missionary Society's annual report is included in the *Yearbook of the Christian Churches*. The periodicals *Leaven, Missionary Tidings*, and *World Call* and their predecessors contain additional material about the mission work in Africa. *The Christian*, formerly named *Christian-Evangelist*, is the newsweekly of the Disciples. There is a three-volume index for the *Christian-Evangelist*, 1863–1958, which has many references to African missions. The Society's Africa mission work is treated in *Congo Crisis and Christian Mission* (St. Louis, Bethany Press, 1961), by Robert G. Nelson. A report of a study commission to review Disciple work in the Congo was prepared in 1963.

INTERNATIONAL MISSIONS

International Missions, Inc., 234 Bergen Avenue, Jersey City 5, New Jersey, was organized as The India Mission in Elyria, Ohio, in 1930 and changed its name to International Missions, Inc., in 1954. Since then International Missions has begun missionary work in Kenya and Tanganyika, where the work is confined to the minority Asian population in the larger cities and towns. The Jersey City office has complete records on its overseas missionary work. The Missions magazine, *Eastern Challenge*, is circulated five times a year free of charge to those requesting it.

LUTHERAN SYNODICAL CONFERENCE OF NORTH AMERICA

The Missionary Board of the Lutheran Synodical Conference was organized in 1874 to coordinate the Negro mission work of the Conference, at present composed of the Evangelical Lutheran Synod (Norwegian), the Synod of Evangelical Lutheran Churches (Slovak), the Lutheran Church—Missouri Synod, and the Wisconsin Evangelical Lutheran Synod. It has had mission work in Nigeria since 1936 and Ghana since 1958. The archives of the Board are at the Historical Institute, Concordia Seminary, 801 De Mun Avenue, St. Louis 5, Missouri. The Institute has the convention reports of the meetings of the Lutheran Synodical Conference and the files of the Missionary Board of the Lutheran Synodical Conference, i.e., correspondence, minutes of meetings, and other papers. Much of this material is of a restricted nature and may be used only by special permission. The Board's annual reports are included in the *Lutheran Annual* and the *Statistical Yearbook*, both published by the Lutheran Church—Missouri Synod. The official monthly, *Missionary Lutheran*, was discontinued in December 1961, owing to a shift in responsibility for mission work within the Conference. Copies of publications for the Nigerian mission include the *Lutheran Witness*, the *Nigerian Lutheran*, and the *Lutheran Herald*. Missionary work in Africa includes the operation of a seminary, a hospital, clinics, and schools. A printshop is maintained in Nigeria, and radio broadcasts are sponsored by the Board.

MARYKNOLL FATHERS

The Catholic Foreign Mission Society of America, Inc. (popularly known as the Maryknoll Fathers), Maryknoll, New York, was founded in 1911 by Fathers James A. Walsh and Thomas F. Price. Mission work was begun in Africa in 1946 in Tanganyika at Musoma, on Lake Victoria, and in the Shinyanga district in 1954. The Society also maintains a house in Nairobi, Kenya.

The archives are at the headquarters in Maryknoll. Materials in the archives include original manuscripts of missioners' letters, diaries, and reports. Among the printed materials held are annual reports, the Society's monthly magazine, *Maryknoll*, and World Horizon Reports on Africa. Maps of the area served by the Society are also available.

MARYKNOLL SISTERS OF ST. DOMINIC

The Maryknoll Sisters of St. Dominic, Maryknoll, New York, the first Catholic missionary sisterhood in the United States, was founded in 1912 by Mary Josephine Rogers. The Sisters started their work in Africa in 1948. Their missions in Africa are all in Tanganyika.

Annual reports on each of the missions are correlated at the Motherhouse, Maryknoll, New York, each year. The Mission Education Secretariat, also at the Motherhouse, has the original history of this mission venture, which is also told briefly in *The Maryknoll Sisters: A Pictorial History* (New York, Dutton, 1962). Most recent coverage of the missions is contained in *Safari by Jet* (New York, Scribner, 1962). In addition, individual stories of the Tanganyikan missions are reported in the *Maryknoll* magazine.

MENNONITE BOARD OF MISSIONS AND CHARITIES

The Mennonite Board of Missions and Charities, 1711 Prairie Street, Elkhart, Indiana, was organized in 1906. It has had its own mission operations in Algeria and Ghana since 1957 and in Nigeria since 1959. The repository for all the Board's archival material is the Mennonite Historical Library, Goshen College, Goshen, Indiana. The archival material includes personal files, correspondence, manuscripts, and pictures. The most recent correspondence and other records are still in the Elkhart office. The Board's official publications are its annual report and the

Gospel Herald, a weekly published since 1907. Two monthlies which also carry material about the African missions are *Christian Living,* published under other names since 1945, and *Mission-Service Newsletter,* which has appeared since 1955.

MENNONITE BRETHREN CHURCH OF NORTH AMERICA

The Mennonite Brethren Board of Missions, 315 South Lincoln Street, Hillsboro, Kansas, was organized in 1885. In Africa it has had mission centers in the Congo (Leopoldville) since 1920. The centers are at Kikwit, Kafumba, Matende, Kipungu, Lusemvu, Gungu, Kajiji, Panzi, and Pai-Kongila. The Board's office files at Hillsboro include correspondence, reports, statistics, publications, pictures, and films. The annual reports are contained in the yearbooks of the Mennonite Brethren Conference. A biweekly, the *Christian Leader,* and a weekly, the *Mennonite Brethren Herald,* also carry material on the mission endeavor.

METHODIST CHURCH

The Board of Missions of the Methodist Church was organized in 1940 as a result of the 1939 reunification of three Methodist churches. Overseas work of the Board is carried on by the Division of World Missions and Woman's Division of Christian Service, Department of Work in Foreign Fields. The original Methodist Episcopal Church was founded in 1784. The Methodist Protestant Church, which never developed mission work in Africa, split off in 1828. The Methodist Episcopal Church, South, which broke off in 1844, started mission work in the Congo (Leopoldville) in 1913. The most extensive missionary work in Africa was carried on by the original Methodist Episcopal Church, which began activity in Liberia in 1833. Other areas of interest are Angola (since 1884), Southern Rhodesia (1898), Mozambique and the Republic of South Africa (1903), Algeria and Tunisia (1908), and the Congo (Leopoldville; 1910). Most of the extensive archives and records of Methodist missionary work in Africa are kept in the Board of Missions of the Methodist Church Library, 475 Riverside Drive, New York, New York 10027. These include various unpublished manuscripts; files of deceased bishops and foreign missionaries containing manuscripts, published writings, newspaper clippings, etc.; special project files on various aspects of mission work in Africa— medical, educational, etc.; and the official publications of the denominations and their mission boards. Among the last are the *Journals of the General Conference* of both the Methodist Episcopal Church and the Methodist Episcopal Church, South, and the *Official Journals and Minutes* of the various societies responsible for mission work in both denominations over the years, including the *Journals and Minutes of the Woman's Foreign Missionary Society of the Methodist Episcopal Church* from 1869 to 1940 and, since 1940, the *Journals and Minutes of the Department of Work in Foreign Fields,* of the Woman's Division of Christian Service. All the official publications of the reunited Methodist Church and its missionary board are available. In addition, the journals of the missions and the annual conferences held in Africa are kept in the library. An extensive collection of the official periodicals published before and after the merger is also available. Three additional sources of archival materials are in the same offices at 475 Riverside Drive, New York. The office of the recording secretary of the Division of World Missions maintains an official dossier of all its mission workers in Africa (past and present). The central records (correspondence files) include the correspondence of individual missionaries of the Division of World Missions. Dossiers of workers related to the Woman's Division of Christian Service are kept in the office of the Department of Work in Foreign Fields of the Woman's Division of Christian Service along with a limited amount of their correspondence. There are stringent regulations limiting access to the dossiers and correspondence of both male and female missionaries.

METHODIST PUBLISHING HOUSE LIBRARY

The Methodist Publishing House Library, Nashville, Tennessee, has 162 items of correspondence and other papers, 1909–1912, which concern the missionary activities of Bishop Joseph Crane Hartzell (1842–1929) in Africa. Among these are lists of donors to the work of the mission as well as information on the Diamond Jubilee of mission work in Africa.

MISSIONARY AVIATION FELLOWSHIP

The Missionary Aviation Fellowship, 3519 West Commonwealth Boulevard, Box 32, Fullerton, California, was first organized (1944) as the Christian Airmen's Missionary Fellowship by Christian airmen in the armed forces during World War II. It was incorporated in 1945 and adopted its present name in 1946 to show its oneness of purpose with a British group of that name. During 1948 the British group conducted a survey of Central Africa which led to the establishment of missionary air service in the Anglo-Egyptian Sudan in 1950. Central and East Africa were resurveyed jointly by the two groups in 1957, and this led to the extension of services by the British group to Kenya (1959), Ethiopia (1961), and Tanganyika (1963). The American group established service in the Congo (Leopoldville) early in 1961. This service was extended to Southern Rhodesia in mid-1964. A further extension to Nigeria was planned for late 1964. The Fellowship maintains an extensive collection of records, past publications, missionary correspondence, etc., in its Fullerton office for the convenience of its officers. The Fellowship issues a monthly publication, *Wings of Praise and Prayer*, which is periodically alternated with a publication entitled *Missionary Aviation*. These publications give news of its work in Africa, Latin America, and Southeast Asia.

MISSIONARY BOARD OF THE BRETHREN CHURCH

The Missionary Board of the Brethren Church, 530 College Avenue, Ashland, Ohio 44805, was founded in 1892. In 1948 the Board entered into an agreement with the General Brotherhood Board of the Church of the Brethren with headquarters in Elgin, Illinois, to work cooperatively in their mission field in Nigeria. Letters, reports, maps, photographs, colored slides, and some study materials and New Testament translations in the dialects are kept on file at the Board's office.

MORAVIAN CHURCH

The Moravian Church, Bethlehem, Pennsylvania, is operator of missions in 'Egypt' and 'Africa.' Its archives date from 1457 and are 53 linear feet in extent.

NATIONAL BAPTIST CONVENTION

The Foreign Mission Board, National Baptist Convention, U.S.A., Inc., at 701–703 South 19th Street, Philadelphia 46, Pennsylvania, was organized in 1880. The Board's first mission station was established in Liberia in 1883. Mission work is currently conducted in Liberia, Sierra Leone, Ghana, Republic of South Africa, Malawi, Rhodesia, Zambia, and Basutoland. The Board publishes a bimonthly report, the *Mission Herald*, along with tracts and maps giving information on the history of its missions. Among the texts available from the Board is *Epoch of Negro Baptists and the Foreign Mission Board* (Central Seminary Press, 1953), by E. A. Freeman.

NATIONAL FELLOWSHIP OF BRETHREN CHURCHES

The Foreign Missionary Society of the Brethren Church, Inc., Box 588, Winona Lake, Indiana, is the foreign mission organization of the National Fellowship of Brethren Churches. The Society, organized in 1900, began its mission work in Africa in 1921 in Ubangi-Shari province, which became the Central African Republic in 1958. Records, missionary correspondence, and historical items are kept in the Winona Lake office. The Society cooperates in furnishing material for one issue per month of the *Brethren Missionary Herald* (a biweekly) and also prints a small monthly publication, *Foreign Mission Echoes*. The field in Africa puts out a Sango-language monthly publication, the *Trompette Évangélique*, and cooperates with other missions in a French monthly, *Vaincre*. Books concerning the Brethren's Africa mission work include *Some African Links* (Winona Lake, Ind., Foreign Missionary Society of Brethren Church, 1953), by Mary L. Emmert; *Undaunted Hope* (Ashland, Ohio, Brethren Publishing Co., 1932) and *Stranger than Fiction* (Winona Lake, Brethren Missionary Herald Co., 1949), both by Florence N. Gribble; and *Conquering Oubangui-Chari for Christ* (Winona Lake, Brethren Missionary Herald Co., 1957), by Orville D. Jobson.

NATIONAL LUTHERAN COUNCIL, DEPARTMENT OF WORLD MISSIONS COOPERATION

The Department of World Missions Cooperation of the National Lutheran Council, 50 Madison Avenue, New York, New York 10010, has archives deposited in the library of the Council. Those dealing with Africa include approximately 5 archives boxes of correspondence and reports; mimeographed reports, annual from 1918 to 1948, semiannual thereafter; and half a file drawer of photographs. These concern Ethiopia, Gold Coast (Ghana), Togoland, Cameroun, Nigeria, Rhodesia, Sudan, Tanganyika, Natal, Orange Free State, Transvaal, Cape Colony, Bechuanaland, Zululand, and Madagascar. They deal with church and government matters as related to the churches and to their 'orphaned mission' status. In later years, they also deal with their transference to the status of indigenous churches.

NEW TRIBES MISSION

The New Tribes Mission, Woodworth, Wisconsin, a Protestant interdenominational foreign missionary organization, was organized in 1942. The Mission's Africa work was started in Senegal in 1955 and in Liberia in 1956. The New Tribes Institute was begun in 1943 for the express purpose of providing the Biblical and technical knowledge necessary in order to work with peoples who speak unwritten languages. The monthly magazine, *Brown Gold*, is published at Woodworth and includes field reports. Back copies are available from the Woodworth office. Surveys of missionary work in Africa are filed at the New Tribes Institute, Box 279, Jersey Shore, Pennsylvania; New Tribes Institute, Fredonia, Wisconsin; New Tribes Institute, 915 North Hartwell, Waukesha, Wisconsin; and New Tribes Institute, Box 398, Oviedo, Florida.

NORTH AMERICAN BAPTIST GENERAL MISSIONARY SOCIETY, INC.

The North American Baptist General Missionary Society, Inc., 7308 Madison Street, Forest Park, Illinois 60130, was organized in 1883 under the name of the General Missionary Society of the German Baptist Churches of North America. Its missionaries have been active in Cameroun since 1891. The Society has files of correspondence at its headquarters. An annual report is issued, and a biweekly, the *Baptist Herald*, carries articles on the mission work in Africa. Publications about the Africa mission work include *Now We Are 82*, about the mission fields and the 82 missionaries serving in Africa in the Federal Republic of Cameroon and elsewhere; *The Call of the Cameroons*, about some earlier work in the British Cameroons, West Africa; *At God's Command*, by Professor George A. Dunger, about the philosophy of missions pertaining to the North American Baptist General Conference and a brief review of some of their work in Africa and elsewhere; and numerous leaflets on Africa.

OBLATES OF ST. FRANCIS DE SALES

The Oblates of St. Francis de Sales, with Congregation headquarters at Via Dandolo, 49, Rome, Italy, and American headquarters at 2200 Kentmere Parkway, Wilmington, Delaware, was founded at Troyes, France, in 1872. The Oblates went to Africa in 1882, assuming charge of the missions in Namaqualand. At present they have charge of two missionary fields: the Diocese of Keimoes, first established in 1884, in the Republic of South Africa, and the Vicariate of Keetmanshoop, erected in 1909, in South-West Africa.

The archives of the missions are at the international headquarters in Rome, although considerable information can be obtained from the archives of the American Province in Wilmington, Delaware. The memoirs of the first Oblate bishop in Africa have been published by Benziger Brothers, New York City, under the title *Bishop for the Hottentots*. News concerning the present American missionaries can be found in the *De Sales World*, published at the American headquarters. More extensive coverage of the Oblates' mission activities can be found in the *Annales Salesiennes*, published at Annecy, France.

OPEN BIBLE STANDARD CHURCHES, INC.

The Open Bible Standard Missions, Inc., 851 Nineteenth Street, Des Moines, Iowa 50314, was organized in 1932. It has participated in mission work in Liberia since 1935 and in Guinea since 1953. The office's files contain a great deal of correspondence from the field. The foreign missions secretary issues an annual report. A monthly official magazine, the *Message of the Open Bible*, and a missionary news service magazine, *World Vision*, carry material about the society's work in Africa.

THE ORDER OF THE HOLY CROSS

The Holy Cross Liberian Mission was founded in 1922 by the Order of the Holy Cross, West Park, Ulster County, New York. The Order of the Holy Cross is a religious order in the Episcopal Church. The archives, located at Holy Cross Monastery, West Park, include original manuscripts, printed material published over the years, photographs, etc. Information about the Mission can be found in the *Hinterland*, a quarterly recently incorporated into the *Holy Cross News*.

ORIENTAL MISSIONARY SOCIETY

The Oriental Missionary Society, Inc., 850 North Hobart Boulevard, Los Angeles 29, California, was founded in 1901 in Japan, with headquarters in Tokyo until 1919. International headquarters were later opened in Los Angeles. The Society's work in Nigeria was started in 1957 in cooperation with the United Missionary Society. All records, journals, missionary correspondence, etc., are kept at the international headquarters offices in Los Angeles. The official organ of the Society is the *Missionary Standard*, published monthly.

PENTECOSTAL HOLINESS CHURCH

The Department of Foreign Missions, Pentecostal Holiness Church, maintains headquarters and archives at Franklin Springs, Georgia. Active in West Africa and the Transvaal since the early twentieth century, the Department currently administers over 300 churches in Nigeria and South Africa. Information on missionary activities is available from the following publications: *Advocate*, the official church organ; *Helping Hand*, the women's auxiliary paper; *Lifeline*, the young people's paper; and brochures and promotional material published annually. All these can be obtained from the Franklin Springs headquarters.

PILGRIM HOLINESS CHURCH

The World Missions Department of the Pilgrim Holiness Church, 230 East Ohio Street, Indianapolis 4, Indiana, was organized in 1897. Mission work was begun under the International Holiness Union in the Republic of South Africa in 1900. The Department started its own mission work there in 1909 and in Northern Rhodesia in 1929. The Department maintains confidential files of missionary correspondence. The official monthly, *World Missions Bulletin*, and occasional publications provide information on the African missions.

PITTSBURGH THEOLOGICAL SEMINARY

The Pittsburgh Theological Seminary Library, 616 North Highland Avenue, Pittsburgh, Pennsylvania 15206, includes the following materials on Africa:

United Presbyterian Church of North America, General Assembly, minutes— Sudan, 1900–1958; Ethiopia, 1920–1958.
United Presbyterian Church in the U.S.A., General Assembly, minutes—Sudan, from 1959; Ethiopia, from 1959.

PRESBYTERIAN CHURCH IN THE UNITED STATES OF AMERICA (NORTHERN)

(Now part of the United Presbyterian Church in the United States of America)

The Board of Foreign Missions of the Presbyterian Church in the United States of America was organized in 1837 and was merged with the Board of Foreign Missions of the United Presbyterian Church of North America in 1958 to form the Commission on Ecumenical Mission and Relations of the United Presbyterian Church in the United States of America, whose offices are at 475 Riverside Drive, New York, New York 10027. In 1837 it assumed the mission work that was begun in 1833 in Liberia by the Western Foreign Missionary Society. Other stations were opened in Río Muni (Spanish Guinea) in 1865, Gabon in 1870, and Cameroun in 1879. An invaluable collection of the diaries, letters, journals, and memoranda of these missions up to 1910 has been catalogued, microfilmed, and filed at the United Presbyterian Mission Library, 475 Riverside Drive, New York. Prints of these microfilms may be ordered from the Presbyterian Historical Society, 520 Witherspoon Building, Philadelphia 7, Pennsylvania. The United Presbyterian Mission Library, which is the repository for the records of these missions since 1910, is microfilming the post-1910 archives. This library also has all the records of the Western Missionary Society, a complete set of the *Minutes and Annual Reports of the Presbyterian Church in the U.S.A.* (which includes the annual reports of the Board of Foreign Missions), and a complete set of the *Home and Foreign Record of the Presbyterian Church in the U.S.A.* (which contains many references to the missionary work in Africa). In addition, a complete file of the monthly Presbyterian missionary magazine, *Concern* (and its predecessor *Outreach*), and the biweekly *Presbyterian Life* (begun in 1948) is available. Of special interest to Africanists in the Mission Library's collection of bound volumes of the periodical of the Presbyterian Church mission in West Africa since 1922, *Drum Call*. Since 1958, official references to the work in Africa can be found in the *Annual Reports of the Commission on Ecumenical Mission and Relations.*

PRESBYTERIAN CHURCH IN THE UNITED STATES (SOUTHERN)

The Board of World Missions of the Presbyterian Church in the United States, 2400 Twenty-first Avenue, South, P.O. Box 330, Nashville 1, Tennessee, was organized in 1861. It began mission work in the Congo (Leopoldville) in 1891. The archival material is divided between the Nashville office and the Historical Foundation of the Presbyterian and Reformed Churches, Montreat, North Carolina. The Nashville office holds only a few manuscripts but has an extensive collection of published material, including bound copies of the annual reports of the Board and of the missionary magazine dating from its origin in 1867. The magazine was known as *Missionary, Missionary Survey,* and *Presbyterian Survey.* An index of missionary letters from the Congo appearing in this publication from 1890 to 1916 is available at the Nashville office, which also has files of missionary letters dating from 1916 to the present. The Historical Foundation possesses the original instructions to the two pioneer missionaries, Samuel Norvell Lapsley and William H. Sheppard, in regard to the establishment of the Congo mission; miscellaneous letters from Sheppard; and the minutes of the Congo mission, 1893–1894 and 1917–1956. The Foundation also has the 1899 diary of William McCutchen Morrison; letters from missionaries in the Congo, 1929–1960; and copies of the *Kasai Herald,* 1901–1916, and the *Lumu Lua Bena Kasai,* 1927–1957, both published in the Congo. Bound volumes of the missionary magazine are also available at Montreat. Numerous books and articles have been written about the Board's mission work in Africa.

PRINCETON THEOLOGICAL SEMINARY

The Princeton Theological Seminary Library, Princeton, New Jersey, holds, in the Synod of New Jersey Collection, records of the American Protestant Mission Church (American Board of Commissioners for Foreign Missions), Gabon (1843–1871), and of the Presbyterian churches in Benito (1866–1886) and in Angom (1892–1902), also in Gabon. (Congregational Christian Churches has a fuller account on the ABCFM.)

PROTESTANT EPISCOPAL CHURCH IN THE UNITED STATES OF AMERICA

The Church Historical Society, 606 Rathervue Place, Austin, Texas 78751, holds files of the Domestic and Foreign Missionary Society of the Protestant Episcopal Church (organized 1820) which contain missionary correspondence from 1820 to the present. The Protestant Episcopal Church began its work in Liberia in 1836, and missionary reports and correspondence from that time are available. The Church Historical Society publishes the *Historical Magazine of the Protestant Episcopal Church*, a quarterly. A limited number of books and pamphlets pertaining to the history of the Protestant Episcopal Church are held in the Austin office.

REFORMED CHURCH IN AMERICA

The Board of World Missions of the Reformed Church in America, 475 Riverside Drive, New York, New York 10027, operates missions in Ethiopia and the Sudan. It has been engaged in mission work in the South Sudan since 1948. This activity has from its beginnings been a cooperative venture with the United Presbyterian Church, which has had missionaries in the South Sudan since the early twentieth century. Publications of the Reformed Church relevant to Africa include the *Church Herald*, official denominational paper; an annual report, with data on all missionary activity; and miscellaneous pamphlets and literature. Primary historical archives of the Board of Missions are maintained in the library of the New Brunswick Theological Seminary, New Brunswick, New Jersey.

REGIONS BEYOND MISSIONARY UNION

The Regions Beyond Missionary Union was founded in England in 1878 and is a member of the Interdenominational Foreign Mission Association. The American headquarters are located at 8102 Elberon Avenue, Philadelphia 11, Pennsylvania. Missionary work was begun in the Congo in 1878 and is currently carried on in the Equator Province of the Congo. Records of the work of the Union are found in its mission magazine, *Regions Beyond*.

SAINT PAUL'S ABBEY

Saint Paul's Abbey, Benedictine Missionaries, Newton, New Jersey, was established in 1924. Originally known as The Little Flower Monastery, it became Saint Paul's Abbey in 1947. The Abbey has missions in Tanganyika and South Africa, and it publishes a quarterly, *Pax*. The archives at Saint Paul's Abbey contain a sizable quantity of original manuscripts, printed matter, maps, and photographs.

THE SALVATION ARMY

The Salvation Army was founded in London in 1878. The U.S.A. headquarters, established in 1880, are at 120–130 West 14th Street, New York, New York 10011.

Missionary work is conducted in the following areas of Africa: South Africa (since 1883), Rhodesia (1891), Zululand (1891), Portuguese East Africa (1916), Nigeria (1920), Kenya (1921), Ghana (1922), Uganda (1931), South-West Africa (1932), Tanganyika (1933), Congo-Leopoldville (1934), and Congo-Brazzaville (1937). Publications include the following: *Year Book*, issued by the international headquarters, London; *War Cry*, official U.S. organ; *Nsango na Kobikisa*, official, Congo-Leopoldville; *Sauti-ya-Vita*, official, East Africa; *Nsangu Zambote*, official, Congo-Brazzaville; *War Cry*, official, Nigeria; and *War Cry (Die Strydkreet)*, official, South Africa.

SEABURY-WESTERN THEOLOGICAL SEMINARY

The Seabury-Western Theological Seminary Library, 600 Haven Street, Evanston, Illinois, holds the following materials on Africa:

Church Missionary Society for Africa and the East, annual reports and proceedings,
    1816/17–1817/18, 1819/20, 1824/25, 1826/27, 1849/50, 1890/91–1916/17,
    1918/19, 1921/22, 1923/24, 1925/26, 1930/31–1936/37, 1938/39–.
Church of England Zenana Missionary Society, annual reports, 1897, 1908,
    1912/14, 1927/28, 1930, 1956/57.

SERVITE FATHERS, OUR LADY OF SORROWS PROVINCE

The Servite Fathers, Our Lady of Sorrows Province, has its headquarters at 3111 West Van Buren Street, Chicago 12, Illinois. The order was founded in 1233 in Florence, Italy; the American foundation was established in 1870 in Wisconsin. Mission work in Africa began in Zululand in 1947. There are currently five mission stations in operation. The archives at Chicago contain letters and reports from the missions. *Novena Notes* carries articles on work in Africa. Two books on Zululand have been written by one of the Servite Fathers: Thomas M. Calkins, *Umfundisi, Missioner to the Zulus* (Milwaukee, Bruce Publishing Co., 1959) and *Kisimusi: The Story of a Zulu Girl* (Milwaukee, Bruce Publishing Co., 1962).

SEVENTH DAY BAPTIST GENERAL CONFERENCE

The Seventh Day Baptist Missionary Society (successor of board established in 1818) was organized in 1842. The records of the Society are kept at its office, 403 Washington Trust Building, Westerly, Rhode Island. The American Sabbath Tract Society (successor of the General Tract Society established in 1831) was organized in 1843. The records of this society are maintained by the Seventh Day Baptist Historical Society, Seventh Day Baptist Building, 510 Watchung Avenue, Plainfield, New Jersey. The Missionary Society sent its first representative to the Gold Coast (Ghana) in 1900. Under the sponsorship of the Tract Society, a Sabbath Evangelizing and Industrial Association was set up and an Industrial Mission established in Nyasaland in 1898. This work was discontinued in 1902. After maintaining occasional contacts over the years, the Missionary Society resumed work in Nyasaland in 1947. The Historical Society has missionary correspondence, letter files, reports, and other documents that relate to its Nyasaland work, including material for the period between 1902 and 1947. Scattered materials contain documents dealing with the African Industrial Mission (1899–1906) and the Blantyre and Livinstonia missions (1908–1910), among them curriculum outlines. Reports of visits to Ghana (1899 and 1910) and southern and central Africa (1910–1912) are also held. A complete file of the Missionary Society's annual reports from 1842 and a file of the official weekly organ, the *Sabbath Recorder*, from 1844 are available. Other information about the missionary work can be found in *Mission Notes*, published by the Seventh Day Baptist Missionary Society.

THE SOCIETY OF CATHOLIC MEDICAL MISSIONARIES

The Society of Catholic Medical Missionaries (the Medical Mission Sisters), 8400 Pine Road, Philadelphia, Pennsylvania 19111, was founded in 1925. The Society's first establishment in Africa was in Ghana in 1948, and the American Province of the Society began work in Uganda in 1963. The archives of the American Province of the Society in Philadelphia contain an extensive collection of original manuscripts, annual reports, records, photographs, indigenous dress, and curios for the use of its members. A bimonthly publication, the *Medical Missionary*, covering the activities of the American Province of the Society in all countries, is issued from Philadelphia.

SOCIETY OF THE DIVINE WORD

The Society of the Divine Word (Divine Word Missionaries), with international headquarters at the Collegio del Verbo Divino in Rome (Cas. post. 5080), Italy, was founded at Steyl, Holland, in 1875 and approved by the Holy See in 1901 as a Roman Catholic foreign missionary society. American provincial headquarters are at Techny, Illinois; Girard, Pennsylvania; and Bay Saint Louis, Mississippi. Missionary work has been conducted in the following African areas: Togoland, 1891–1917; Accra, Ghana, since 1939; Banningville, Congo, since 1951; and Yendi, Ghana, since 1958. Missionary letters, diaries, and reports are in archives located at the Provincial Residence, 201 Ruella Avenue, Bay Saint Louis, and at the Provincial and Mission Procure Residence, Divine Word Seminary, Techny. Publications of the Society having articles on African mission work include *Divine Word Missionaries*, Techny, and *Divine Word Messenger*, Bay Saint Louis.

SOCIETY OF MARY (MARIANISTS)

The Society of Mary (Marianists), a religious congregation of the Roman Catholic Church, is engaged principally in education on the secondary and college and adult levels. Since its founding in France in 1817 the Society has established itself throughout the world, including four provinces in America. The Cincinnati Province, Mount Saint John, 4100 Patterson Road, Dayton, Ohio 45430, opened schools in Nigeria in 1957 and 1964, Malawi (Nyasaland) in 1960 and 1963, and Kenya in 1961 and 1963. The archives of the Cincinnati Province contain material on the African missions, letters of the first missionaries, and some photographs. The Marianist Mission publishes a four-page *Marianist Bulletin*. Other information can be found in circular letters from provincial superiors giving news items on work in Africa and in official reports sent to the Superior General of the Society of Mary at Rome.

SOUTHERN BAPTIST CONVENTION

The Foreign Mission Board of the Southern Baptist Convention, 3806 Monument Avenue, P.O. Box 6597, Richmond 30, Virginia, was organized in 1845. Mission work has been carried on in Liberia from 1846 to 1875 and since 1960, Nigeria since 1850, Sierra Leone from 1857 to 1875, Ghana since 1946, Southern Rhodesia since 1950, Kenya and Tanganyika since 1956, Nyasaland and Northern Rhodesia since 1960, and Uganda since 1963. During 1960 an attempt to begin work in Guinea was abandoned. The Board's library in Richmond has missionary correspondence, diaries, biographies, and other materials, including a complete set of the *Southern Baptist Foreign Mission Board Magazine*, now titled *The Commission*, from 1845 to 1964. Previous issues of the Board's annual report, *The Field Is the World*, as well as press releases concerning its work in Africa, are available at the library. A monthly missionary family publication, *Missionary Intercom*, was inaugurated in 1960. The Historical Commission of the Southern Baptist Convention has issued a catalogue of archival material which has been microfilmed by the library. The library of the Board contains a number of books on Southern Baptist mission work in Africa.

SOUTHERN BAPTIST THEOLOGICAL SEMINARY

The Southern Baptist Theological Seminary, 2825 Lexington Road, Louisville, Kentucky 40206, has manuscript holdings relating to the Baptist missions from 1854 to 1953. Of special interest are the accounts of the travels and explorations of William H. Clarke in Nigeria, 1854–1859, and a history of Methodism in Eastern Nigeria by H. G. Brewer.

Related to the above manuscript collection are typed theses on witchcraft, on religious education, and on the history of missionary work with present and future opportunities.

The collection also contains several printed works related to many phases of missionary endeavor—medicine, language, biography—the greater part of them on Nigeria, where Southern Baptists began work in 1850 and have continued it to the present time with the exception of a few years in the earlier period.

SOUTHERN METHODIST CHURCH

The Southern Methodist Church Board of Missions and Church Extensions, with headquarters at Southern Methodist College, 760 Broughton, S.W., P.O. Box 413,

Orangeburg, South Carolina, was created by the General Conference of the Southern Methodist Church in 1945 for the purpose of propagating missions from the Southern Methodist Church. All its missionaries go out under the independent boards after being approved by their board. Missionary work in Africa began in Kenya in 1945, the Congo (Leopoldville) in 1948, and Nigeria in 1953. The record of the General Conference Board of Missions and Church Extensions is kept in the annual journals of the various conferences of the Woman's Missionary Work and of the Church. Prayer letters from missionaries are occasionally sent to its entire body.

SUDAN INTERIOR MISSION

The Sudan Interior Mission was organized in Toronto, Canada, in 1893. The American home office is at 164 West 74th Street, New York, New York 10023. Other home offices are in Canada, England, New Zealand, South Africa, Australia, and Switzerland, with field offices in Africa. Fields of service and dates of entry are as follows: Nigeria, 1893; Niger, 1924; Ethiopia, 1927; Upper Volta, 1930; Sudan, 1936; Dahomey, 1946; Liberia, 1952; Somalia, 1954; and Ghana, 1956. Home offices maintain correspondence and record files, together with historical works, for the use of their own officers. Quarterly publications include *Sudan Witness* and *Africa Now*. Pamphlets giving information on mission work are also available from the home offices. Books published include James H. Hunter, *A Flame of Fire: The Life and Work of R. V. Bingham* (Toronto, Sudan Interior Mission, 1961), and Helen M. Willmott, *The Doors Were Opened: The Remarkable Advance of the Gospel in Ethiopia* (London, Sudan Interior Mission, 1961).

SUDAN UNITED MISSION

The Sudan United Mission, an international and interdenominational body, was organized in Britain in 1904. The North American branch, founded in 1926, has offices at 89 Quincy Street, Brooklyn 38, New York; 5537 North Glenwood Avenue, Chicago, Illinois 60640; and 189 High Park Avenue, Toronto 9, Ontario, Canada. Missionary work is conducted in Northern Nigeria, Cameroun, and Chad. Records are maintained in the North American offices, but the London headquarters are the major repository. The *Lightbearer* carries articles on the work of the Mission.

UNEVANGELIZED FIELDS MISSION

The Unevangelized Fields Mission, 306 Bala Avenue, Bala-Cynwyd, Pennsylvania, was founded in London in 1931 by 32 missionaries who had previously served with the Worldwide Evangelization Crusade. Congo and Brazil were the original fields, with headquarters in Stanleyville, Oriental Province, Congo, and in Belem, Para, Brazil. A collection of records, journals, correspondence, maps, photographs, and films is held in the Bala-Cynwyd, London, and Melbourne offices. The Mission publishes a quarterly magazine, *Lifeline*, informative brochures, and booklets concerning fieldwork, copies of which can be obtained from the Bala-Cynwyd office.

UNITED LUTHERAN CHURCH IN AMERICA
(Now part of the Lutheran Church in America)

The Board of Foreign Missions of the United Lutheran Church in America, 231 Madison Avenue, New York, New York 10016, was organized in 1919. In 1962 it was merged with the mission boards of the Augustana Lutheran Church, the American Evangelical Lutheran Church, and the Suomi Synod (Finnish) in the Board of World Missions of the Lutheran Church in America. The United Lutherans have sponsored missionary work in Liberia since 1860 and in Ethiopia since 1960. In 1955 the Board published a master's thesis, *Lutheran Mission in Liberia*, written by Harold Vink Whetstone in 1954 while he was a student at the Kennedy School of Missions of the Hartford Seminary Foundation. Pastor Whetstone, who served as a missionary in Liberia from 1950 to 1952, included in his thesis an extensive bibliography of the pamphlets, letters, journals, periodicals, official documents, and other materials available for research purposes.

UNITED MISSIONARY SOCIETY

The United Missionary Society, 1819 South Main Street, Elkhart, Indiana, is the foreign board of the United Missionary Church, formerly called Mennonite Brethren in Christ Church. The Church sent its first missionaries to Nigeria in 1901. In 1905 the Mennonite Brethren in Christ Missionary Society was organized for work in Nigeria. In 1921 this board was reorganized to unite and enlarge the foreign missionary work of the several districts of the Church. Bound copies of the *Gospel Banner*, which records the early years of the Society, and bound copies of the *Missionary Banner*, monthly publication of the United Missionary Society (since 1938), are available at the Elkhart headquarters. Also available are copies of the original minutes and printed journals of the Society since its inception.

UNITED PRESBYTERIAN CHURCH OF NORTH AMERICA
(Now part of the United Presbyterian Church
in the United States of America)

The Board of Foreign Missions of the United Presbyterian Church of North America was organized in 1858 and was merged with the Board of Foreign Missions of the Presbyterian Church in the United States of America in 1958 to form the Commission on Ecumenical Mission and Relations of the United Presbyterian Church in the United States of America, with offices at 475 Riverside Drive, New York, New York 10027. Its mission work began in Egypt in 1854. The Board started its own mission work in the Sudan in 1900 and in Ethiopia in 1924. The Pittsburgh Theological Seminary Library, Pittsburgh, Pennsylvania 15206, possesses typed manuscripts of the histories of the mission work in Egypt and the Sudan, as well as the minutes of the annual meetings of the Egyptian Missionary Association, 1910–1955, and the Sudan Missionary Association, 1911–1913, 1915–1916, 1918–1920, and 1949–1950. The seminary library also contains a complete set of the *Women's Missionary Magazine of the United Presbyterian Church*

(1887–1953) and its successor, *Missionary Horizons* (1953–1958), and an incomplete set of the *Minutes and Annual Reports of the United Presbyterian Church of North America*, which included the annual reports of the Board of Foreign Missions. Most of these published reports are also available at the United Presbyterian Mission Library, 475 Riverside Drive, New York. Since 1958, official references to the work in Africa can be found in the *Annual Reports of the Commission on Ecumenical Mission and Relations*.

THE UNITED WORLD MISSION

The United World Mission, 800 East Welch Causeway, St. Petersburg, Florida, was organized in 1946. Its primary purpose was to serve the interdenominational church, but many of the denominational churches have joined forces with the Mission in work throughout the world. The United World Mission began work in the Republic of the Congo in 1949, in Mali in 1954, and in Senegal in 1960. In the Mission's headquarters are letters, reports, and pictures. The Mission publishes bimonthly the *UWM Reports*.

THE WESLEYAN METHODIST CHURCH OF AMERICA

The Department of World Missions of The Wesleyan Methodist Church of America, Box 2000, Marion, Indiana 46955, was organized in 1862. It began work in Sierra Leone in 1889. The available records consist largely of letters, reports, and articles published in the *Wesleyan Methodist*, a weekly, and the *Wesleyan Missionary*, a monthly. Bound copies of these magazines are in a vault at the church headquarters in Marion. Scrapbooks of clippings covering the history of each of the fields during the past twenty years have recently been compiled. A review of the Church's missionary work in Sierra Leone is contained in Ira F. McLeister, *History of The Wesleyan Methodist Church* (rev. ed. by Roy S. Nicholson, Marion, Ind., Wesley Press, 1959).

THE WHITE FATHERS OF AFRICA

The White Fathers (Society of Missionaries of Africa), whose U.S. headquarters are at 1624 21st Street, N.W., Washington 9, D.C., are an international Roman Catholic missionary society of priests and brothers working exclusively in Africa. The Society, founded in 1868, began missionary activity in Algeria in 1873; Tunisia, 1875; Uganda and Tanganyika, 1878; Congo (Leopoldville), 1883; Nyasaland, 1889; Urundi, 1891; Mali, 1895; Northern Rhodesia, 1895; Guinea, 1896; Ruanda, 1900; Upper Volta, 1900; Ghana, 1906; Nigeria, 1944; Mozambique, 1946; and Senegal, 1947. The Society's official archives of original manuscripts and all printed materials are in Rome (Via Aurelia, 269). In Washington, information files contain current documentation and some historical data.

Besides internal organs, the White Fathers publish *White Fathers Magazine*, Washington, D.C., 9 issues a year, 1963– (successor to *White Fathers Missions*,

1943–1962, which in turn succeeded *African Missions of the White Fathers*, Montreal, 1908–1943).

WOMEN'S MISSIONARY ASSOCIATION, GENERAL CONFERENCE MENNONITE CHURCH

The Women's Missionary Association, organized in 1917, is an auxiliary of the General Conference Mennonite Church, 722 Main Street, Newton, Kansas. As an auxiliary, the Association is not a sending agency but rather promotes the General Conference mission program. The General Conference is affiliated with other Mennonite groups in the Congo Inland Mission work in Africa, with home offices at 251 West Hively Avenue, Elkhart, Indiana. The Mission publishes a field paper, the *Congo Missionary Messenger*, and a newssheet, *Congo Contact*, which keeps the mission constituency informed on recent Congo developments. Mission work in the Congo, as well as General Conference mission work in other areas, receives publicity through the *Missionary News and Notes*, publication of the Women's Missionary Association.

WORLD GOSPEL MISSION

The World Gospel Mission, 123 West 5th Street, Marion, Indiana 46953, was first organized as the National Holiness Missionary Society in 1910. The present name was adopted in 1948. About that time plans were begun for the merger of Peniel Missions with the World Gospel Mission. The first work in Africa was begun by Peniel Missions in 1897 in Egypt. Since then fields have been opened in Kenya (1932) and Burundi (1939). The World Gospel Mission keeps its records, missionary correspondence, etc., at the Marion office. It publishes two monthly magazines, the *Call to Prayer* and the *Junior Call*. The Burundi field publishes *Burakeye*. The story of the work of the World Gospel Mission is given in Laura Trachsel, *Kindled Fires in Africa* (Marion, Ind., World Gospel Mission, 1961).

WORLD MISSIONS, INC.

World Missions, Inc., 1486 Gaviota Avenue, P.O. Box 2611, Long Beach, California, was organized in 1958. Work in Africa was organized and incorporated in Johannesburg, South Africa, in 1960. Five major areas are covered by aerial distribution of literature, with headquarters now in Durban. Records are kept on file in the Long Beach office. World Missions issues a quarterly report and a monthly publication, *The Challenge*.

THE WORLDWIDE EVANGELIZATION CRUSADE

The Worldwide Evangelization Crusade, P.O. Box A, Fort Washington, Pennsylvania, was founded by C. T. Studd. He pioneered his way into the northeast corner of the Belgian Congo in 1913 and founded a mission known as the Heart of Africa

Mission. When the work began its global expansion some years later, it took the name Worldwide Evangelization Crusade. The Mission is an interdenominational society drawing workers from many denominational backgrounds. The work has been expanded to Spanish Guinea (1933), Ivory Coast (1934), Senegal (1936), Liberia (1938), Upper Volta (1939), Ghana (1940), Portuguese Guinea (1940), and Chad (1962). Field reports and missionary correspondence and surveys are on file at the Fort Washington office. The Mission publishes a bimonthly magazine, *Worldwide,* and occasional bulletins in the form of prayer-grams, copies of which are available from Fort Washington.

XAVERIAN BROTHERS

The Congregation of the Brothers of St. Francis Xavier (Xaverian Brothers), founded in Belgium in 1839, began its work in the United States in 1854. The American Northeastern Province, 601 Winchester Street, Newton Highlands 61, Massachusetts, has missions in Uganda and Kenya. The archives for the work of the Brothers in Africa are at the Massachusetts Provincialate, and they consist mainly of copies of contracts, correspondence, and a few bulletins and pictures.

ART AND ETHNOGRAPHIC COLLECTIONS

Note: The surveys marked with an asterisk (*) were compiled by the author, Peter Duignan. All other data on art and ethnographic collections were supplied by Professor Roy Sieber and Mr. René Bravmann of Indiana University.

ALBION COLLEGE ART MUSEUM

Albion College Art Museum, Albion, Michigan; Chairman of Art Department, Vernon L. Bobbitt; 100 pieces; Guinea coast, Congo.

THE AMERICAN MUSEUM OF NATURAL HISTORY,* NEW YORK

The American Museum of Natural History, Central Park West at 79th Street, New York, New York 10024, has an African collection of some 30,000 pieces. The collection was begun at the end of the nineteenth century and has been growing steadily ever since. There was no curator for the African collection until 1959, but Miss Bella Weitzner and Mr. Philip Gifford went through the entire collection and arranged it by area. At that time certain gaps became evident, and Dr. H. L. Shapiro, chairman of the Department of Anthropology, set out to fill those gaps whenever the opportunity arose. The Museum relied mainly on donors for 'art' pieces and used such funds as it had for the purchase of field collections.

Even in 1959 the collection was already extraordinarily representative. The weakest areas were the western and eastern Sudan; in particular, there were no more than half a dozen Nilotic items. That has now been largely rectified through the close cooperation and generosity of the governments of the Sudan, Chad, and Mali.

The Congo collection is probably the strongest, forming about a third of the total collection and representing the entire Congo area from the coast, through the Kasai and Ubangi areas, to the East African borders. Much of this collection was made in the field, and it includes some fine specimens and an unusually large and comprehensive collection of Pende masks.

Through a number of large private donations the Museum has acquired splendid examples of West African craftsmanship, and from that general area Nigeria is probably the best represented, including the northern territory (from which the Museum has two large field collections) and a collection of Yoruba material made by Dr. William Bascom.

There are examples of most of the tribes of West Africa, though from tribes such as the Dogon and Bambara and the Baga and Bobo the collection is restricted to the so-called 'art' pieces, no opportunity having developed to acquire a more respresentatively ethnographic collection. In all other areas, however, the collection is more truly ethnographic, and the Museum's interest in 'art' pieces is primarily in their ethnographic significance.

The Museum has approximately 1,000 musical instruments. There is a general catalogue, and a classified index is being prepared. The Congo is best covered. The musical collection includes all classes of instruments: aerophone, idiophone, membranophone, and chordophone, from all over Africa, with a few from Madagas-

---

* In this section the surveys marked with an asterisk were compiled by the author, Peter Duignan. All other data on art and ethnographic collections were supplied by Professor Roy Sieber and Mr. René Bravmann of Indiana University.

car. The collections date back to about the turn of the century, so that none of these instruments is likely to be as much as a hundred years old, although one, a sansa made entirely of bark with bamboo tongues, may be older.

ARIZONA STATE MUSEUM

Arizona State Museum, Tucson, Arizona; Assistant Curator, Wilma Kaemblein; 300 pieces; Congo, East and South Africa.

THE ART INSTITUTE OF CHICAGO*

The Art Institute of Chicago, Michigan Avenue and East Adams Street, Chicago 3, Illinois, holds approximately 60 pieces of African art ranging from gold weights and masks to headdresses and sculptured pieces, all from West Africa. Six items of Bambara sculpture are described in the *Art Institute of Chicago Quarterly*, Vol. LVI, No. 1 (March 1962). A catalogue of the Institute's collections, *Primitive Art in the Collections of the Art Institute of Chicago* (Chicago, 1965, 52 pp.), illustrates many of their African pieces.

THE BALTIMORE MUSEUM OF ART*

The Baltimore Museum of Art, Baltimore, Maryland, was presented with the Wurtzburger Collection of African Sculpture in 1954. The collection includes 10 pieces from the Sudan (Bambara, Bobo, Dogon, and Mossi); 63 from the Guinea coast (Ashanti, Baga, Baule, Bron, Guro, Kissi, Mende, Ngere, the Poro Society [Liberia], and Toma); 22 from Nigeria (Benin, Ekoi, Ibibio, Ibo, and Yoruba); 6 from the Camerouns; and 42 from Central Africa (Bakongo, Bakota, Baluba, Bapende, Basonge, Batchioke, Bateke, Bayaka, Bena Lulua, Bushongo, Fang, Mangbetu, Mayombe, Ogowe River Region, and Warega).

The wooden pieces and the sculpture date from the nineteenth century, with a few Benin bronzes and stone and terra-cotta sculptures dating from the sixteenth and seventeenth centuries. Noteworthy specimens in the collection are the Baga dance headdress, the Bambara dance headpiece, the Baule female figure, an Ibibio mask, the Fang male ancestor figure (Gabon), the Baluba neckrest, the Mossi dance headpiece, the Guro mask, and the Benin bronze head of a king. According to scholars in the field, the Baga dance headdress and especially the Fang male ancestor figure (Gabon) are pieces outstanding in quality. The collection also includes a bronze relief with serpent from Benin, an elephant mask from the Sudan, probably Bambara, and a large, very fine Senufo standing female figure (Ivory Coast).

For a detailed description and pictures of the collection see *The Alan Wurtzburger Collection of African Sculpture* (2d ed., Baltimore, Baltimore Museum of Art, 1958, 30 pp.).

BAYLOR UNIVERSITY, STRECKER MUSEUM

Strecker Museum, Baylor University, Waco, Texas; Museum Curator, Dr. Bryce C. Brown; 50 pieces; North Africa, Congo, Natal.

BELOIT COLLEGE MUSEUM

Beloit College Museum, Beloit, Wisconsin; Director, Dr. Andrew Whiteford; over 100 pieces; Sahara, Congo.

BIRMINGHAM MUSEUM OF ART

Birmingham Museum of Art, Birmingham, Alabama; Director, Richard Howard; 750 pieces; Congo.

BROOKLYN CHILDREN'S MUSEUM

Brooklyn Children's Museum, 185 Brooklyn Avenue, Brooklyn 13, New York; Curator, Paul C. Hooks; about 200 pieces plus more than 100 volumes; North, South, East, and West Africa, Congo.

THE BROOKLYN MUSEUM*

The Brooklyn Museum, Eastern Parkway, Brooklyn 38, New York, contains a good collection in the field of African art, including masks, sculptures, costumes, weapons, tools, utensils, ornaments, games, stools, doors, etc., made of wood, metal, ivory and bone, textile fiber, stone, and ceramic. African areas and tribes represented in the collection include: *Angola*—Badjowke (wooden snuffbox in the form of a seated female figure); *Congo*—Bakongo (mother and child sculptures of wood, stone sculpture, masks, wooden sculptures); Bapende (ivory charms from Katanga); Baluba (ivory amulets, bow rests, twin figures, stools, utensils, staffs, wood sculptures); Bushongo (royal portrait of Bom-Bosh, wooden cups and boxes, masks); Bateke, Bambala, Babwende, Warega, Makonde, Bayaka, and Mangbetu (wooden masks, sculptures, utensils, stools, ceramic jars, maternity figures); *Gabon*—Fang (wooden sculptures, etc.); Bakota; *Gold Coast*—Ashanti (stools, copper weights); *Guinea*—Baga (Nimba masks, polychrome wood carvings); *Ivory Coast*—Baule, Senufo, Guro (wooden doors, masks, utensils, gold pendant); *Liberia*—Dan (Poro Society masks); *Nigeria*—Ife (clay head); Benin (carved elephant tusks, ivory cups, bronze sculptures); Yoruba (wooden doors, masks, etc.); Ibo (masks); Mende, Bambara, Dogon, Bobo, Mossi (wooden figures, masks).

BUFFALO MUSEUM OF SCIENCE

Buffalo Museum of Science, Buffalo, New York; Curator of Anthropology, Virginia Cummings; over 1,000 pieces; Guinea coast, Congo.

UNIVERSITY OF CALIFORNIA, BERKELEY, LOWIE MUSEUM OF ANTHROPOLOGY*

The Lowie Museum of Anthropology, University of California, Berkeley, California, under the direction of William Bascom, has over 2,000 pieces in its collection of masks, sculptures, and other African objects from the western Sudan, the Guinea coast, and the Congo. It is in constant demand for research study and campus display.

UNIVERSITY OF CALIFORNIA, LOS ANGELES*

The Ethnic Collection of the University of California, Los Angeles, California, has been growing steadily over the past few years, and its African Art and Ethnology Section now contains some 4,300 items representing, among others, the Batutsi, Sebei, Bambara, Dogon, Mossi, Mende, Ashanti, Yoruba, Bini, and Bakota. In 1963 a splendid Congo collection was purchased from M. Jean Hallet—approximately 3,000 pieces covering 38 tribes—consisting of musical instruments, artifacts, ceremonial sculptures, fetishes, instruments of war, and other objects. The Balega group, numbering 768 items, is one of the most comprehensive in existence and is rich in artistically outstanding carvings in wood, bone, and ivory.

CARNEGIE MUSEUM, PITTSBURGH

Carnegie Museum, Pittsburgh 13, Pennsylvania; Curator, James L. Wauger; over 790 pieces, mostly ethnological.

CHICAGO NATURAL HISTORY MUSEUM*

The Chicago Natural History Museum (formerly the Field Museum of Natural History), Roosevelt Road and Lake Shore Drive, Chicago 5, Illinois, has African ethnological collections of approximately 11,000 specimens in the Department of Anthropology. The largest collection is of Camerouns artifacts, with more than 1,800 pieces. The Benin collection, numbering 391 pieces, is the most valuable; the Chicago Natural History Museum's holdings and the recently acquired Capt. A. W. F. Fuller Collection combine to make this the largest collection in the United States and one of the largest in the world. A third important collection, numbering about 500 pieces, is from Angola and is the only collection in the Museum's African holdings made by an ethnologist, the late Dr. Wilfrid D. Hambly, former curator of African ethnology.

The remaining 8,300 pieces of the African ethnological collections are divided among other peoples and areas of Africa, including about 1,400 from the Sudan, 1,500 from the Congo area, 2,600 from South and East Africa, and 1,100 from the East African Horn area.

All the material mentioned above is of relatively recent origin, most of it falling into a time range of 30 to 100 years ago. The Benin material has a historical time range of from 70 to 300 years ago, the main part from about a hundred years back.

There are also miscellaneous archaeological materials from North Africa (1,250), South Africa (250), and East Africa (500). And there are extensive Egyptian holdings, numbering about 3,300 pieces and ranging over Egyptian historical and prehistorical time periods.

The above collections, totaling 16,300 pieces (African ethnological, 11,000; African archaeological, 2,000; Egyptian, 3,300), and the Museum Library are available for study by qualified students.

For a complete catalogue of the Museum's Benin holdings see Philip Dark, *The Art of Benin* (Chicago, 1962); see also Wilfrid D. Hambly, *The Ovimbundu of Angola* (Chicago, 1934; Fieldiana Anthropology, Vol. XXI, No. 2, Publication 329).

CHILDREN'S MUSEUM, NASHVILLE

Children's Museum, Nashville, Tennessee; Director, Philbrick M. Crouch; 100 pieces; Guinea coast, Congo.

CHILDREN'S NATURE MUSEUM OF YORK COUNTY, SOUTH CAROLINA

Children's Nature Museum of York County, Rock Hill, South Carolina; over 100 pieces; Congo, East Africa.

CINCINNATI ART MUSEUM

Cincinnati Art Museum, Cincinnati, Ohio; Registrar, Carolyn K. Shine; over 100 pieces; Congo.

CLEVELAND MUSEUM OF ART

Cleveland Museum of Art, Cleveland, Ohio; Associate Curator of Decorative Arts, William B. Wixom; 75 items; western Sudan, Guinea coast, Congo.

COMMERCIAL MUSEUM, PHILADELPHIA*

The African ethnological materials in the storage vaults and display cases of the Commercial Museum, Philadelphia, Pennsylvania, number some 3,000 specimens. In the 1890's three collections of African ethnological specimens were acquired. Two of these collections, comprising specimens chiefly from Muslim North and Northeast Africa, with a much smaller number from the Guinea coast region, were originally in the Berlin and Imperial Austrian (Vienna) Ethnological Museums and were exchanged by the German and Austrian governments, respectively, for duplicate botanical specimens at the Commercial Museum; the third was a collection of specimens displayed by the Liberian government at the Columbian Exposition in Chicago, 1893.

The largest single acquisition of African materials came, however, from the Paris International Exposition of 1900. It is noteworthy that French colonial exhibits at that time, roughly half of which eventually reached the Commercial Museum, incorporated much older specimens from the earlier French Colonial Exposition of 1889. The African specimens in this distinguished collection came for the most part from Senegal, French Guinea, French Sudan, Middle Congo, and French Somaliland (Djibouti), with a very few specimens from the Ivory Coast, Gabon, and Ubangi-Shari.

Specimens from German East Africa were acquired similarly, as a gift of the German government, after the Louisiana Purchase Exposition held in St. Louis in 1904.

Until 1930, a considerable number of African materials continued to be added, primarily by purchase from private individuals; these rounded out the Commercial Museum's African collections by specimens of note from Northern Rhodesia and French Middle Congo, Nigeria, and elsewhere. In time the greater part of the continent has come to be represented, if in some areas only very modestly.

Fortunately the great bulk of the Museum's specimens comes from that part of Africa that has contributed most significantly to the population and culture of the United States: from Senegal and the western Sudan, from Nigeria and Dahomey, and from the greater Congo region. For full description and pictures of the collection see *A Handbook of the African Collections of the Commercial Museum, Philadelphia* (Philadelphia, 78 pp.), by Harold D. Gunn.

The African musical instruments of the Commercial Museum have come chiefly from the Senegal region of French West Africa, but items from the Congo, Gabon, Tanganyika, and Madagascar are also held. Over 25 drums, lutes, fiddles, and flutes are in the collection. See Joseph Barone, *A Handbook of the Musical Instrument Collection of the Commercial Museum, Philadelphia* (Philadelphia, 1961, 63 pp.).

DARTMOUTH COLLEGE MUSEUM

Dartmouth College Museum, Hanover, New Hampshire; Curator of Anthropology, Alfred F. Whiting; about 500 pieces; East Africa.

DENVER ART MUSEUM*

The Chappell House Branch (1300 Logan Street) of the Denver Art Museum, West 14th Avenue and Acoma Street, Denver, Colorado, has 296 African objects in its collections. These objects were collected from the point of view of arts and crafts. Represented are a Benin bronze plaque and several other Benin objects, wood sculpture, and metalworks, including figures, masks, panels, boxes, and utilitarian objects characteristic of such tribes as Dogon, Bambara, Baga, Karumba, Senufo, Baule, Ashanti, Yoruba, Ibibio, Gaboon, Bakota, Bushongo, Bateke, Bapende, and others.

The Douglas Library of the Denver Art Museum contains several hundred publications on African art and anthropology. Museum publications on African art include *The Backgrounds of African Art* (Denver, 1945), by Melville J. Herskovits, and *The Art of Africa* (Denver, 1964), handbook written by Cile M. Bach.

DETROIT INSTITUTE OF ARTS*

The Detroit Institute of Arts, Detroit 2, Michigan, holds African art objects in the following categories:

Sculpture, approximately 18 pieces. Included are warrior masks, fertility symbols, female figures, a headdress, and a crucifix; materials used are wood, copper, and bronze. These figures originated in Benin (seventeenth century), Cameroun (nineteenth century), Nigeria (nineteenth century), Upper Volta and West Africa (nineteenth century), Gabon (date undetermined; nineteenth century), French Guinea (date undetermined), and Angola–southern Congo (date undetermined).

Ivory carving, 3 pieces: knife case, amulet, and carved boar's tusks.

Textiles, 6 pieces: colored materials, tunic, and embroidered panel, originating in Morocco, North Africa, and West Africa, nineteenth and twentieth centuries.

Costume accessories, 18 items: necklaces, armbands, and bracelets, nineteenth and twentieth centuries.

EVERHART MUSEUM, SCRANTON

Everhart Museum, Nay Aug Park, Scranton, Pennsylvania 18510; Director, R. L. Shalkop; about 125 pieces exclusive of North Africa; West Africa, Congo.

FISK UNIVERSITY*

Africa-related materials at Fisk University, Nashville, Tennessee, include the Baldridge Collection and several hundred African museum pieces. The Baldridge Collection, which is on exhibit in the lobby and third-floor halls of the Fisk University Library, consists of 68 drawings by Cyrus Leroy Baldridge. Because of the broad scope of their subject matter and their authentic portraiture, they form one of the most complete records in America of African life and African types. The drawings were a gift from Samuel Insull of Chicago. The museum pieces, housed and exhibited in the Social Science Division Library, include such items as coiled basketry from the Mende of Sierra Leone, gourd rattles, ivory tusks, and African brasswork.

UNIVERSITY OF FLORIDA, FLORIDA STATE MUSEUM

Florida State Museum, University of Florida, Gainesville, Florida; 400 pieces; Congo, Sierra Leone.

FORT WORTH CHILDREN'S MUSEUM

Fort Worth Children's Museum, Fort Worth, Texas; Director, William G. Hassler; over 100 pieces; West Africa.

UNIVERSITY OF GEORGIA, GEORGIA MUSEUM OF ART

Georgia Museum of Art, University of Georgia, Athens, Georgia; Director, A. H. Holbrook; 250 pieces; Camerouns.

HAMPTON INSTITUTE COLLEGE MUSEUM

Hampton Institute College Museum, Hampton, Virginia 23368; Director, Friedrich J. Gronstedt; over 100 pieces; North, South, East, and West Africa, Congo.

HARVARD UNIVERSITY, PEABODY MUSEUM OF ARCHAEOLOGY AND ETHNOLOGY

Peabody Museum of Archaeology and Ethnology, Harvard University, Cambridge, Massachusetts; Director, J. O. Brew; 45,000 pieces; Sahara, western Sudan, Guinea coast, Congo, South Africa.

HERRON MUSEUM OF ART, ART ASSOCIATION OF INDIANAPOLIS*

The Art Association of Indianapolis of the Herron Museum of Art, 110 East 16th Street, Indianapolis, Indiana, has a small but growing collection on Africa.

HOWARD UNIVERSITY*

The art gallery located in the new Fine Arts Building of Howard University, Washington, D.C., has a rapidly growing collection of African artifacts. It consists primarily of the Alain LeRoy Locke Collection of African Sculpture and contains 400 objects representing some of the major art-producing centers of West African culture. Many of the objects are of wood, ivory, or brass, but the largest number consists of a diversified group of gold weights from Ghana and the Ivory Coast. Other items of less importance, such as handicrafts and musical instruments, illustrate in a limited way decorative and industrial art as practiced today among the Vai, Temne, and Mende tribal groups in Liberia and Sierra Leone. During the past four years numerous examples of the high tribal arts of West Africa and the handicrafts of both East and West Africa have been added by gift, purchase, or loan.

Also of interest are the Art Department's collection of 500 photographs of African art and architecture given by the Museum of Modern Art of New York and the Carnegie Art Teaching set of photographic reproductions of representative artifacts and historical monuments of ancient Egyptian and Arabic civilizations. There are several hundred slides devoted to African art. The Department of Art now offers a course on the art and architecture of Black Africa and a course on Negro art which includes the related African-American experience in painting and sculpture.

ILLINOIS STATE MUSEUM OF NATURAL HISTORY

Illinois State Museum of Natural History, Springfield, Illinois; Curator of Anthropology, Joseph R. Caldwell; 100 pieces; East and West Africa.

INDIANA UNIVERSITY MUSEUM

Indiana University Museum, Bloomington, Indiana; Director, Dr. Henry Hope; 500 pieces; western Sudan, Guinea coast, Congo, South Africa.

KALAMAZOO PUBLIC MUSEUM

Kalamazoo Public Museum, Kalamazoo, Michigan; Director, Alexis Praus; about 250 pieces; West Africa, Congo.

LA JOLLA ART CENTER

La Jolla Art Center, La Jolla, California; Assistant Director, Don Dubley; 100 pieces; western Sudan, Guinea coast.

LINCOLN UNIVERSITY*

Lincoln University, P.O. Lincoln University, Chester County, Pennsylvania; their library materials are supplemented by a large and growing collection of African art and artifacts.

LONG BEACH MUSEUM OF ART

Long Beach Museum of Art, Long Beach, California; Educational Curator, H. J. Weeks; 158 pieces; Liberian contemporary.

LOS ANGELES COUNTY MUSEUM

Los Angeles County Museum, Los Angeles, California; Curator of Anthropology, R. M. Ariss; over 1,000 pieces; Guinea coast, Congo.

MASSILLON MUSEUM

Massillon Museum, Massillon, Ohio; Curator, Albert E. Hise; 100 pieces; Abyssinian pieces solely.

UNIVERSITY OF MICHIGAN MUSEUM OF ANTHROPOLOGY

University of Michigan Museum of Anthropology, Ann Arbor, Michigan; 100 pieces; Kenya.

MICHIGAN STATE UNIVERSITY*

The University Museum, Michigan State University, East Lansing, Michigan, has in its custody over 400 items of jewelry, weapons, musical instruments, pottery, sculpture, masks, and other art objects. Most of these are from West Africa, chiefly Nigeria and Liberia.

The Kresge Art Center has additional items, such as old Egyptian-Coptic sculpture and Benin bronzes.

MILWAUKEE PUBLIC MUSEUM*

The Milwaukee Public Museum, 800 West Wells Street, Milwaukee 3, Wisconsin, has an extensive East African collection, gathered in the early 1930's on a museum expedition. There are items from such tribes as the Ikoma, Kikuyu, and Masai. It is a well-balanced collection of material culture and includes weapons.

The Museum has only miscellany from other regions of Africa, though it does have a good ethnographic collection (emphasizing the art of wood carving) from the Camerouns, a collection which the Museum has had for some ten years. (See William R. Bascom and Paul Gebauer, *West African Art*, edited by Robert Ritzenthaler [Milwaukee, 1954; Milwaukee Public Museum Popular Science Handbook No. 5, 75 cents].)

MINNEAPOLIS INSTITUTE OF ARTS*

The Minneapolis Institute of Arts, 201 East 24th Street, Minneapolis, Minnesota, has collections of African art.

UNIVERSITY OF MISSOURI MUSEUM OF ANTHROPOLOGY

University of Missouri Museum of Anthropology, Columbia, Missouri; Director, Dale R. Henning; 200 pieces; East Africa.

MUSEUM OF AFRICAN ART, WASHINGTON, D.C.*

The Museum of African Art, 316 A Street, Northeast, Capitol Hill, Washington, D.C. 20002, sponsors rotating exhibitions of African art in the Washington area. Most pieces are on loan from private collections and museums throughout the country—each exhibition is changed approximately every three months. The Museum has a study lounge, library resources, and reproductions and slides illustrating the relationship between African and modern art.

MUSEUM OF FINE ARTS, BOSTON*

The Museum of Fine Arts, Boston 15, Massachusetts, holds a collection of approximately 30 African musical instruments. Most of these materials have not, however, been catalogued and are not available to the student or the public.

MUSEUM OF PRIMITIVE ART, NEW YORK*

The Museum of Primitive Art, 15 West 54th Street, New York, New York, has approximately 600–650 pieces of African art and ethnographic material (textiles, weapons, figures, masks, jewelry, etc.) from the western Sudan, the Guinea coast, and the Congo regions. The material is mostly wood but includes some brass, ivory, and gold from the areas where these materials have been traditionally worked. There are also a few textiles: Bambara, Ashanti, and Bakuba pile clothes. With reference to age, the collection contains some early Benin pieces (sixteenth century); the wooden pieces, however, can only be credited with a tentative date, the nineteenth century.

The following museum publications contain material held by the Museum in whole or in part: *Traditional Art of the African Nations in the Museum of Primitive Art* (1961, 70 pp., 77 illus., boards, $6.00), Introduction by Robert Goldwater; *Sculpture from Africa in the Collection of the Museum of Primitive Art* (32 pp., 24 illus., paper, 75 cents); *Bambara Sculpture from the Western Sudan* (1960, 64 pp., 112 illus., boards, $3.50), by Robert Goldwater; *The Great Bieri* (1962, 8 pp., 4 illus., paper, 25 cents), by Robert Goldwater; *Sculpture from Three African Tribes: Senufo, Baga, Dogon* (1959, 32 pp., 22 illus., paper, $1.50), Introduction by Robert Goldwater; *Senufo Sculpture from West Africa* (80 pp., 186 illus., boards, $8.95), by Robert Goldwater.

The Photographic Archive of the Museum of Primitive Art was founded in 1957 as a research facility and also to provide a sizable body of comparative material for use of the staff of the Museum and students and scholars in the field of primitive art.

At present the Archive offers a good working collection of roughly 20,000 documented black-and-white photographs covering African, Oceanic, and North, Central, and South American objects. The aim has been to collect as many previously unpublished examples as possible. There is also a collateral collection of color slides as well as one of color transparencies. No effort has been made to have unphotographed objects photographed for the Archive. This will be a project for the future.

The African section of the Archive represents approximately 6,500 documented black-and-white photographs arranged according to geographic area, tribal style, and type of object. Of this number approximately 5,500 have been completely processed. To the African section are added every year roughly 1,000 photographs, as gifts, through purchase from private collectors and museums, and through exchange. The Museum's own collection is, of course, a part of the Archive.

Some photographs came from private sources that include Eliot Elisofon, Paul Wingert, Douglas Fraser, and Ladislas Segy. Selections from most of the major museums are represented (British Museum, Brooklyn Museum, American Museum of Natural History, etc.), and the Museum is negotiating for picture collections in specialized areas, such as the Benin group collected by Dark and Nigerian objects by Sieber and Fagg.

THE NATURAL SCIENCE MUSEUM, CLEVELAND*

The Natural Science Museum (formerly the Cleveland Museum of Natural History), University Circle, Cleveland 6, Ohio, has roughly 800 specimens of

African ethnological materials. The bulk of this collection was acquired in the 1920's. The largest single accession comprises more than 300 artifacts, chiefly from Liberia and Nigeria, with smaller amounts from Senegal, the Congo, and Sudan, and was purchased from the Philadelphia Commercial Museum in 1922. The same year the Museum received 92 specimens from the Congo, donated by a private individual; this acquisition was supplemented in 1928 by a gift of 130 specimens from the Ituri forest by the African Art Sponsors, the Gilpin Players. In the remainder of these early years the Museum acquired another 100 specimens, representing mostly Kenya and East Africa, from private individuals.

No material was acquired between 1933 and 1951. In the last thirteen years the Museum has received small donations from Nigeria, Ethiopia, and the Liberian-Guinean border.

The artifacts themselves represent a cross-section of items—clothing, woven materials, war weapons, musical instruments, ornaments, carvings, and masks. Currently most of it is not on display, being housed in the Museum's storage vaults. A portion is on loan.

NEW YORK PUBLIC LIBRARY, SCHOMBURG COLLECTION OF NEGRO LITERATURE AND HISTORY*

The Schomburg Collection of Negro Literature and History, kept at a branch of the New York Public Library on 135th Street near Lenox Avenue, New York, New York, includes art objects and musical recordings. The art collection was started by Alain Locke, who had about half the Blondeau-Theatre Arts Collection deposited there. Over 250 African weapons and arms, mainly from south of the Sahara, are in the Eric de Kolbe Collection.

THE NEWARK MUSEUM*

The collection of African material of the Newark Museum, 43–49 Washington Street, Newark 1, New Jersey, includes approximately 1,200 objects from the area south of the Sahara. Material from the Yoruba and other peoples of Nigeria was in large measure collected in the 1890's. The Museum has a good collection of materials, especially baskets and mats from the lower Congo region (probably mostly Bakongo), gathered before World War I. A representative collection from the Bambuti Pygmies, the Mangbetu, and the Azande of the upper Congo and some East African material collected by Mrs. Delia Akeley in the 1920's (about 200–250 items) are also held. The Museum has scattered holdings from other tribes and areas. The collection was supplemented in the 1950's by the purchase of a small group of African sculptures.

The only available publication on this material is an article written by Professor Paul Wingert on the art objects and published in the Museum's quarterly publication, *The Museum*, Vol. VI, No. 4 (Fall 1954).

About 150 African items are in the Museum's extensive lending collection. All objects in the collection are available to teachers of the area for use in classrooms and may also be borrowed by certain individuals and clubs for group meetings. Although a few pictures may be included, the collection is made up almost entirely of actual three-dimensional objects.

OBERLIN COLLEGE, ALLEN MEMORIAL ART MUSEUM*

The Allen Memorial Art Museum of Oberlin College, Oberlin, Ohio, has a small but valuable collection (8 pieces) on African art. Most of these African items are described and reproduced in the *Allen Memorial Art Museum Bulletin*, Vol. XIII, No. 2 (Winter 1955–1956). Seven of the art objects are from West Africa and one is from the Bapende in the Congo.

PEABODY MUSEUM, SALEM*

The Peabody Museum, East India Marine Hall, Salem, Massachusetts, holds over 2,300 African artifacts. The collections consist largely of materials from East and West Africa, with scattered items from all over the continent—among other things wearing apparel, weapons, textiles, religious items, tools, household items, money, musical instruments, baskets, gold weights, and horse equipment. Some of the early-nineteenth-century material relates to the Salem trade with Zanzibar and West Africa. The Congo items include a collection from the Pygmies, and there are early drawings of the Hottentots and Bushmen.

UNIVERSITY OF PENNSYLVANIA, UNIVERSITY MUSEUM*

The University Museum, University of Pennsylvania, 33d and Spruce Streets, Philadelphia 4, Pennsylvania, contains a large ethnological collection—eight to ten thousand pieces—from all of sub-Saharan Africa. Over two-thirds of the collection is from West Africa and the Congo and includes many musical instruments and wood carvings—masks, figures, fetishes, boxes, cups, headrests—besides such purely ethnographic material as weapons, tools, household equipment, and cloth. Much of the sculpture is of especially fine quality. From South Africa and East Africa the collections are entirely ethnographic in character.

The J. F. G. Umlauff Collection, which includes a large number of specimens collected by L. Frobenius in the Congo, and the W. O. Oldman Collection, which contains many important pieces from Benin (approximately 1,000), comprise a large part of the University Museum's African collection.

A great deal of the ethnographic material was collected for the Museum by missionaries and others working in Africa mainly before 1930. The Museum also contains a collection from Sherbro Island off Sierra Leone collected by Mr. H. U. Hall in 1937 for a Museum-sponsored expedition.

The Museum has the largest and most varied collection of African sculpture in the United States. The material is largely from West and Central Africa. Especially valuable items are three great helmet masks from the Yoruba, masks and figures from the Senufo of the Ivory Coast, Dogon figures from the Sudan, a helmet mask and a cult object from the Mende of Sierra Leone, bronze heads with tusks from Benin, Nigeria, Bakota funerary figures, and an Ibo dance mask.

There is a descriptive catalogue. Published surveys appeared in 1945 and 1957: H. A. Wieschhoff, 'The African Collections of the University Museum,' *The University Museum Bulletin*, March 1945 (76 pp.), and Margaret Plass, 'African Negro Sculpture,' *The University Museum Bulletin*, December 1957 (79 pp.). From a library of 45,000 volumes a large selection of African ethnographical and archaeological literature complements the Museum's collections.

PRINCETON UNIVERSITY ART MUSEUM*

The Art Museum, Princeton University, Princeton, New Jersey, has 149 objects from Africa (excluding ancient Egyptian material as well as Ethiopian). Most of the material came as a group in 1953, presented to the Museum by the widow of an alumnus who had lived in the Belgian Congo. Holdings include: 55 textile and basketwork objects from Batshok, Bakuba, and Baluba, also British West Africa; 68 wooden objects (masks, vessels, ornamental figures, musical instruments, arrows, etc.) from Bampedi, Batshok, Bakuba, and Baluba; 13 metal objects (jewelry, weapons, etc.) from Bakuba, Baluba, Batshok, and Bashila; 9 miscellaneous objects, chiefly ornamental, from Batshok, British West Africa, Belgian Congo generally; 1 seated wooden figure from Baule; 3 brass gold-dust weights from Ashanti.

PRINCETON UNIVERSITY MUSEUM OF NATURAL HISTORY

Princeton University Museum of Natural History, Princeton, New Jersey; Curator of Vertebrate Paleontology, Glenn L. Jepsen; over 100 pieces; Camerouns.

READING PUBLIC MUSEUM AND ART GALLERY

Reading Public Museum and Art Gallery, Reading, Pennsylvania; Director, Samuel C. Gundy; over 100 pieces.

ROCHESTER MUSEUM OF ARTS AND SCIENCES

Rochester Museum of Arts and Sciences, Rochester, New York; Associate Curator of Anthropology, Charles F. Hayes III; over 170 pieces; West, East, and South Africa, Congo.

ST. GREGORY'S COLLEGE, GERRER MUSEUM

Gerrer Museum, St. Gregory's College, Shawnee, Oklahoma; Director, Stephen Gyermek; 120 pieces; North Africa, Somaliland.

ST. LOUIS, CITY ART MUSEUM

City Art Museum, St. Louis, Missouri; Curator, Thomas Y. Hoopes; 98 pieces; western Sudan, Guinea coast, Congo.

SEGY GALLERY FOR AFRICAN ART, NEW YORK*

The Segy Gallery for African Art, 708 Lexington Avenue, New York, New York, is one of the largest private collections of African art. It was founded in 1950.

SMITHSONIAN INSTITUTION, UNITED STATES NATIONAL MUSEUM*

The United States National Museum, Smithsonian Institution, Washington 25, D.C., contains one of the largest African ethnological collections in the country. It has not attempted to specialize in any particular region, but rather specimens came from many parts of Africa and were acquired as gifts from missionaries, travelers, and others.

The most extensive collection of specimens comes from the Congo. This is comprised chiefly of the Herbert Ward Collection (which includes a great many knives and spears), augmented by artifacts collected by official United States representatives sent to the Congo as observers in the 1880's and other items gathered by missionaries in the early part of this century. All of these add up to perhaps the most representative ethnological collection from the Congo in this country. Besides weapons, there are many masks, figures, baskets, items of clothing, and household utensils.

The Smithsonian also contains a West African collection gathered primarily by Capt. C. C. Roberts in the 1920's. Other smaller collections include the specimens collected by Theodore Roosevelt's expedition to East Africa in 1909–1910, the Hoffman Phillip Collection from Ethiopia, the Talcott Williams Collection from Morocco, and, in recent years, the collection made by Ethnology Division Associate Curator Gordon D. Gibson of artifacts from the peoples of Bechuanaland, South-West Africa, and Northern Rhodesia.

UNIVERSITY OF SOUTH DAKOTA MUSEUM*

The University of South Dakota Museum, Vermillion, South Dakota, has African art holdings totaling about 100 pieces from North Africa and Kenya and including wood carvings, textiles, and weapons.

UNIVERSITY OF TEXAS, TEXAS MEMORIAL MUSEUM

Texas Memorial Museum, University of Texas, Austin, Texas; Director, W. W. Newcomb, Jr.; over 100 pieces; West Africa, Congo.

TUSKEGEE INSTITUTE, GEORGE WASHINGTON CARVER MUSEUM*

The George Washington Carver Museum, Tuskegee Institute, Tuskegee, Alabama, has an extensive collection of African art—over 100 pieces, from the western Sudan and the Congo. It also has 20 dioramas depicting Negro contributions to civilization, and in the Etta Moten African Literature Corner there are more than 1,000 photographs of life in Ghana and Nigeria.

WILSON MUSEUM, CASTINE, MAINE

Wilson Museum, Castine, Maine; Director, Mrs. N. W. Dondiet; under 10 pieces; Congo, East and South Africa.

UNIVERSITY OF WISCONSIN*

The Department of Art History, University of Wisconsin, Madison, Wisconsin, has in its custody a collection of 14 pieces of African art. These are of West African provenance and are chiefly masks and sculpture.

WITTE MEMORIAL MUSEUM, SAN ANTONIO*

The Witte Memorial Museum, 3801 Broadway, Brackenridge Park, San Antonio 9, Texas, holds approximately 617 items in its African collection, of which 381 are from a single collection made in Southeast Africa. Holdings also include 141 photographs from the Southeast Africa collection, Ethiopian material with Coptic items from Aksum, and ethnic items from the Kanama tribe, Barentu, Eritrea.

YALE UNIVERSITY ART GALLERY, LINTON COLLECTION*

The collection of African sculpture of Dr. Ralph Linton, former professor of anthropology at Yale University, New Haven, Connecticut, is one of the finest in the United States. It consists of approximately 250 pieces, which were given to Yale University after Dr. Linton's death in 1953. A catalogue of selected items (153) in the Linton Collection was prepared for an exhibition in 1954. The masks, headpieces, sculpture, artifacts, etc., exhibited were from Sudan (36), the central Guinea coast (22), Nigeria (16), the Camerouns (4), Central Africa (68), and East Africa (7). (See *The Linton Collection of African Sculpture: An Exhibition, March 13 through April 18, 1954, Yale University Art Gallery* [New Haven, Yale University Press, 1954, n.p.].)

The Art Gallery has other African anthropological materials. A large African anthropological collection in the Yale University Peabody Museum is catalogued and available to researchers.

PRIVATE U.S. COLLECTORS

The list below gives only those with holdings of 25 or more pieces.

Allen Alperton, 45 Ford Drive, West Amityville, Long Island, New York; 50 pieces; western Sudan, Guinea coast.

Dr. Mark Altschule, McLean Hospital, Waverley, Massachusetts; 31 pieces; Congo.

Ernst Anspach, 118 West 79th Street, New York, New York; 62 pieces; western Sudan, Guinea coast, Congo.

Herbert Baker, Highland Park, Illinois; 26 pieces; western Sudan, Congo.

Frank Barton, 55 Third Avenue, New York, New York; about 25 pieces; West Africa.

Dr. Otto Billing, Nashville, Tennessee; 25 pieces; West and East Africa.

Arthur A. Cohen, 103 East 86th Street or 1457 Broadway, New York, New York; 150 pieces; western Sudan.

Justine N. Cordwell, 925 Winona, Chicago, Illinois; 40–50 pieces; Guinea coast.

Eliot Elisofon, 1133 Park Avenue, New York, New York; about 200 pieces and over 3,000 negatives of art objects in Africa, Europe, and the United States; western Sudan, Congo.

Chaim Gross, 30 West 105th Street, New York, New York; 250–300 pieces; western Sudan, Guinea coast, Congo.

Robert Haines, 370 Arguello Boulevard, San Francisco 18, California; 100 pieces; West Africa, Congo.

Irwin Hersey, 106 West 69th Street, New York, New York; over 100 pieces.

Jay Leff, Uniontown, Pennsylvania; 249 pieces; western Sudan, Guinea coast, Congo.

Earl Loran, c/o Art Department, University of California, Berkeley, California; 38 pieces; western Sudan, Guinea coast, Congo.

Everett McNear, 1017 Ridge Court, Evanston, Illinois; 25 pieces; western Sudan, Guinea coast, Congo.

Alan P. Merriam, 2010 Arden Drive, Bloomington, Indiana; 300 pieces; Congo.

Raymond L. Myrer, 11 Louisburg Square, Boston, Massachusetts; 100 pieces; western Sudan, Guinea coast, Congo.

Bill Pearson, 1816 Union Street, San Francisco, California; 125 pieces; western Sudan, Guinea coast, Congo.

Mrs. Webster Plass, Barclay Hotel, Philadelphia, Pennsylvania; over 100 pieces; West Africa, Congo.

J. Bernard Reis, 252 East 68th Street, New York, New York; 50 pieces; western Sudan, Guinea coast, Congo.

Harold E. Rome, 415 East 52d Street, New York, New York; over 1,000 pieces; West Africa, Congo.

Gustave Schindler, 140 East 19th Street, New York, New York; 80 pieces; western Sudan, Guinea coast, Congo.

E. Clark Stillman, 24 Gramercy Place, New York, New York; 350 pieces; western Sudan, Guinea coast, Congo.

D. Tengbergen, 7 Sunnybrook Road, Bronxville, New York; 53 pieces; western Sudan, Guinea coast, Congo.

Benjamin Weiss, 200 East 66th Street, New York, New York; about 40 pieces; Congo.

Raymond J. Wielgus, 5550 South Dorchester, Chicago, Illinois; 30 pieces; western Sudan, Guinea coast, Congo.

BUSINESS ARCHIVES

FARRELL LINES

The Farrell Lines, 1 Whitehall Street, New York, New York, has been engaged in American-African shipping trade since the late 1920's. Ports of call include most of Africa south of the Sahara. The company maintains a library with holdings of 2,000 to 3,000 volumes covering areas of the line's operations, and it receives an extensive number of periodicals. The Farrell Lines also issues the *African News Digest*, a monthly. Private records of the company are not usually available to persons unconnected with the firm. Inquiries should be directed to Mr. James A. Farrell, Jr. There is a history of the company by Robert G. Albion, *Seaports South of Sahara: The Achievements of an American Steamship Service* (New York, Appleton-Century-Crofts, 1959, 316 pp.).

FIRESTONE TIRE AND RUBBER COMPANY LIBRARY AND ARCHIVES

In the Library and Archives of the Firestone Tire and Rubber Company, Akron, Ohio, are many noncurrent records of permanent value created since the company was founded in 1900. Some of these records deal with Liberia after the company's entry into that country in 1924. Permission to use the records must be requested.

FIRST NATIONAL CITY BANK OF NEW YORK

The First National City Bank, 399 Park Avenue, New York, New York, maintains or has maintained the following branches and affiliates in Africa: (1) a branch, The First National City Bank of New York, Cairo, Egypt (established April 1955, closed March 1961); (2) an affiliate, The Bank of Monrovia, Monrovia, Liberia (established September 1955); (3) an affiliate, The First National City Bank of New York (South Africa), Ltd., Johnnesburg (established December 1958), with branches in Cape Town and Durban. Regular banking records are not open for scholarly research. The head office maintains an up-to-date financial library with periodicals, reports, and monographs dealing with monetary and commercial affairs in Africa. Researchers may use these facilities on request. The bank has also published studies on various African states, among them *Liberia, Federation of Nigeria, Republic of South Africa, Ethiopia*, and *African and Malagasy Union*.

TRANS WORLD AIRLINES

Trans World Airlines, 380 Madison Avenue, New York, New York, maintains one file cabinet of records dating from 1945 and covering its air service to Africa. These materials include the following:

Ethiopia, economy, government, tourist information, and Ethiopian airlines records, reports, and literature.
Nigeria, commerce and industry, economy, government, trade index, customs and duties, investment information, and tourism.

In *TWA's Services to Ethiopia* (Washington, D.C., National Planning Association, 1959, 80 pp.) Theodore Geiger describes one of the airline's major African ventures. Permission to use the TWA materials should be obtained from Mr. James O. Plinton, Jr., Manager, Special Group Sales.

INDEX